The Organizational
Revolution

THE PRESBYTERIAN PRESENCE:
THE TWENTIETH-CENTURY EXPERIENCE

Series Editors

Milton J Coalter

John M. Mulder

Louis B. Weeks

The Organizational Revolution: Presbyterians and American Denominationalism

Edited by
Milton J Coalter
John M. Mulder
Louis B. Weeks

Essays by
Louis B. Weeks, Richard W. Reifsnyder,
Lewis L. Wilkins, Jr., Scott Brunger,
Robin Klay, D. Scott Cormode,
Joan C. LaFollette, Dale E. Soden,
Gary S. Eller, David B. McCarthy, and
Craig Dykstra and James Hudnut-Beumler

Westminster/John Knox Press
Louisville, Kentucky

Chapter 1 appeared in a slightly different version under the title "The Incorporation of American Religion: The Case of the Presbyterians" in *Religion and American Culture,* vol. 1, no. 1 (Winter 1991), a publication of the Center for the Study of Religion and American Culture, IUPUI, © Indiana University Press.

Book design by Gene Harris

First edition

Published by Westminster/John Knox Press
Louisville, Kentucky

PRINTED IN THE UNITED STATES OF AMERICA
9 8 7 6 5 4 3 2 1

Library of Congress Cataloging-in-Publication Data

The Organizational revolution : Presbyterians and American
denominationalism / edited by Milton J Coalter, John M. Mulder,
Louis B. Weeks ; essays by Louis B. Weeks ... [et al.]. — 1st ed.
     p.   cm. — (The Presbyterian presence)
  Includes bibliographical references and index.
  Contents: The incorporation of the Presbyterian Church / Louis B.
Weeks — Managing the mission / Richard W. Reifsnyder — The
American presbytery in the twentieth century / Lewis L. Wilkins, Jr.
— A financial history of American Presbyterian giving, 1923–1983 /
Scott Brunger and Robin Klay — Changing priorities / Robin Klay —
Global and local mission / Scott Brunger — A financial history of
Presbyterian congregations since World War II / D. Scott Cormode —
Money and power : Presbyterian women's organizations in the
twentieth century / Joan C. LaFollette — Men and mission / Dale E.
Soden — Special interest groups and American Presbyterianism / Gary
S. Eller — The emerging importance of Presbyterian polity / David
B. McCarthy.
  ISBN 0-664-25197-8

  1. Presbyterian Church—United States—History—20th century.
2. Presbyterian Church—United States—Government. 3. Presbyterian
Church—United States—Finance. I. Series.
BX8937.074 1992
285′.1′0904—dc20
                                     90-23330

Contents

Series Foreword

This series, "The Presbyterian Presence: The Twentieth-Century Experience," is the product of a significant research project analyzing American Presbyterianism in this century. Funded by the Lilly Endowment and based at Louisville Presbyterian Theological Seminary, the project is part of a broader research effort that analyzes the history of mainstream Protestantism. By analyzing American Presbyterianism as a case study, we hope not only to chronicle its fate in the twentieth century but also to illumine larger patterns of religious change in mainstream Protestantism and in American religious and cultural life.

This case study of American Presbyterianism and the broader research on mainstream Protestantism arise out of an epochal change in American religion that has occurred during the twentieth century. Mainstream American Protestantism refers to those churches that emerged from the American Revolution as the dominant Protestant bodies and were highly influential in shaping American religion and culture during the nineteenth century. It includes the Presbyterians, Episcopalians, Methodists, Congregationalists (now the United Church of Christ), Disciples, and American or northern Baptists.

In this century, these churches have been displaced—religiously and culturally—to a significant degree. All have suffered severe membership losses since the 1960s. All have experienced significant theological tensions and shifts in emphasis. All are characterized by problems in their organization as institutions. And yet they remain influential voices in the spectrum of American religion and retain an enduring vitality in the face of a massive reconfiguration of American religious life.

The result is a complex phenomenon that is not easily described. Some would say the term "mainstream" or "mainline" is itself suspect and embodies ethnocentric and elitist assumptions. What characterized American religious history, they argue, was its diversity and its pluralism. Some groups may have believed they were religiously or culturally dominant, but the historical reality is much more pluralistic. Others would maintain that if there was a "mainstream," it no longer exists. Still others would propose that the mainstream itself has changed. The denominations of the evangelical awakening of the nineteenth century have been replaced by the evangelical churches of the late twentieth century—Southern Baptist, charismatic, Pentecostal.

Some propose that the term "mainline" or "mainstream" should be dropped in favor of talking about "liberal" Protestantism, but such a change presents additional problems. Like "evangelical," the term "liberal" is an extremely vague word to describe a set of Christian beliefs, values, and behavior. Furthermore, virtually all the "mainstream" churches contain large numbers of people who would describe themselves as either evangelical or liberal, thus making it very difficult to generalize about them as a denomination.

Despite the debates about terminology and the categories for analyzing American Protestantism, there is general agreement that American culture and American Protestantism of the late twentieth century are very different from what they were in the late nineteenth century. What has changed is the religious and cultural impact of American Protestantism. A study of American Presbyterianism is a good lens for examining that change, for in spite of their relatively small numbers, Presbyterians are, or were, quintessential mainstreamers, exerting a great deal of influence because of their economic, social, educational, and cultural advantages.

When did the change occur? In a pioneering article written more than fifty years ago, Arthur M. Schlesinger, Sr., pointed to the period from 1875 to 1900 as "a critical period" in American religion. In particular, American Protestants confronted the external challenges of immigration, industrialization, and urbanization and the internal challenges posed by Darwinism, biblical criticism, history of religions, and the new social sciences.[1] Robert T. Handy has maintained that the 1920s witnessed a "religious depression." The result was a "second disestablishment" of American Protestantism. When the churches lost legal establishment in the U.S. Constitution, they attempted to "Christianize" American culture.[2] But by the 1920s, it was clear that both legal and cultural establishment had been rejected. Sydney Ahlstrom points to the 1960s as the time when American religion and culture took a "radical turn" and the "Puritan culture" of the United States was shattered.[3] Wade Clark Roof and William McKinney build on Ahlstrom's argument, proposing that the 1960s and 1970s represent a "third disestablishment," in which mainstream churches lost their religious dominance.[4]

These diverse interpretations underscore the fact that the crises of mainstream Protestantism did not appear suddenly and that the developments within one tradition—American Presbyterianism—are mirrored in other denominations as well. While some of our studies reach back into the late nineteenth century, most of our studies focus on the period after the fundamentalist controversy within Presbyterianism during the 1920s and 1930s. For a variety of reasons, that became a watershed for Presbyterians and ushered in the twentieth century.

The value of this substantial Presbyterian case study can be seen from at least two perspectives. First, this research is designed to write a chapter in the history of American religion and culture. It is the story of the attempt of one tradition—its people and its institutions—to respond to the crosscurrents of the twentieth century. Second, it is an attempt to illumine the problems and predicaments of American Presbyterianism so that its members and leaders might better understand the past as a resource for its future direction.

The series title was carefully chosen. Presence is more than passive existence, and it connotes the landmark that we hope these groups of studies provide for comparing the equally important pilgrimages of other mainline Protestant denominations through the past century. Missiologists have characterized the Christian responsibility as one of "profound presence" in the world, patterned on the presence of God in providence, in the incarnation, and in the work of the Holy Spirit. In the words of missionary and theologian John V. Taylor, Christians "stand" in the world in the name of Christ to be "really and totally present in the present."[5]

Has the Presbyterian presence declined into mere existence? Have the commitments of Presbyterians degenerated into lifeless obligations? What forces have informed, transformed, or deformed our distinctive presence within the Christian community and the society? And can changes in Presbyterianism invigorate their continued yearnings to represent Christ in the world today? These are the questions posed in the series.

More than sixty researchers, plus students at Louisville Seminary and generous colleagues in seminaries, colleges, and universities throughout the United States, have cooperated in the research on American Presbyterianism. Many are historians, but others are sociologists, economists, musicians, theologians, pastors, and lay people. What has excited us as a research team was the opportunity of working on a fascinating historical problem with critical implications for the Presbyterian Church and mainstream Protestantism. Animating our work and conversations was the hope that this research might make a difference, that it might help one church and a broader Christian tradition understand the problems more clearly so that their witness might be more faithful. It is with this hope that we issue this series, "The Presbyterian Presence: The Twentieth-Century Experience."

Milton J Coalter
John M. Mulder
Louis B. Weeks

Acknowledgments

The management of the Louisville research project on American Presbyterianism would have been impossible without the assistance of our secretaries—Elna Amaral, Beverly Hourigan, Kem Longino, Jean Newman, Dana Cormack, and Ingrid Tanghe. They took care of a mountain of correspondence and frequent phone calls and kept everything orderly amidst many other responsibilities.

We are also grateful to our colleagues at Louisville Seminary for their encouragement and support, and to the Board of Directors for generously allowing each of us time to carry out the research and planning for this series.

We are equally thankful to the scores of people who have listened to the results of our research and offered helpful suggestions and criticisms that have influenced the final result. The researchers themselves have been a wonderful group of people with whom to work. They have been unfailingly patient with our suggestions for revision and extremely cooperative in meeting deadlines. Others have been generous with their time in reading drafts and offering new insights. The Louisville research project created new friendships, and in the process the researchers became not only a community of scholars but a community of faith as well.

We are also grateful to the staff at Westminster/John Knox Press, especially our editor, Alexa Smith, Editorial Director Davis Perkins, Publisher Robert McIntyre, and Director of Publicity Sally Telford. Their personal interest in this series has encouraged and sustained us.

This project would not have been possible without the financial support of the Lilly Endowment and the creative stimulation provided by Dr. Robert Wood Lynn, Senior Vice President for Religion. Bob retired in mid-1989, but it was his vision that prompted the research on American mainstream Protestantism. For his wise advice, patience, and encouragement we are deeply grateful. He has been and continues to be a perceptive mentor and a discerning critic.

The Louisville research project on American Presbyterianism assumed new dimensions in the fall of 1990 with the establishment of the Louisville Institute for the Study of Protestantism and American Culture. Funded by the Lilly Endowment, the Louisville Institute will plan and stimulate further research and leadership education programs in mainstream Protestantism. We are delighted to be working with Dr. Craig Dykstra, Vice President for Religion at the Lilly Endowment, in creating the Louisville Institute, and with James W. Lewis, the Executive Director of the Louisville Institute. We hope this series, The Presbyterian Presence: The Twentieth-Century Experience, and the Louisville Institute will offer new insights into American religion and provide new perspectives on the renewal of mainstream Protestantism.

Contributors

Scott Brunger teaches economics at Maryville College in Tennessee. He holds a doctorate in economics from the New School for Social Research in New York. The son of a Presbyterian minister working in the international YMCA, he grew up in Hong Kong and Beirut and has served for five years in West Africa as part of a Presbyterian volunteer program. His research interests include the economies of less-developed countries.

D. Scott Cormode is a doctoral candidate in American religious history at Yale University. He is a graduate of the University of California, San Diego, and Fuller Theological Seminary and is a candidate for ordination in the Presbyterian Church (U.S.A.).

Craig Dykstra is the vice president at the Lilly Endowment responsible for its Religion Division. Dykstra was previously Professor of Christian Education at Princeton Theological Seminary and editor of *Theology Today*. He has also taught at Louisville Presbyterian Theological Seminary and was assistant minister at the Westminster Presbyterian Church of Detroit. Dykstra is the author of *Vision and Character*, a book on moral formation, and of a Presbyterian General Assembly study paper entitled, "Growing in the Life of Christian Faith."

Gary S. Eller is pastor of Providence Presbyterian Church in Charlotte, N.C. He holds a Ph.D. from Vanderbilt University and has contributed to several publications, including *The Dictionary of Pastoral Care* and *Life-Span Growth and Development*.

James Hudnut-Beumler is a program associate in Lilly Endowment's Religion Division. Hudnut-Beumler is by training a specialist in the history of American religion and is the author of a number of articles on church-state relations and the social teachings of the Presbyterian Church U.S.A. He is a Presbyterian minister and holds a Ph.D. from Princeton University.

Robin Klay is Associate Professor of Economics at Hope College. She holds degrees from Whitman College and Princeton University, with a Ph.D. in economics. She spent two years in West Africa as part of a teaching and research project sponsored by the University of Michigan. Among her publications are *Counting the Cost: The Economics of Christian Stewardship*.

Joan C. LaFollette is pastor of Immanuel Presbyterian Church in Binghamton, N.Y. She is a graduate of Oberlin College and Harvard Divinity School.

David B. McCarthy is a graduate of Carleton College, Duke University, and Harvard Divinity School. He is pastor of the John Hus Presbyterian Church in Binghamton, N.Y.

Richard W. Reifsnyder is pastor of the First Presbyterian Church of Oyster Bay, N.Y. He is a graduate of Duke University, Yale Divinity School, and Princeton Theological Seminary, where he received a Ph.D. in the history of Christianity.

Dale E. Soden is Associate Professor of History at Whitworth College. He received his Ph.D. in American intellectual history from the University of Washington. He is the author of several articles on American religious history and recently published *A Venture of Mind and Spirit: An Illustrated History of Whitworth College*.

Louis B. Weeks is Dean and Paul Tudor Jones Professor of Church History at Louisville Presbyterian Theological Seminary. He is a codirector of the Louisville research project on American Presbyterianism in the twentieth century. He has written many articles and books on theology and church history, the most recent of which is *The Presbyterian Source: Bible Words That Shape a Faith.*

Lewis L. Wilkins, Jr., is General Presbyter of Palo Duro Presbytery in Texas. He is a graduate of Southwestern at Memphis (now Rhodes College), Austin Presbyterian Theological Seminary, and McCormick Seminary. He did four years of graduate study at the University of Mainz and translated Wolfhart Pannenberg's *Jesus—God and Man.* He has served in several executive positions in the Presbyterian Church and ecumenical organizations.

Introduction

When Presbyterians settled in the American colonies, most assumed that it would be desirable and even possible to re-create a state church modeled after the Church of Scotland or other Reformed churches in Europe. This ideal embodied the union of church and state—the formal recognition of one church as the church of the land. Like colonists of other religious persuasions, they eventually recognized that Old World patterns could not be repeated in the New World. What emerged was a presbyterian system of government, organized first in congregations, then in presbyteries, then in synods, and finally in a General Assembly in 1789.

What also emerged was the separation of church and state and a new form of the church—the denomination. This development marks the most significant change in the nature of the church since the age of Constantine. The "denomination" was not understood as the only true church because conscientious Christians could in fact differ in their understandings of various nonessential aspects of the Christian faith and still be Christian.[1]

The American soil proved fertile for the blossoming of churches transplanted from Europe as denominations and new churches indigenous to American culture. To some observers in the twentieth century like H. Richard Niebuhr, the denominational pattern represented a moral failure of Christianity. First, the denominations fractured the unity of the body of Christ, and second, the divisions were often rooted in race, class, ethnicity, geography, or nationalism.[2] Others, however, have emphasized the vibrancy of faith that denominations have brought to American religious life and their contributions to a common ecumenical mission.[3]

The study of American religion has long relied on the idea of denominations as a way of organizing the religious pluralism of American culture. Denominational studies, such as this one, have provided insight into the dynamics of a particular tradition and the opportunity for comparison with other churches. Notably absent, however, is sustained attention to denominations *as organizations* and their puzzling varieties.[4] Some examples: Despite a hierarchical church polity, American Catholics have virtually no national structures of any significant size or power. American Presbyterians have retained the same basic polity since the founding of the General Assembly more than two hundred years ago, but church organization and mission have changed significantly. Religion receives nearly half of all money contributed to charitable causes in the United States; in 1989, individuals gave religious organizations more than $54 billion.[5] Yet there is not a single adequate study of the history of church finances in America.

The essays in this volume are a modest beginning toward addressing the organizational aspect of American religious history. While they are only beginnings, they point toward a tentative but very significant conclusion. The Presbyterian Church has been undergoing an organizational revolution. The roots of this revolution seem to have preceded the dramatic decline in membership that began in the mid-1960s. The revolution is closely related to the transformation of other mainstream Protestant church organizations and American religious institutions in general. It also coincides with dramatic alterations in the organization of other institutions in American culture.[6]

Louis Weeks's essay, "The Incorporation of the Presbyterians," sets the stage for the rise of the twentieth-century denomination. During the late nineteenth and early twentieth centuries, Weeks argues, American Presbyterians adopted the imagery, structures, and practices of the modern business corporation and applied them to the organization of the Presbyterian Church as a denomination. The impulse for doing so was part of the broader "search for order" in American social, economic, and political life that characterized the progressive period in American history.[7] Many Presbyterians were part of the restructuring of American economic organizations into modern corporations, and their middle- and upper-class economic status made them likely participants in the reshaping of American institutions as corporations. Consequently it is scarcely surprising that the values and ideals of the modern corporation exerted a profound influence on the Presbyterian Church as it "incorporated."

Weeks's essay demonstrates the far-reaching examples of how the Presbyterian Church was changed by adopting the model of a corporation for organizing its life. Loosely knit and quasi-independent mission groups and agencies were finally united in one denominational structure with defined areas of responsibility and lines of authority. The primary administrative officer of the church, the Stated Clerk, moved from part-time to full-time employment with a staff. "Efficiency" and "businesslike methods" were the rallying cries of the early twentieth-century leaders who sought to bring the corporation to the church. "Experts" appeared for specialized tasks; "departments" emerged with "directors" or "managers" responsible for effective and efficient administration.

The process of incorporation also affected congregations in both dramatic and subtle ways. The pastor became less the spiritual guide and director of a flock and more the manager or supervisor of congregational employees—sextons, secretaries, and staff for specialized ministries. Even the terminology for physical space changed. The "pastor's study," used for the preparation of sermons, retained its name but also became the "pastor's office," the place where the congregation's "business" was managed. The session increasingly assumed the role of a board of directors; the Sunday school became hierarchical, with a bureaucracy for administration.

The examples could be multiplied, but the result has been dramatic and overwhelming. The church became a corporation, and the implications have been both positive and negative. On the one hand, Weeks argues, the incorporation of the church did make it more efficient and effective in carrying out mission to the world, in ecumenical relations, and in programs of nurture and education. On the other hand, incorporation bred the alienation so noteworthy in corporate economic life, encouraged a preoccupation with structures rather than mission, and fostered a fragmentation of the church's identity. Weeks concludes that the "incorporation" of American Presbyterianism tied the church to a broader cultural pattern. As corporate structures thrived or suffered, so went the Presbyterian Church.

While Weeks argues for the ascendance of a corporate ideal in twentieth-century American Presbyterianism, Richard Reifsnyder shows that different forms or models of a corporation shaped the organizational character of the church as a denomination. The Presbyterian Church in the U.S. (PCUS) developed somewhat differently from the Presbyterian Church in the U.S.A. (PCUSA) and The United Presbyterian Church in the U.S.A. (UPCUSA). Reifsnyder argues that the differences, rooted in theological principles and influenced by cultural factors, are less striking than the similarities.

The first chapter in this transformation occurred in the 1920s, when "national bureaucracies" appeared. In the PCUSA the plan was largely formulated by a lay administrator, Robert E. Speer. He proposed four boards, for Christian education, national mission, global mission, and ministerial support, coordinated by a general council. The Stated Clerk's office was also given broad latitude and greater responsibilities. In its distrust of national agencies, the PCUS adopted this model less completely and more slowly, but by the 1950s the PCUS agencies were very similar to those of the PCUSA.

The 1960s and 1970s brought a "managerial revolution" to the organization of American Presbyterianism. Theories of business management, previously only implicit in the formation of the national bureaucracy, were explicitly used in the sixties and seventies. Reacting to what was perceived as the independence and autonomy of the national boards, Presbyterians attempted to decentralize the administration of the church and redistribute decision-making power. The reunion of the two main branches of American Presbyterianism in 1983 brought yet another round of restructuring, based largely on the values that shaped the reorganizations of the 1970s. Reifsnyder's insightful chronicle of these organizational efforts demonstrates their significance in determining not only how Presbyterians conducted their mission but what they decided their mission was.

While Reifsnyder focuses on the organization of the General Assembly, Lewis Wilkins changes the lens to examine the presbytery, the distinctive feature of Presbyterian government. Colonial Presbyterians imported the model of the presbytery from the Church of Scotland, with two functions. One was liturgical—the ordination of ministers. The other was governmental—the organizing and ordering of congregational life. Wilkins argues that an open frontier transformed the presbytery into an agency of mission. Throughout the nineteenth century the presbytery retained its first two purposes but added a crucial third purpose—evangelizing the American people and bringing them into the Presbyterian Church as members.

The division of American Presbyterianism spawned by the Civil War created two types of presbyteries in the late nineteenth and early twentieth centuries. Southern presbyteries became what Wilkins calls "Home Missions Presbyteries," with powerful boards; presbyteries in the PCUSA were weaker organizations, staffed by national administrators who coordinated national programs. Both patterns were dramatically affected by the social turmoil of the post–World War II era. The mission of the presbytery became less a matter of extending Presbyterian membership in the West and more a task of ministering to the inner cities of America and reaching out to racial ethnic minority groups. The image of the frontier was transformed from the American West to the cities. The presbytery's mission moved away from "settlers" to suburbanites and those affected by urban and ghetto blight.

The redefinition of the frontier produced new organizational forms for presbyteries—the "Congregational Mission Support Presbytery" with a relatively small staff designed to meet the needs of congregations and the "Comprehensive Program Presbytery" with a large staff capable of administering a wide-ranging agenda of mission concerns. Reorganizations in the 1970s strengthened the role of presbyteries, but both patterns failed to address an erosion of clarity about the concept of mission itself. Nothing seemed to replace the powerful nineteenth-century images of the frontier and evangelization that had inspired the mission of presbyteries before the mid-twentieth century.

Wilkins concludes, "The era of the American evangelical denomination as a connected, coherent, and potent mission enterprise is over. . . . A generation of efforts since World War II to find surrogate frontiers to pull the denominational mission wagon have failed." Wilkins suggests that Presbyterians reject efforts to find yet another frontier and proposes that the church recover the "parish" concept of a presbytery, based on a geographical area and the image of the "settled church." The presbytery and its congregations would attempt to embody all the marks of the church and to participate with other areas of the church in cooperative forms of mission and ministry.

The organizational revolution in twentieth-century American Presbyterianism can also be traced in the denomination's financial history. In comparison with other Western cultures, American philanthropy stands out as one of the distinctive features of American society.[8] Religious freedom in the United States brought with it not only the freedom to join the church but a unique method of funding the church's mission—freewill offerings. Yet why church members give, what they support, and how money is managed and allocated are subjects that are inadequately studied and understood.

The essays by Scott Brunger, Robin Klay, and D. Scott Cormode clear away some of the mystery surrounding Presbyterian benevolences, and their findings demonstrate the tremendous change that has swept through American Presbyterianism in the twentieth century.

In their essay on Presbyterian giving since the 1920s, Brunger and Klay conclude that fluctuations in the American economy are critical in determining how much money Presbyterians will give to their church. Increases in per capita income generate more donations. Inflation causes donations to suffer. Membership increases bring more dollars for denominational mission, and declines have a negative effect. Interestingly, however, changes in American business cycles seem to have little effect on contributions.

Theological controversies apparently have little effect on how much Presbyterians choose to give to the church. But Brunger and Klay do suggest that controversies may play a role in how money is allocated. In separate essays they analyze the dramatic redistribution of funds in the PCUSA/UPCUSA and the PCUS during the twentieth century.

Klay shows in her paper on the PCUS that the first blow to the financing of Presbyterian mission came during the Great Depression. Real (that is, inflation-adjusted) total contributions fell by 36 percent, and benevolences suffered even more, falling by 49 percent. Although real contributions in the PCUS eventually exceeded the levels of the 1920s, benevolences never recovered from the Great Depression, falling from 35 percent of contributions in 1928 to 25 percent in 1950–1967 to 20 percent by the 1980s. Despite growing strength among PCUS General Assembly agencies prior to the 1970s and then the reorganization of the church's mission to the regional level, the long-term pattern of PCUS benevolences since the Depression reveals a steady decline in allocating funds beyond the congregation.

Klay's explanation focuses on the disenchantment of Americans with "large and remote bureaucracies," but adds a distinctive twist based on PCUS history and Southern culture. She argues that the debates over allocations at the General Assembly level finally took their toll in the 1950s. If PCUS members could not be confident that their money would be used by the General Assembly as they designated, they would allocate their money in different ways. In the 1960s, membership began to decline, and in the 1970s the church shifted program and budget away from the General Assembly to synods and presbyteries. The cumulative effect of these developments severely weakened General Assembly agencies and their capacity to carry out mission. Klay emphasizes the role of regionalism in the South and the desire for local control in explaining why priorities shifted away from the General Assembly to local causes.

Brunger's analysis of the PCUSA and UPCUSA confirms the same decline in support for General Assembly causes and increases in support for synods and presbyteries, congregational expenses, and designated causes. The change in the PCUSA/UPCUSA has been even more dramatic because it had a much stronger tradition of unified budgets and nationally organized mission. For example, in 1963 the UPCUSA allocated $10.9 million for synod and presbytery mission and $29.9 million for General Assembly mission causes. Twenty years later, in 1983, synod and presbytery mission had more than tripled to $36.5 million, while giving to General Assembly causes actually declined to $24.7 million.[9] The reorganization of the UPCUSA, which shifted power to presbyteries and synods, exacerbated the trend.

Brunger's explanation of this change lies not in regionalism but in a series of factors. Dissatisfaction with General Assembly priorities, especially administrative expenses, may have played a role in the decline, but Brunger finds no way of correlating decline in funding with controversies over social action. Reorganizations have a negative effect on General Assembly giving. Membership decline has affected General Assembly support, but Presbyterians have become increasingly generous, partially offsetting the impact of the decline. Brunger also suggests that increasing congregational expenses for salaries and benefits, program, and utilities are also part of the explanation.

The seismic shift in Presbyterian finances began as early as the Great Depression, but took an even more dramatic turn in the 1950s. Congregations began to allocate their money in different ways, and here D. Scott Cormode's analysis of congregational finances since World War II is particularly helpful. Combining figures for both the PCUS and the PCUSA/UPCUSA, Cormode concludes that there are three distinct periods of change. From 1950 to 1965, despite inflation, congregational receipts grew steadily. From 1965 to 1980, a period of very high inflation, congregational receipts remained basically the same. From 1980 to the present, congregational receipts returned to a pattern of significant growth.

Cormode also notes the shifting priorities of congregations as they reduced support for General Assembly causes and diverted funds to local causes and congregational needs. He tests three hypotheses to explain the change: controversies over social action (the Angela Davis case), redistribution (the decentralization of administration), and increasing pastoral compensation. None of these, he concludes, explains why congregations have reduced support for General Assembly causes.

The answer, he proposes, lies in the complexities of local ecclesiastical factors and in a broader process of alienation from institutions that are seen as distant and remote. As the concept of Presbyterian mission became more variegated and unfocused, Cormode maintains, congregations became uncertain about the direction of the denomination and less likely to support its General Assembly causes. In contrast, the mission of the congregation triumphed at the Assembly's expense, as did appeals for specific causes and organizations with clearly defined goals and affinities to congregations.

These financial studies of the organizational revolution in American Presbyterianism confirm other research on the declining power of denominationalism.[10] These studies reveal that members overwhelmingly identify themselves with congregations, not denominations. Furthermore, congregations increasingly behave as mini-denominations— charting their own courses independently of denominational programs and priorities and establishing their own mission causes. The voluntaristic principle, which was long checked by the twentieth-century denomination, now appears not only when people choose to become members but also in how congregations spend their resources. Whether Christian mission itself has been weakened is a fascinating question, but it is certain the church's *denominational* mission has been radically altered.

One of the characteristics of American denominationalism has been the phenomenon of organizations formed for special purposes. These organizations are sometimes within the formal structure of the denomination, or independent but closely related to the denomination. Historically women's organizations have been the most powerful and resilient of these groups, and Joan LaFollette traces the uneasy relationship between women's organizations and the Presbyterian denominations during the twentieth century.

Women have comprised the majority of church membership in America since at least the early eighteenth century, but their participation in the government of churches has been severely restricted until the twentieth century and the rise of the modern women's movement. In the PCUSA, the denomination approved the ordination of women as elders in 1930 and as ministers in 1956. In the PCUS the decision to ordain women as elders and ministers came in 1964.

In the face of this delayed acceptance of women's participation in the life of the church, women in many Protestant denominations organized during the early nineteenth century separate societies for study, prayer, fellowship, and mission. Presbyterian women were no exception. The enduring dilemma for them and for the Presbyterian denominations was their status. Should they be fully a part of the church, or should they remain separate and retain their independence?

The dilemma was real because of the numerical and financial strength of the women's organizations, and it was viewed differently by the women who supported their own organizations and the men who controlled the denomination. For example, in 1890 in the PCUSA women gave more to home missions than all the congregations combined. In 1912 gifts from PCUS women paid for half of the entire debt of the foreign missions program. Men feared that such generosity would bring calls for power and control, and it did.

Although the chronology differs in the PCUSA/ UPCUSA and the PCUS, the history of women's organizations is remarkably similar. The first step was formal recognition as an independent organization, followed eventually by separate incorporation. After a relatively short period of autonomy, the women's organizations were once again subsumed under the authority of the denominations. At every stage the women continued to give generously, and at least in the PCUSA/UPCUSA much of their giving remained unrestricted and supported the overall mission of the denomination. Yet cries were still heard that women's contributions drained money from congregational budgets and the denomination's overall support.

LaFollette notes that women's giving in both the PCUS/ UPCUSA and the PCUS has never recovered from the impact of the Great Depression, and support from women has fallen as a percentage of total giving since the 1930s. She also expresses concern about the increasing age of women involved in the Presbyterian women's organizations and the challenges posed by women's changing roles in society. Yet she concludes that these groups, which have exercised significant power against entrenched opposition, will endure and flourish in new ways.

Dale Soden's essay paints a very different picture of Presbyterian men's organizations during the twentieth century. Noting that historians have neglected the study of men's organizations even more than of women's groups, Soden shows how the men's movement ebbed and flowed in vitality and popularity in this century. Its shifting fortunes demonstrate, he argues, the flaws of the movement and illuminate the larger story of mainstream Protestantism in American culture.

The century opened for men's organizations with promise and vitality. Presbyterian men could and did draw on significant financial and human resources. Thousands attended national and regional meetings, and their speakers were prominent men of the day—Theodore Roosevelt, Woodrow Wilson, William Jennings Bryan, William H. Taft, and others. They flocked together for inspiration and commitment to mission, both foreign and domestic. Soden argues that the reforming instincts of a moderate social gospel appealed to Presbyterian men of the early twentieth century, and as long as the social gospel's heady optimism prevailed, the men's organizations thrived.

World War I and the decade of the twenties sent these organizations into decline until after World War II, when they recovered amidst the postwar "religious revival." Their renewal, Soden maintains, represents the infusion of a sense of mission fueled by the rhetoric of the Cold War and American civil religion. Men rallied to the cause of the church because of its calling to resist communism and protect democracy. The ethos of the 1950s seemed to encourage a cultural consensus about American society and the need for religion, but when this consensus came under attack in the 1960s, men's organizations again withered and nearly disappeared. Soden concludes that Presbyterian men's organizations flourished when American culture was relatively stable and when they were able to identify with the prevailing cultural ethos. When the cultural ethos became fragmented and even turned hostile to the church and religious values, men's organizations declined. The price of identification with the culture and the power of

American society in shaping the church were part of the fabric of mainstream Protestantism's experience in the twentieth century. The history of Presbyterian men's organizations tells that story in microcosm.

Besides women's and men's organizations, mainstream Protestant denominations have become increasingly aware of the influence of other special-purpose organizations. Their predecessors were the benevolent societies, such as the American Bible Society, formed in the early nineteenth century for special mission causes. As part of the incorporation of American Presbyterianism, the PCUSA formally recognized these groups in a section of the church's constitution, approved in 1902. Gary Eller's essay illuminates how these organizations have reflected the conservative/liberal split in American Presbyterianism and have increasingly affected the denomination itself.

Eller argues that the special-purpose or special-interest groups have flourished and multiplied in the wake of debate and dissension since World War II. Some of the groups are organized for spiritual renewal and growth, but many more have specific political agendas, ranging from conservative to liberal issues. Eller demonstrates that these groups frequently exert an influence on the denomination far out of proportion to the size of their membership because of their skills in organization and lobbying. In one light, they are in-house critics and reformers; in another, they are disruptive forces, sapping the energy of the denomination and fragmenting its unity and mission.

The exploding number of special-purpose groups is a reflection of the diversity and pluralism of American Presbyterians and other mainstream Protestant denominations. They also exemplify the heightened political sensitivity of American Protestants and the phenomenon of single-issue politics which characterizes the American political landscape.[11] In 1990 the General Assembly of the Presbyterian Church (U.S.A.) voted to recommend to the presbyteries a constitutional change that would eliminate denominational recognition of such groups, but their role and influence, regardless of their legal status, will undoubtedly

endure as long as the denomination itself remains in conflict over its priorities. In dealing with these groups, the
denomination confronts a difficult dilemma of trying to
maintain the allegiance and support of dissenting groups
while also forging a common sense of direction. The 1990
action suggests that the denomination may have recognized its inability to control the special-purpose organizations along with its desire not to lose their voices.

A prevailing theme of this volume of essays has been the
nature of the church as an organization and the changing
character of political power in a denomination. As part of
the Reformed tradition, Presbyterians have affirmed that
the church is not only an organization that orders the life
of the people of God but also one that is bound together by
a common confession of faith. Until the mid-twentieth
century, the Westminster Standards served as that common confessional and doctrinal basis for American Presbyterians. At the same time, Presbyterian history has been
marked by lively debates about the meaning of Westminster and the degree to which its doctrines are binding on
the church.

As other essays in this series make clear, Presbyterian
theology in the twentieth century gradually became more
pluralistic in responding to changes in the Christian
church, American culture, and the world.[12] David B. Mc-
Carthy's essay maintains that the embrace of pluralism has
meant that polity, rather than theology, has emerged as the
basis for Presbyterian unity.

McCarthy's argument is based on an analysis of several
decisions by the permanent judicial commissions of the
UPCUSA and the PCUS during the 1970s and 1980s. In
three of these cases, he argues that the denomination in
effect sidestepped theological issues and resolved disputes
by relying on the church's polity. In two other cases, the
denomination reaffirmed theological principles over those
of polity. In short, McCarthy suggests, the Presbyterian
Church (U.S.A.) is still ambivalent about the role of theology and the church's confessions in determining its identity, but when conflict arises, issues tend to be resolved on

the grounds of polity and procedure. McCarthy recognizes that there are significant theological issues undergirding Presbyterian polity, including order, equality, and accountability. He concludes that "in an era of increasing theological pluralism and growing ecumenical relationships with other churches, the enduring contribution of the Presbyterian Church may well lie in its polity."

McCarthy's assessment suggests a further transformation and truncation of American Presbyterianism as a denomination. Wilkins argued that the functions of the colonial presbytery were liturgical and legislative, and the goal of mission was added in the nineteenth century. If the denomination's mission and theology are both severely fragmented, the only remaining functions of a denomination as an organization in the late twentieth century are legislative and judicial in nature.

Craig Dykstra and James Hudnut-Beumler suggest just such a conclusion by offering in the final essay a set of metaphors, each of which epitomizes a significant stage in the organizational metamorphosis of Protestant denominations in American history. Dykstra and Hudnut-Beumler propose that in the early national period, denominational governance resembled the constitutional confederacy being developed in the larger political system of the new United States. Although a national framework for coordinating interchange was created in both churches and the state during this era, the absence of national programmatic agencies and bureaucracy left much to be decided by local option.

During the late nineteenth and early twentieth centuries, this arrangement was transformed by a new working model, that of the corporation. In an age of "trusts, collectives, and, above all, vertically integrated corporations," denominations followed a parallel course of bureaucratization, consolidation, and rationalization of time, personnel, and resources. But in the process, the function of the denomination changed dramatically. Now, like corporations, the business of denominations became the provision of goods and services such as Sunday school curricula, publications, and organized methods of financial pledging.

In recent decades, particularly since 1960, denominations built in the corporate image changed their line of products and services based on new understandings of the Christian gospel and the world situation. Congregational consumers were frequently dissatisfied with the resulting "new and improved" offerings, and, to compound the problem, membership dropped at about the same time. Drooping support led to cuts in the number of goods offered, which in turn provided the opportunity for a range of ecclesiastical "cottage industries" to enter the market of church programs and training where denominations had formerly dominated.

Facing dwindling resources and rising competition from nondenominational entities of such different sorts as the Alban Institute, the Pony Express stewardship program, the Religious Coalition for Abortion Rights, and twelve-step, Jungian, or spiritual formation groups, denominations adapted by following the pattern of modern-day regulatory agencies. Rather than services and goods, now rules, policies, and procedures threatened to predominate.

Dykstra and Hudnut-Beumler caution that the contemporary regulatory trend may hold more menace for the denominational regulators than for those being regulated. They acknowledge that declining funds and personnel, alongside obstinate opposition to well-grounded gospel imperatives, make regulation appear more attractive and time-efficient than the labor-intensive efforts of educating and persuading the membership. But however well-intentioned, regulation invariably carries the explosive element of coercion, which is both contrary to the very discipleship the gospel intended and often a trigger for a negative reaction of potentially destructive force.

The conclusions drawn in the essays by McCarthy and by Dykstra and Hudnut-Beumler certainly have profound and troubling implications for the future of denominations like the Presbyterian Church (U.S.A.). Nevertheless, there are heartening countersigns that balance their disturbing assessments. In 1990, for instance, the Presbyterian General Assembly did approve a new "Brief Statement of

Faith," evidence that there are in fact grounds for a common affirmation of the church's theology. Furthermore, this volume's essays on the Presbyterian denominations in the twentieth century demonstrate the remarkable flexibility and the adaptability of these institutions to new challenges and demands such as we face today.

If these studies of Presbyterian churches as organizations are applicable to other Protestant denominations, then the conclusion remains: The American denomination is undergoing an organizational revolution. What once was a highly effective bureaucracy capable of delivering goods and services to congregations and mobilizing support for mission domestically and globally is now severely weakened and fragmented. And yet, the denomination as an organization will not disappear: given the complexities of American society and the diversity of American religious life, the denomination would have to be reinvented.

This volume should not be read with nostalgia for the days that are gone but with anticipation of what lies ahead. It is impossible to predict the outcome of a revolution in midcourse. The future of the denomination as an organization is unclear, much like the future of other institutions in the current metamorphosis of American society. But given current trends, the denomination must be and is being transformed. In the maelstrom of change and fluidity, the temptation to long wistfully for days gone by will be strong. But the transformation should also be the occasion for seeing new opportunities and challenges. The peculiar genius of the American denominations and the Christians who have sustained them has always been their ability to adapt structures to the leading of the Holy Spirit and the changing needs of the world.

1

The Incorporation
of the Presbyterians

Louis B. Weeks

Presbyterian denominations and congregations changed thoroughly when captured by societal forces of "incorporation" in the United States during the last part of the nineteenth century and the early decades of the twentieth. Because of their patterns of governing at several levels in overlapping responsibilities, their propensity for focusing on structures and complex connections, and their special place in the demography of American life, Presbyterian churches seem to have been especially susceptible to the process, which also radically affected other American denominations.[1]

It seems ironic that the Presbyterians embraced the principalities of incorporation so pervasively, because they already perceived themselves as a "body" by theological and institutional self-definition. Not only did they proclaim themselves a part of "the body of Christ," but they fashioned a pattern of representative and shared leadership which permitted a sense of "ownership" of the communion on the part of many members of the body.[2] Reformed theology, emphasizing God's sovereignty over all matters, meant that final ownership and direction of the church belonged to no human being. Moreover, the offices of "ruling elder" and "teaching elder" defined leadership in terms of function more than in terms of hierarchy or control.[3] God's gifts, according to tenets of the faith, extended to all people. In sum, Presbyterians for the most part held an organic ecclesiology.

Although it may have been ironic that the social forces of "incorporation" exercised such influence among the Presbyterians, it should not be surprising. The Christian church, including all its various branches, has been consistently susceptible to the influences forming or changing a culture. Scholars claim this adaptability has been extremely important in the rise and spread of Christianity. In the American environment Protestants formed voluntary associations, attracting people individually and by family groups.[4] This environment actually shaped "denominations" even during the colonial period; and Presbyterians, it has been shown, pioneered in the forming of a communion that existed as neither a "state church" nor a "dissenting" church body.[5] Thus, as the United States experienced industrialization and the consequent growing complexity of economic and cultural patterns, the denominations were affected by those same forces. They naturally became what came to be termed "nonprofit corporations," subject to the limitations and problems of such organizations but reaping the benefits as well.

This essay explores the process of the movement toward "incorporation" on the part of the Presbyterians, both in microcosm and in macrocosm. It considers both congregations and denominations, drawing conclusions on the basis of other historical data.[6] The essay also offers opinions on the meaning of "incorporation" today among the Presbyterians. Perhaps this preliminary effort may spur other thought about the implications of "incorporation" among Presbyterians and other denominations, as well as ways to mitigate its negative effects.

The Rise of the Corporation

The power of the process of bureaucratization has long been recognized as significant in Western societies during the period of industrialization.[7] More recently, though, scholars have pointed to the development of the "corporation" itself as an influential component in modern life.[8] In America after the Civil War, extended families as centers of meaning and their "island communities" gave way to a wider "search for order."[9] Bureaucracies emerged along with other trends of the time, such as compartmentalized urban life and the beginning of industrial centers. With bureaucracies came new values. For example, business-related values such as "healthy competition," efficiency, and regularity replaced traditional values such as familial continuity.

In business, single-unit enterprises gave way to the modern, complex, hierarchical enterprise of the present century.[10] The concept and the reality of the "manager" emerged, especially that of the "middle manager," who coordinated a portion of the business in a particular place or provided oversight of a distinct stage of production or distribution. Managers came to be linked with others in similar functions and those of equal rank in the same company, and American economic life came to be governed by corporate systems.[11]

According to several scholars, especially Alan Trachtenberg, who has used literature as well as history to demonstrate his thesis, the image and the reality of the "corporation" as an entity seized the imagination of Americans during the last decades of the nineteenth century. The image and the effects permeated not only the nation's economic life, but also its cultural and political life. A tightly structured society emerged, with what one scholar has termed "hierarchies of control" operating in many spheres of activity.[12]

For example, the idea of ownership changed in subtle ways. The corporation was dominated by two minorities: the company was owned by stockholders, who were a minority in society; and a few executive managers exercised practical ownership, with authority to control workers, investments, and many other aspects of corporate life. Real participation in directing the company belonged usually to only a few "directors" among the board, and alleged alternative influences such as stockholder votes usually proved a fiction.[13]

Privatization of the purpose and identity of the corporation was largely a new phenomenon. Before the Civil War, corporations had been regarded as public, or at least quasi-public, economic entities, existing in behalf of the common welfare. As the process of incorporation evolved, this "mixed enterprise" increasingly became a "private enterprise," and the legislatures of governments sought only general control over the kinds of activities undertaken by them. By the turn of the twentieth century, a majority of businesses had still not made the transition to become corporations, but a "successful elite" had thoroughly adapted.[14]

At the same time, an elitism evolved in American cultural and economic realms. Arts and industries that had flourished in small-town environments among the people became specialized in the burgeoning cities. Many Americans, rich and poor, agreed that fine arts and other kinds of cultural emphases represented a higher sphere of life, not of interest to or necessary for lower classes. Some scholars also speak of a concurrent, growing feminization in cultural movements that coincided with that elitism. Sports, on the other hand, even at a professional level, grew to accommodate the interests of people not included in the cultural elite, especially "working men."[15] Middle- and upper-class Americans distinguished themselves from the masses more thoroughly than in previous eras. Aggravation between labor and the growing number of capitalists increased. Whereas "unions" at least communicated something of human solidarity and equality, "corporations" by their very existence demonstrated unequal authority, responsibilities, and rewards. Neighborhoods evolved in towns and cities as a reinforcing influence to separate and define people by rank and class.[16]

These cultural and economic forces did produce for many, perhaps most, people an increasing sense of alienation from the institutions that previously had provided participation, if not a portion of human identity itself. Adversarial relationships in the urban, complex, industrial, "corporate" environment meant that workers felt (and indeed were) often left out of most decisions and ownership. Of course, most managers felt left out as well, though they may have shared a bit in the process of decision making. Even stockholders who were not among the board of directors felt removed from control, and those on the board who were not on executive committees felt somewhat powerless.[17] A sense of alienation also grew concerning political participation, cultural decisions, ownership of the sports teams, and a wide range of other components of American life.[18]

All these forces operated on religious organizations. The ethos of worship and church participation changed. The Presbyterians in many congregations and even throughout many communities were also some of the same people who formed the cultural elite, the emergent "class" of managers and capitalists that controlled the wealth of corporations.[19] Interlocking leadership that marked other institutions also characterized the churches. In fact, given the voluntary environment of American religious institutions, cultural tendencies might even have been exaggerated among denominations. "Working people" felt increasingly alienated from the Presbyterian Church in particular, and from Protestantism in general.[20]

A sense of alienation from religious institutions accompanied other forces at work during the period. As organization increased among the Presbyterians, efficiency became a prized value. The hierarchies of control increased, techniques from corporate management were applied wholesale, and the very nature of a denomination changed, both for better and for worse. The "captains of industry"— John Wanamaker, Andrew Carnegie, Cleveland Dodge, and other corporate giants—were involved in the mutations. Thousands of Presbyterians who were or became "middle managers," professional people who shared corporate ideals and were perceived by others to share power with the giants, played a significant part in the change.

Poor but aspiring people who became Presbyterians, and even those who chose to dissociate themselves from the Presbyterian churches—all participated in the "incorporation" of the Presbyterians.[21]

The Presbyterian Patterns of Incorporation

How thoroughly did the Presbyterians "incorporate" themselves during this period? It is extremely difficult to answer this question, for many currents affected all the churches. For example, in the Presbyterian Church in the U.S.A. the Office of the Stated Clerk changed from a part-time position as late as 1890 to a full-time one. By 1910 the office included several secretaries and some other "professionals" on a part-time basis. The Stated Clerk himself, William Henry Roberts, became during that period an "expert" in both "travel efficiency" and legal matters affecting denominations.[22] Record-keeping multiplied, and reports from an increasing number of agencies became more complex as well, all in the name of efficiency and evangelism.[23]

In the same period, the PCUSA thoroughly organized the Sunday schools, the Foreign and Home Missions programs, the Women's and the Men's programs, the "Systematic Benevolence," and many other enterprises.[24] Several major public issues received the considered attention of the Presbyterians through the work of specific committees, special and sometimes permanent in nature. New "departments" mushroomed—for example, in immigration and social service. To name concurrent events and processes does not prove they were connected. But all these had in common characteristics of tighter organization, developing hierarchies, multiplication of "offices" and "officers," stringent controls of prospective funding, and other hallmarks of incorporation.[25]

These Presbyterians had already been well organized at the time of the reunion of Old and New Schools in 1869, but during the late nineteenth and early twentieth centuries they began to use the methods and structures of

American "corporations." Their innocence in using the language of the corporations, and of American business more generally, now seems quaint and amusing. But when members of the Committee of Benevolence and Finance advertised their work as attractive to "men of influence," they were not joking. The committee sought business leaders "of acknowledged skill" to comprise its membership.[26] There are explicit references to the wisdom of having boards and agencies in "friendly competition" for the allegiance of Presbyterians.[27]

The terms comprising a "vocabulary of incorporation" had already existed in the English language. But words such as "efficiency," "department," and "expert" took on new meanings during this time. Those responsible for offices at the Assembly level (Roberts, for example) became the "experts." Seldom were ministers termed "experts" on anything. "Expert" took on a patina of science, as did the word "efficiency." Soon books and articles on "Efficient Ministry," "The Efficiency of the Congregation," and even "Efficient Preaching" gained currency among Presbyterians.[28] As early as 1871, the Board of Education of the PCUSA employed mechanical analogies unabashedly to speak of its plan for educating scholars in Sunday schools:

> *Sources of Efficiency of the Plan.* We can speak of the powerful engine of a great mill. What does it mean? That the pipes, and wheels, and beams have any inherent energy? No? But that they are suitable in their adaptation as to form and strength, for the exertion of power through them. . . . What, corresponding to these, does the Church's plan of education need?[29]

Answers to its question included the power of the Holy Spirit and the "Hearty Interest of the Membership," among other things. Though this language proved more crass than most, it characterized much of the conversation and even the later advertising copy for the church.

The PCUSA, according to Richard Reifsnyder, offers the most thorough example of a Reformed denomination's succumbing to the vocabulary and referents of a corporate culture. The other two major Presbyterian bodies seem to have experienced similar tendencies. They lagged in instituting "corporate" measures from want of resources, not from a lack of will to do so.[30]

Fascinating, and less well explored, is the same process that prevailed among congregations of Presbyterians at the same time. Pastors, for example, became supervisors in new and different ways. They had long supervised the administration of church discipline, a practice in which the session or other governing body sat as a court to judge the merits of complaints against members for grossly sinful behavior. Discipline of members almost ceased during this period. Instead, pastors began to exercise supervision of sextons, secretaries, organists, and choir directors, and sometimes associate ministers and/or directors of education.[31] Those congregations that could not afford to pay people in those capacities sought volunteers to occupy the positions (or else seemed to feel guilty for not having them).

The "pastor's study," historically a kind of retreat for reading and for preparing sermons, may have retained its name, but it came to function as an "office," a place for gathering meetings, seeing people in crisis, and scheduling programs.

In common parlance of Presbyterians, the "ruling elder" came to mean a person in business or in one of the major professions, instead of the paterfamilias, the father or head of an extended family, as previously. Generally elders ceased making periodic visits among the congregation of Presbyterians to test morality or theology.[32] Among many, if not most Presbyterian congregations, they came to function as a "board of directors" for the "corporation."

The organization of the Sunday school in Presbyterian congregations took on the character of the corporation as well. A superintendent oversaw the various parts of the organization—including the "Beginners," "Primary," "Intermediates," "Seniors," and usually several other "departments," each with its own superintendent, teachers, substitutes, and officers among the members. "Assemblies" would be followed by classes, and recognition for attendance, learning, money given, and various activities took place in a regular, hierarchical fashion.[33]

The Sunday school movement, and the early institutions that supported it, began as para-church organizations. A host of such structures grew to offer training and sustenance for Presbyterians and others involved. Not only did the American Sabbath School Union offer conferences and other resources in systematic fashion after its rejuvenation in the 1870s, but it also spurred a national and then an international Primary School Union specializing in the Christian education of younger children. A Chautauqua Institution sprang up, with enormous influence not only at its Jamestown, New York, location, but throughout the country. For young Presbyterians, Societies of Christian Endeavor provided inspirational, service-oriented evangelicalism. These and many more associations, unions, and institutions existed to serve mainstream Protestantism, and Presbyterians exercised highly visible leadership in almost every case.[34]

Women's and men's organizations also contained highly structured, tightly controlled units. In "efficient" congregations, the boards of deacons and elders were likewise organized into a number of committees with chairs and secretaries and such.[35]

The marked "successes" of revivalist Dwight L. Moody, together with those of a host of lesser lights, also demonstrated the influences of the American ethos of tighter structures, hierarchies of control, and other elements of incorporation. "Scientifically" designed "tabernacles" usually held the special services, following carefully planned organization of the religious community that would hold the revival.[36] Nearby communities contracted for special trains to carry the faithful to the meetings, sometimes designated by special segments of society—men, women, youth, "workingmen," Black people, and so on. Subsequent congregational revivals carried on the spirit of

enthusiasm engendered in the mass meetings. The Presbyterian denominations cooperated with, even depended on,
these para-church organizations for enlistment of new
members as well as for energizing present members.[37]

Another area of immense change and radical restructure
can be found in the music of the Presbyterian churches.
Informal singing gave way during this period to the hiring
of directors of music in congregations that could afford
them. To contract with professional singers for services—
usually a quartet of voices, two male, two female—became
fashionable. Quartets, professional and/or volunteer, came
to present anthems and special musical "offerings."[38]
Choirs also gave leadership to congregational singing, and
they presented pageants, recitals, and other kinds of programs. The overall supervision, of course, belonged to the
pastor, who had the assistance sometimes of a committee
from the session or the diaconate.[39]

Patterns for congregational funding also changed, as
family-oriented, traditional practices of paying pew rents
annually and "subscriptions" for special needs declined.
Instead came a "free" system in which annual pledges
would be paid in weekly installments. For the first time,
the "offering" became a liturgical rubric for Presbyterians.
In 1902, the Directory for Worship was amended to require all collections of offerings to be approved by the
session (GA, PCUSA, 1902, p.120). Assembly agencies,
and committees in some lower courts, began to publish
"benevolence ratios," identifying the percentage of money given to others as a portion of total congregational
giving.[40]

One classic study of the PCUSA, written in the early
1890s, lamented all the changes. Robert Ellis Thompson
decried what is here termed the process of "incorporation":

> In the actual working of our Presbyterian churches generally
> this evil has reached an extreme development. The habit of
> speaking of a congregation as Dr. A's or Mr. B's church is
> but an expression of the fact. Practically the pastor carries
> the undivided work on his own shoulders, the sexton being

the official next in importance. The Scriptural diaconate for men has been replaced by trustees, who have only the duties of collecting the pew rents, paying the salaries and the bills, and keeping the church building in repair. The diaconate for women has disappeared altogether, or is feebly represented by the Dorcas societies. . . . Lastly, the eldership . . . is tending to become little more than association with the pastor in a religious committee. . . . [The pastor] has to do all the preaching, all the pastoral visiting, all the presiding, all the work of administration except the financial, and often a good deal of that.[41]

Thompson proceeded for several pages to comment on the state of affairs. He saw it as reducing the rich Presbyterian tradition of representative church leadership. He saw it as unnecessarily simplifying Presbyterianism. It did simplify as it also increased the complexity of the enterprise, a structural anomaly.

Interestingly, a number of other leaders saw the subtle mutations at work, and some complained or tried to resist the changes. Most blamed outside forces—greed among capitalists, atheism among socialists, immigrants, Roman Catholics, or all of these—for destroying the fiber of historic Presbyterianism. Few noticed changes in themselves, their language, their goals, or the means employed to seek those goals.[42]

Nor did the changes come without institutional resistance. At several points, the various General Assemblies refused some moves in the direction of centralization. PCUSA retrenchment in the 1910s required elimination of several departments and the consolidation of some others. In congregations, relatively independent Sunday school and women's organizations frequently resisted attempts to subsume their work in the regular lines of congregational authority, as exercised by the pastor(s), staff, and session.[43]

Overall, however, Presbyterians seem to have found tighter structures, well-defined responsibilities, "efficiency," and other types of control to their liking. Resistance was generally overcome, and Presbyterian "incorporation" proceeded.

The Results of "Incorporation"

The movement of Presbyterians toward methods and images drawn from "incorporation" as it occurred in American culture set a direction that has persisted until the present. One might even argue that the incorporation of American Presbyterians has become more thorough and determinative throughout the twentieth century and that subsequent decisions on structures and personnel have proven the point time and again. The adoption of similar methods and images by other denominations subsequently would argue for Presbyterian influence on their structures. Hierarchies established during the era became "triumphant" in the PCUSA reorganization in the 1920s, and they became even more complex after that. The United Presbyterian Church in North America and the Presbyterian Church in the U.S. may have remained a bit less rigidly structured, with fewer and more tenuous hierarchies, but examination of their actions and operations suggests differences in quantity rather than quality of control. Managers predominated in all the major streams of what has become the Presbyterian Church (U.S.A.), and governing bodies in the years since 1983 have relied heavily on a corporate model in selecting "executives" and designing "flow charts."[44]

Important to remember are some of the benefits and successes of incorporation. The membership of all the major Presbyterian denominations increased in numbers between 1880 and 1915.[45] The Sunday schools flourished. Women's organizations particularly augmented the regular work of the Presbyterians in missions at home and abroad. Professional musicians increased the quality of church music. Church secretaries enabled more programs and better communication, and usually increased the efficiency of pastors. Remunerated custodians may have taken their responsibilities more seriously and certainly were considered more accountable.

Fund drives at first succeeded, and many have provided substantial increments for denominational and congregational efforts ever since. The Reunion Thanksgiving Gift of the PCUSA set the denominational tone in 1870–1871. "Objects properly to be embraced" in the range of gifts were determined by a committee of oversight. Presbyterians gave more than $7.5 million for repair and erection of some churches and manses, the retiring of mortgages on others, and the strengthening of colleges and seminaries (GA, PCUSA, 1919, p.182).

Though total giving to PCUSA causes did not equal such heights again until the occasion of the Victory Fund Campaign and accompanying New Era Movement in 1919, regular giving and bequests apparently did increase throughout most of the period. Other statistics, meticulously gathered and interpreted in a 1927 publication, showed a cyclical "evangelistic index," a healthy growth in the number of Sunday school membership, and a drop in Assembly monies for "church erection" throughout the 1880–1915 period. In the PCUS, parallel movements occurred during that time.[46]

Incorporation also permitted the Presbyterians to bring to bear informed, if not always "expert," leadership and insights regarding the issues and problems in the modern world. The departments of the PCUSA most involved in addressing many crises of American life—oppression of the urban, usually minority, poor; needs for workers to organize countervailing structures to combat inordinate demands by employers, especially on women and children; pervasive alcoholism—were also those that pioneered in implementing corporate methods and ideas.[47]

Contrary to popular notions, the incorporation of the Presbyterians seems to have attracted generally competent and creative leaders as managers. Sheldon Jackson, E. O. Guerrant, Mrs. Richard Haines, Robert E. Speer, Charles Stelzle, and Francis J. Grimké are just a few of the notable Presbyterians who held responsibility in the communions during the period. All proved excellent administrators and charismatic leaders.[48]

By 1905, the PCUSA possessed a *Book of Common Worship,* and it served to direct public services more thoroughly than standards had done in the past. Even before it was formally adopted, the Board of Publication had offered *A Manual of Forms,* edited by A. A. Hodge, and *Forms for Special Occasions,* by Herrick Johnson.[49]

The incorporation of the Presbyterians also meant ecumenical relations came more easily. Who could provide continuity in dialogues and make plans on behalf of annually reconstituting Presbyterian Assemblies? Stated Clerks, members of the bureaucracies, and the people they named. Though not the exact equivalent of bishops, who represented and designated representatives for the majority branches within the Christian church, administrators began to function that way in many situations of joint action and cooperation. For example, Presbyterians could help formulate a Federal Council of Churches by using people in such administrative offices. Permanent, professional managers of the Presbyterian denominations came to "speak for" the church, at least in limited fashion.[50]

Both foreign missions and home missions efforts increased enormously as incorporation occurred. Although many of the projects and relations became increasingly "Presbyterian" in places and among people where sixteenth-century Protestant history mattered little, regular ties between denominational officials and officers in national and colonial administrations opened vast areas of service for evangelical, educational, medical, and other mission activities. Churches came to be strong in many locales, movements for freedom in many colonies were encouraged, and ties were firmly established with emerging leaders of Christians in Asian, African, and Latin American countries. Within the United States, new churches grew among people in Appalachia, Western towns, Alaska, and various Native American nations on account of the efficient and systematic work of denominational leaders and emergent leaders among the groups of new Presbyterians. Allegiance to these efforts soared on the part of Presbyterian members.[51]

At the same time, the incorporation of the church proved costly. What might be termed a fragmentation in Presbyterian identity on the part of members and even ministers seems to have been the most expensive price. Interestingly, even the leaders, both lay and clergy, expressed frustrations with the growing hierarchies, their own apparent lack of voice, and other complaints. As time passed, it seemed Presbyterians came to belong not to an integral and single congregation in an integral and single denomination, but rather to a distinct age, sex, racial, or socioeconomic group within that denomination (or even a combination of those categories). Members and leaders also seemed to identify with a portion of the "program"— the choir, a Sunday school class, a service group, a theological perspective, a mission endeavor, or a combination of such parts—rather than with the whole of the life of the church. One can sense these sentiments emerging as early as the turn of the twentieth century.[52]

The potential for alienating some members and leaders seems to be a distinguishable result. Just as workers in corporations rightly would sense themselves as distant and powerless in matters affecting them, so members would come to feel that they were not participating in decisions concerning their Presbyterian Christianity. As Thompson lamented that the session of many congregations had degenerated into "little more than association with the pastor in a religious committee," even members of the session could sense their role limited in a heavily organized congregation.

Another result was that Presbyterians came to spend vastly more time and energy on institutional matters than had previously been the case. Not only did they keep more records, "more" was termed "better" records of everything. With the numbers of new organizations, probably a larger portion of the member's time was consumed in meetings than had been spent a century before in the extended worship services, which began to disappear. Though church discipline waned during the period under consideration, the number of demands on members increased—to teach Sunday school, to go to women's or men's meetings, to attend youth functions and choir recitals, to support first para-church and then congregational or ecumenical affairs, and so on.

What had been extremely informal and family-oriented congregations, linked together in a denomination that resembled a state church (the pattern remembered by many Presbyterians), became tightly structured, hierarchically oriented congregations managed by pastors with staffs, regulated thoroughly by a denomination that resembled a major corporation. The congregation came to be viewed by ministers, members, elders, the denominational authorities, the state, and the general society alike as a small (or medium-sized) corporation, closely held and linked to others. The session frequently, but not universally, served as a board of directors; the pastor became chief executive officer. The various staff and sometimes the committee members comprised the work force. To stretch the image, small groups within a larger congregation acted as semiautonomous units within the larger body.[53]

The denomination emerged as another corporate entity in macrocosm. In this setting, department and agency heads more nearly resembled the board of directors, with executive secretaries and perhaps the Stated Clerk as major managers. Elected representatives for annual General Assemblies became more like the stockholders than would the members of the denomination, who might be said to correspond to "consumers." Such an image might do some violence to the knowledge and expectations of many Presbyterians, but it also seems to correspond to the expectations and actions of many more. Moreover, it would seem that this image, both in macrocosm and in microcosm, began to exert subtle pressures on the Presbyterians during the time when corporations came to dominate American life.

Conclusions

The metamorphosis described in this essay may have been more or less inevitable. In addition, people in the midst of it could scarcely be blamed for not perceiving its results. Doubtless from a distance of three generations it is still difficult to see all the implications of "incorporation" or other similar movements.

Certainly it proved compatible with other elements in American society. Benefits accrued almost immediately from the incorporation of the Presbyterians. When the American corporations flourished, as in the 1950s, the Presbyterians and other well-organized religious bodies apparently did as well. Membership and contributions multiplied, external signs of health within a corporate (and also frequently within a traditionally Christian) perspective.

Fascinating, and somewhat puzzling, was the increase of voiced disaffection on the part of many Presbyterian leaders during the fifties with American corporations. The observer today becomes tempted to apply psychological categories, such as "reaction-formation" or "passive-aggressive" to the behavior to explain it. For one thing, the corporations in many cases had become transnational in character by this time, but had controls become tighter? Had corporate morality waned? At any rate, criticism of corporate and bureaucratic hierarchies did multiply, though seldom did church people apply such criticism to their own structures and methods.

Subsequently, criticisms of the incorporation of the Presbyterians have grown in numbers and volume, voiced largely by those neglected or deliberately excluded from management at denominational levels. Occasionally, even denominational executives have expressed in public their disaffection for the structures. "Trust the Holy Spirit" has been the alternative proposed by one such official critic. Pay less attention to organization and management. "Recognize [that] God is the ultimate manager."[54]

The problem with this critique, valuable though it may be in interpreting the extent of the Presbyterian dilemma, is that it juxtaposes the organizational structures of the church with a high ecclesiology that remains "disembodied." Much as Presbyterians might affirm a doctrine of the church that centers on "the body of Christ," "the work of the Holy Spirit among people," and God's sovereignty, they still contend with and exist within an American environment of voluntarism and corporation-induced values. How to balance necessary organization with self-conscious distance from a complex, pervasive atmosphere of incorporation will itself be a complicated task. It seems one worth the effort, however, if a Presbyterian identity remains important within the Christian family.

2

Managing the Mission:
Church Restructuring
in the Twentieth Century

Richard W. Reifsnyder

During the 1920s and again in the 1960s and 1970s, Presbyterians and nearly all major Protestant denominations restructured their organizations in ways deeply influenced by models drawn from the world of business and management science. In the wake of the reunion in 1983 of The United Presbyterian Church in the U.S.A. and the Presbyterian Church in the U.S., Presbyterians reorganized yet another time.[1] What prompted these restructurings? What influenced the shape they took? What do they suggest about the nature and purpose of the church that has emerged in the last decade of the century?

Developing a National Church Bureaucracy:
The 1920s

Developments in the Presbyterian Church
in the U.S.A.

In 1923 the Presbyterian Church in the United States of America (hereafter PCUSA) adopted the organizational structure that would endure through a half century of great expansion. Ten semiautonomous boards and four permanent Assembly committees, each of which had been established independently to perform a certain specialized task for a growing church, were consolidated into four new boards: the Board of Foreign Missions, the Board of National Missions, the Board of Christian Education, and the Board of Relief and Sustentation. In addition, the reorganization gave new responsibilities to the Stated Clerk of the General Assembly and created a General Council to coordinate the work of the boards. This development represented the culmination of the church's transformation into a large-scale bureaucratic organization with a national focus.[2]

Early efforts at coordination.   During the previous half century the church had grown haphazardly. Specialized agencies dealt with such diverse concerns as foreign missions, Sabbath Day observance, and administration of church colleges. Their boards drew their members from a narrow geographical area and kept close control of the operation. Moreover, the boards competed for the limited funds from the churches. Consequently, boards duplicated efforts, and areas of responsibility overlapped.

During the late nineteenth and early twentieth century, tentative steps were taken to plan more systematically for the church's growth. As administrative duties expanded under Stated Clerk William Henry Roberts, his office became a full-time position. As a way of providing a more rational approach to finances, the General Assembly promoted "systematic beneficence" by which church members would make weekly pledges and donate through a double envelope system.[3]

Not until the first decades of the twentieth century were circumstances ripe for a major organizational explosion in the Presbyterian Church. The progressive era, with its emphasis on organizational reform, specialization of professional tasks and functions, and the virtue of efficiency changed the face of the church in significant ways. The church mirrored what was a society-wide "search for order." The transformation was accompanied by the development of a bureaucratic structure with more formal operating procedures and lines of authority.[4]

A new emphasis on "expertise" appeared often in church documents, as did the language of the efficiency movement, pioneered by time-and-motion expert Frederick W. Taylor. In 1912 the PCUSA even hired an efficiency expert of its own. A committee appointed to evaluate structure following the merger with the Cumberland Presbyterian Church in 1906 argued that the PCUSA administrative machinery was woefully lacking, especially in executive power. Few modifications were made, but the suggestion that the church needed strong executive direction was a remarkable development, especially given Presbyterian polity (GA, PCUSA, 1906, p. 83; 1908, pp. 155, 247; 1912, p. 228).[5]

Finances provided the driving force toward administrative centralization. The boards were reluctant to relinquish control over securing funds by deferring to a central planning agency. Yet the desire to ensure a steady income so they could expand, combined with weariness of the competition for funds, led the Assembly to adopt a budget plan in 1908, establishing a fixed budget for each board. Churches were urged to adopt an every-member pledge system to secure benevolent offerings. This represented a significant shift in decision making, from the local to the national level (GA, PCUSA, 1908, pp. 146, 149; 1909, pp. 96–100).

Following World War I, the PCUSA undertook wholescale reorganization. Presbyterians adopted a vast fundraising and promotional scheme called the New Era Movement and joined with other denominations in the ill-fated "Interchurch World Movement." Although results of these efforts proved to be disappointing, the urgent desire to expand the wartime mission provided the context in which the church reorganized. This brought to a culmination a twenty-five-year trend toward administrative centralization and bureaucratic solutions to the church's problems.

The appointment of a special committee on reorganization.
In 1920 the General Assembly appointed a Special Committee on the Reorganization and Consolidation of Boards

and Agencies (hereafter SCRCBA), chaired by the Reverend John Timothy Stone, pastor of the Fourth Presbyterian Church in Chicago. A former Moderator of the PCUSA, Stone commanded wide respect across the church. Significantly, in an era when business was elevated to a quasi-salvific role in American culture, Stone was described by a popular Christian journal as "a business man in religion."[6]

The committee consisted of five elders and five ministers, who were predominantly pastors of large churches. Although they established subcommittees to receive suggestions, consider constitutional and legal questions, and develop preliminary plans for reorganization, the most significant thing that happened at the first meeting was Stone's reading of a memorandum sent to him from Robert E. Speer, Secretary of the Board of Foreign Missions. The influential Speer had the remarkable capacity to combine the roles of church administrator and missionary evangelist. An eloquent speaker, he could move both heart and mind. At the same time, he was the epitome of an efficient administrator, who would translate the missionary vision into effective action. He personified the transition the church was making from a traditional mission structure, loosely organized and staffed by clergy who viewed themselves as pastors, to a modern bureaucratic and hierarchical church structure with a centralized administration staffed by experts. Because of his particular personal gifts, Speer made the change seem painless to all but a few.[7]

A mark of his administrative genius was that Speer had a specific plan for reorganization when no one else did. Although judicatories set policy, according to Presbyterian polity, his initiative revealed an increasing reliance on experts in the church bureaucracy. Conscious that there might be objection to a plan coming from one board, Speer sent his plan to his friend John Stone. Yet by his action Speer ensured that the foreign board would receive full consideration. Speer remained concerned about the overall church, but he understood the importance of the administrator's role in a large-scale organization.[8]

Speer suggested the creation of a central council. It was
not designed as a centralized administration so much as a
"board of spiritual counsel." It would provide continuity,
respond to new concerns, advise the Moderator, and promote efficiency. He also proposed consolidating the entire
work into four boards—a board of foreign missions, a
board of home missions, a board of education, and a board
of relief and sustentation. Stone reported to Speer the
SCRCBA's conviction that it was "one of the sanest and
strongest papers which could possibly be prepared and will
be invaluable to us."[9]

Although the committee heard a number of options, it
evaluated all other proposals against Speer's memorandum. Stone's progress report to the General Assembly in
1921 received a thunderous ovation. The directive to pro-
ceed with full-scale reorganization was passed overwhelmingly. Some dissenters, like noted conservative Maitland
Alexander, pastor of the First Presbyterian Church of
Pittsburgh, lamented the eagerness to "take from big business a lesson for the church."[10]

The die was cast. The SCRCBA was reappointed and
expanded to fifteen members. It met four times between
the General Assemblies of 1921 and 1922. Subcommittees
were formed to recommend the composition and responsibilities for each of four operational boards.[11]

Many of the smaller boards objected vigorously to the
direction the committee was heading. The committees on
Sabbath Observance, Evangelism, and Temperance feared
losing their visibility. The Board of Missions for Freedmen
argued heatedly that interest in Black Americans would diminish and be seen as unimportant. "We pray for deliver-
ance," a resolution sent to the SCRCBA read, "and a
chance to maintain our identity." The prayer fell on deaf
ears. Stone had a rather heated exchange with Dr. John M.
Gaston, the board secretary, accusing him of "class spirit"
rather than "college spirit" in opposing the reorganization.[12]

The women's organizations also expressed reservations.
The Woman's Board of Home Missions argued that
women would not maintain the same interest in second-

mile giving should the General Assembly merge them.
Margaret Hodge, speaking for the Woman's Board of
Foreign Missions, was willing to go along with the merger
provided women received at least one third of the representation on the new board.[13]

The SCRCBA was not to be swayed from its vision of
bureaucratic centralization. It subsumed specialized agencies encouraging the ministry of Blacks and women, arguing that this was no more anti-women or anti-Black than
was the elimination of the Church Erection Fund intended
to be anti–church building.[14]

After a five-hour debate, the General Assembly of 1922
adopted the SCRCBA's proposals. Moreover, it gave the
committee the task of implementing the plan, including
naming the personnel of the new boards, subject only to
final approval of the Assembly (GA, PCUSA, 1922, pp.
129–131, 144–181).[15]

Reorganization accomplished. The reorganization accomplished in 1923 consolidated and confirmed changes
that had been taking place for a quarter of a century. All
boards and agencies were reorganized into the four new
boards. These boards were semiautonomous in nature,
overseeing their own funds and securing their own staff,
subject to approval of the Assembly. The reorganization
was a reform in the direction of a more nationally oriented
church. Whereas the older boards were usually managed
by a small group of men in a particular geographical area,
the new boards were geographically representative. In the
view of the SCRCBA, administrative centralization would
enable the church to see the whole work and provide a
national focus. Not only was the reorganization committee
institutionalizing hierarchical, bureaucratic values, but it
was also looking to organizational change to facilitate the
transition to a national orientation.

In significant ways, the church mirrored other expanding, large-scale organizations, particularly business.
In *Strategy and Structure,* Alfred D. Chandler, Jr., argues
that following World War I some American businesses

found a centralized, departmentalized structure inadequate to their expanding needs. They responded by adopting a multidivisional, "decentralized" structure. In this type of organization, a general office plans, coordinates, and appraises the work of a number of operating divisions. These have responsibility and command the resources for handling one major line of products or set of services over a wide geographic area. Each division is responsible for its overall success.[16]

In creating the fourfold board structure, the Presbyterian Church in the U.S.A. created a similar, decentralized (in this business sense) structure. Each board was responsible for one piece of the overall work, including the recruiting of personnel, the development and promotion of the service, and the oversight of financial responsibility. A General Council was established, and its job, like that of a central office, was to help coordinate and evaluate the work of the boards. Although there is no evidence in the SCRCBA records to indicate that it made any study of contemporary business techniques, it is likely that the committee was influenced by the contemporary state of the art of administration. One committee member argued explicitly for reorganization "as for example in some of the big corporations." Chandler points out that the companies that were pioneers of this form in the 1920s had no patterns to imitate, but were innovators. As a strategy for responding to changing circumstances they created a new type of structure. The church, adopting this structure early in the decade, not only reflected the culture, but was a harbinger of the change.[17]

Reorganization as a response to theological tension. A small but vocal minority of Presbyterians opposed the reorganization plan precisely because they believed it centralized power and violated church polity. The conservative weeklies, *The Presbyterian* and *The Presbyterian Banner,* feared that the increased bureaucracy would make the church more dependent on "experts" removed from the local church. Stone was impatient with this analysis

and felt those objecting to the plan were simply obstruc-
tionist.[18]

Advocates of reorganization believed they were creating
a more effective vehicle for expanding the church's mission. The reorganization occurred in the midst of a re-
emerging theological dispute. Since the 1890s a group of
centrists within the PCUSA focused on the mission of the
church as a way of defusing theological tensions. Robert
Speer desired reorganization to create a more effective instrument to spread the gospel. He personified a pragmatic
spirit which deemphasized theological precision in order
to secure the widest possible consensus for the work of
evangelizing the lost. The militant conservatives saw in the
reorganization an emphasis on consensus in mission at the
expense of doctrinal precision, which increased their sense
of dissatisfaction.

Reorganization was more than a matter of simplifying
and economizing. Because the larger, nationally oriented
boards could no longer give monthly supervision to each
aspect of a board's work, it was natural for professional
staffs to become more of an "expert" managerial class.
Moreover, the creation of centralized organization and the
use of images of efficiency and economy, borrowed from the
business world, made it easier to define success by criteria
that could be tabulated and evaluated by experts. From
there it would be an easy but dangerous step to identifying
faithfulness with more money or more missionaries.

Administrative efficiency is not the most pressing problem for large-scale organizations. Leadership—and in the
church's case, spiritual leadership—is the most important
aspect of organizational strength.[19] During the half century
following reorganization, strong leaders were chosen to
head the boards. These individuals not only knew how to
use the platform given them to promote a program, but
they also reflected the elitist and optimistic outlook of a
church that expected to expand and influence the values of
a nation whose influence was expanding as well.

For forty years, the structure for mission remained the
same, with only minor changes taking place in 1958 fol-

lowing the merger with the United Presbyterian Church of North America. One significant development was the formation of the Committee on Ecumenical Mission and Relations (COEMAR) to replace the two foreign mission boards and three committees dealing with interchurch relations. COEMAR, the brainchild of Charles Leber, the general secretary of the PCUSA Board of Foreign Missions, reflected a shift in mission philosophy from a sending-receiving perspective to a partnership with the now independent Christian communities throughout the world. There was one mission on six continents, as the popular slogan put it, and the structure sought to reflect that change in strategy.[20]

Developments in the Presbyterian Church in the U.S.

The development of large-scale bureaucratic organization in General Assembly agencies took on a somewhat different shape in the Presbyterian Church in the United States (PCUS). It was not simply a matter of a time lag behind the PCUSA but also a result of a different theological concept of the organization of the church.

James Henley Thornwell, a major nineteenth-century theological architect of the PCUS, believed that the church should not add anything to its theology, polity, or worship not specifically or by good inference derived from scripture. "Where God has not commanded, the church has no jurisdiction," he wrote. Mission boards, in his view, were unscriptural. Moreover, he argued that the church's mission was solely to promote the glory of God and human salvation and had nothing to do with voluntary associations for civil and social purposes. This doctrine of the "spirituality of the church" deeply influenced the denomination well into the twentieth century.[21]

Thus the PCUS, believing that the courts or governing bodies of the church themselves undertake mission directly, established executive committees of the General Assembly. Both the members and staff of the executive committees were elected by the Assembly for one-year terms. A passionate commitment to create decentralized structures as a way of preventing power from gravitating to the center led the church to disperse the executive committees geographically.[22]

Despite these deeply rooted principles, the PCUS could not resist some of the impulses toward large-scale bureaucratic organization. As in the PCUSA, stewardship needs provided an impetus. Churches pressed for systematic giving for local mission through the use of envelopes, but they also continued to receive special offerings on designated Sundays for the Assembly's benevolence causes. The number of special collections created confusion. In 1910 the General Assembly created the Permanent Committee on Systematic Beneficence to meet with the secretaries of the executive committees and assess the needs. The General Assembly would then recommend a quota to the synods, who would likewise recommend quotas to presbyteries and then to sessions. Opposed by some as a radical innovation, the plan soon met with widespread approval because it accomplished the goal of supporting the mission of an expanding church.

At the same time, the various executive committees were regrouped into four—Foreign Missions, Home Missions, Ministerial Education and Relief, and Publication and Sabbath School. The executive committees were strong advocates of the Every Member Canvass. Despite the quotas, they still had to raise their own funds. Theoretically the mission agencies were tied directly to the governing bodies, but in fact the executive committees were functionally independent.[23]

The PCUS took a rather dramatic step toward greater "efficiency" and "economy" when it established in 1927 a forty-four-member Committee on the Assembly's Work. Its job was to coordinate the entire benevolent work of the church. The former executive committees became subcommittees. The experiment lasted only three years because it was perceived as centralizing too much power and contributing to declining receipts.[24]

By 1947, a proliferation of executive committees and permanent committees led the General Assembly to undertake a comprehensive study of church structures. A business engineer was hired to look objectively at the church's needs for greater efficiency. Acknowledging the current reality, but nevertheless overturning nearly a century of tradition, the Assembly established five boards—World Missions, Church Extension, Education, Annuities and Relief, and Women's Work. All executive secretaries were elected directly by the boards. Moreover, an Office of the General Assembly was created, as well as a General Council, whose tasks included stewardship, budgeting, program coordination, publicity, and research.[25]

Thus the PCUS adopted the "decentralized" form of structure, borrowed from business, with relatively autonomous operating divisions responsible for organizing and carrying out a portion of the church's program. Despite the denomination's suspicion of centralized power, the boards gained authority not only because they had become necessary instruments for an expanding church, but also because their leaders were widely known and respected figures in the PCUS.

The Managerial Revolution and the Reshaping of the Church: The 1960s and 1970s

The 1960s and 1970s were a decisive period of transition in American religious life. Efforts to reshape national and regional church structures, part of deeper shifts in American culture, swept through the major denominations. In the Presbyterian churches, these changes reflected and contributed to the creation of a transformed religious landscape.

In both the UPCUSA and the PCUS, the reorganizations of the early 1970s represented an intentional response to what was perceived as a new cultural situation. Many factors converged to make reorganization seem necessary, although even during the process of reorganization, the perception of those factors changed. The ecclesiastical and cultural ethos in which decisions were made varied in the UPCUSA and the PCUS yet the reorganizations took substantially the same shape.[26]

Reorganization in the United Presbyterian Church in the U.S.A.

New emphases in mission revealed strains in the structures. COEMAR was the forerunner. Old geographic distinctions between overseas and national missions seemed obsolete. Moreover, the church had begun to take more initiative in responding to the needs of society, especially regarding the challenges of urbanization, poverty, and race relations.

In the early 1960s, the Board of National Missions took the lead in challenging the church. General Secretary Kenneth Neigh assembled a staff of creative administrators such as Bryant George, Max Browning, Daniel Little, and David Ramage, who sought to redirect the church's program toward addressing the needs of the cities and rectifying racial injustices. Crucial to this strategy was an effort to shift mission coordination and implementation from a national staff to synods and presbyteries.[27]

The work of the Committee on Regional Synods. The General Assembly in 1963 appointed a nine-person Special Committee on Regional Synods and Church Administration (hereafter SCRSCA). Initially the task seemed simple: to look at a structure that "creaks at some points," and to untangle the bureaucratic jumble caused by confusing and overlapping relationships among presbyteries, synods, and General Assembly agencies.[28] Before the reorganization was complete in 1973 two more committees would be involved in the process.

At the beginning of this ten-year period, the church appeared institutionally vital. Church membership had increased steadily, if not spectacularly, to over three million, as Presbyterians had benefited from the postwar baby boom and the move of the middle classes to the suburbs. Yet during this decade of reorganization, the religious and cultural situation changed dramatically. The UPCUSA found itself severely challenged, from both within and without. Some within the church proclaimed the death of God and lauded "the secular city." At the same time the UPCUSA sought to respond faithfully to the social ferment generated by gender and racial injustices and the Vietnam War. That context transformed the rationale for reorganization and the eventual outcome.

The Reverend William C. Schram, a pastor from Pelham, New York, who had initiated the overture for the special committee, headed the SCRSCA. The Reverend David Ramage, an urban-mission expert with the Board of National Missions staff, was hired as a consultant. When the committee unveiled its plan in 1965, the General Assembly's *Daily News* declared that "radical reorganization of the United Presbyterian Church is the aim."[29] Decentralized planning through regional synods, having common characteristics, interests, and problems, was deemed the best structural way of responding to changing circumstances. Major metropolitan areas such as New York, Philadelphia, and Chicago would be constituted as separate synods in order to enhance urban strategy. In language similar to the Confession of 1967, which was then under consideration, the SCRSCA argued that "church structures . . . exist for mission and must be designed for mission," defined as proclaiming "God's message of reconciliation." Judicatories were agents of mission, not simply units of church government for the preservation of faith and doctrine (GA, UPCUSA, 1965, pp. 270–273, 303–388).

The committee was encouraged by more than one hundred responses it received from presbyteries to its preliminary work. It recognized it would have to consider more intensively the structure and function of the General Assembly agencies. In 1966 the SCRSCA requested approval to expand the committee to fifteen and extend its work for two years (GA, UPCUSA, 1966, pp. 163–171).

The Design for Mission. By 1968 a sense of urgency prevailed when the SCRSCA presented its long-awaited report, "A Design for Mission." Tensions were evident regarding the nature of the church's mission in a turbulent society. Presbyterians United for a Biblical Confession and the Presbyterian Lay Committee opposed the theological perspective of the Confession of 1967, which stated that responding to social and political issues was central to the church's mission. A committee appointed by the three program boards admitted that "many Presbyterians are deeply troubled about the role our church is playing in public affairs." They published a report, *Why Is the Church in the World?*, which sought to provide a "theological basis for the corporate involvement of the church in the world." But a clear consensus about the nature of the mission was not forthcoming.[30]

After a year of discussion and some modification, the Design for Mission was passed by a 3–1 margin in 1969 at the General Assembly meeting in San Antonio. The Design listed a number of problems impeding the church's mission which it implied could be solved by better administration. Synod boundaries split metropolitan areas. General Assembly agencies had confusing staffing relationships with lower judicatories. There was no way to develop comprehensive mission strategy. Budgets were determined without considering mission priorities. While disclaiming any naive belief that organizational effectiveness alone was the solution, the committee believed that clarity of administrative relationships and better churchwide planning were the organizational keys to the church's renewal for mission.

The SCRSCA proposed that a sense of unified mission could be created from the diversity apparent within the denomination. It proposed a process for all elements of the church to participate in the planning, budgeting, and evaluating of the mission. Each judicatory was to be an agent of mission, but each would develop and execute its specific proposals in light of the strategy and guidelines developed by the next higher judicatory.

On the one hand, the plan stressed the traditional connectional and representational nature of Presbyterian church government and sought to resolve some traditional tensions in Presbyterian polity by tying mission more closely to the judicatories. Each judicatory, from the session through the General Assembly, was both a structure of ecclesiastical government and an agent of mission accountable for initiating, implementing, and evaluating the mission.

On the other hand, the Design for Mission also incorporated the language and style of contemporary management techniques. Arthur M. Adams, dean of Princeton Theological Seminary and a prominent advocate of better church administration, wrote a paper that influenced the thinking of the SCRSCA. Adams argued that for a large and multifaceted organization like the church to express its oneness in mission, it was essential to develop a more sophisticated communication and decision-making network.

Happily, in Adams' view, the Presbyterian Church was representational and lent itself to maximum participation in decision making. The Design for Mission offered an "improved" process, which accepted the organizational theory that participating in the process offered "more significant representation" than voting on the final stage of a decision. The unspoken assumption was that organizational process would enable everyone to be involved in supporting the denominational mission.[31]

It was precisely this consensus on the nature of the mission that was breaking down in the UPCUSA and mainstream Protestantism.[32] The Design suggested organizational and managerial solutions to create a unified church mission. Skilled administrators would facilitate communication and ensure that decisions would be made in light of the mission priorities of the whole church.

As organizations in every field became more complex in the twentieth century, the scientific study of management and organization flourished as well. According to the historian Alfred D. Chandler, Jr., in business "the visible hand of management replaced what Adam Smith referred to as the invisible hand of market forces." In the church, the need for management and for planning and process tended to overshadow at times the more invisible role of the Holy Spirit to provide direction and power. Peter Drucker, an influential management theorist, argues that the emergence of management as a distinct and essential institution has been a pivotal event in twentieth-century social history. The church, as a large-scale organization, was increasingly conscious of the need for effective management. Administrative leaders such as former Board of National Missions General Secretary Kenneth Neigh acknowledged their appreciation for Drucker, but it was not always clear how the principles derived from business could be applied to a quite different and in some ways more complex organization like the church.[33]

To veteran church administrator Richard G. Hutcheson, Jr., the approach of management science, which stressed the importance of goal setting and management by objective, was only one aspect of the "organization mindedness of the contemporary church." Equally important were organizational sociology, which focused on functional analysis and a systems approach to organization, and the human relations movement, which emphasized process and the importance of collegiality and flexibility in decision making. The Design for Mission went far beyond realigning a few synods by utilizing a management model for structural reorganization as a way of enabling the church to deal with diversity and conflict.[34]

In adopting the Design for Mission, the church committed itself to revamping the General Assembly boards and agencies to fit into a participatory, decentralized scheme of planning and facilitating the support of a unified mission. The General Assembly agencies would coordinate and engage in mission at a national and global level.

The reorganization accomplished. A Special Committee on General Assembly Agencies (hereafter SCGAA), which had been recommended by the SCRSCA, began its work in 1969 under the leadership of Orley B. Mason, a businessman from Ohio. This committee undertook its task in a period of great tension within the church, especially regarding the church's response to racial and social justice issues. Under the pressure of circumstances, restructuring was shaped in ways unexpected by the board staffs or the regional synod committee.

In no sense was the SCGAA starting from scratch. Former Moderator Ganse Little chaired a subcommittee of the SCRSCA which had been studying the General Assembly structure since 1966. When the general secretaries were invited to raise concerns, Kenneth Neigh asserted that while he agreed with Drucker about the necessity to continually reorganize or die, he was concerned about how it was to be accomplished. John Coventry Smith reminded the subcommittee he had been through a major restructuring in the formation of COEMAR. Management consultant Frank Martin had worked closely with the staff, forcing them to define first of all "what business they were in" before tackling structure. Smith was not enthusiastic about consultants being used this time.

Although the board staffs agreed that restructuring was probably necessary, they could not reach a consensus on its shape. The subcommittee had suggested that any new structure be laid out along functional rather than geographical lines. Smith and Neigh assumed that the SCGAA would lay out the general shape of the new structure and then allow the General Council to work out the details with the full consultation of those involved. Much to their surprise, Stated Clerk William P. Thompson ruled the General Assembly had authorized wholesale restructuring.[35]

A desire for greater accountability provided major impetus toward restructuring. For some that meant greater financial accountability. Several laymen on the General Council who had been associated with the Presbyterian Men's organization felt the Council was too weak. They were frustrated by their inability to oversee the funds controlled by the semiautonomous boards. For others it was a matter of discomfort with the power of the general secretaries and a desire to curtail the influence of a small group of individuals. One often-quoted incident took place at the turbulent 1970 General Assembly. John Coventry Smith

and Kenneth Neigh, sensing a critical moment, seized the
initiative from the General Council and made a proposal
to provide $1.25 million from their reserves to initiate the
Fund for the Self-Development of Peoples. This act fueled
the resentment of some. A member of the SCGAA sitting
on the stage vowed "to produce a structure that will never
again produce another Ken Neigh." Although reorganization did not begin with the intent of squelching powerful
leaders, it was shaped in such a way as to diminish the
possibility of individuals' gaining a base of influence and
visibility. To James I. McCord, president of Princeton
Theological Seminary, "what began as restructuring
wound up a palace coup."[36]

The Mason committee, while well intentioned, was
faced with the almost impossible task of creating a new
structure without the direct involvement of those who
were doing the mission work. In part that was deliberate.
Not only in the church but throughout the culture there
was a suspicion of those in power and a conscious desire to
reduce the hold of the elites and to open the process to
those who had previously been marginalized. Although the
SCGAA consulted with the executives of the old boards,
many lamented that they were not really being heard.
James Gailey, who had taken over as general secretary of
the Board of Christian Education in the middle of restructuring, felt that although he could not modify the basic
shape of the new structure, he could and did fight for certain changes crucial to the education task.[37]

A management consultant proposed a threefold agency
structure, divided according to function. One agency
would unify all the programmatic aspects of mission (a
program agency), a second would focus on recruitment,
training, and oversight of personnel (a vocation agency),
and a third would provide support services (a support
agency). Considerable controversy arose concerning the
merits of unifying all mission programs in one agency.
Donald Black and others at COEMAR fought to unify national and global mission in one agency. Others agreed
with Arthur Adams, who complained when he saw the

shape of the new organization, "It was a mistake." It was no easy task for the Mason committee to discern what the consensus of the church was.[38]

The most controversial aspect of the proposed new structure was the consolidation of all the programs of COEMAR and the Boards of Christian Education and National Missions in the Program Agency as the visible embodiment of the one mission ideal. The uninspiring name provided little identity to which the church could relate. Kenneth Neigh declared bluntly that "the most important mission force in thirty-five years was destroyed by reorganization."[39]

At the heart of the plan was the General Assembly Mission Council, whose task was to coordinate the work of the agencies. The complaint that the old General Council was too weak, especially in the oversight of finances, was answered by giving the GAMC planning, budgeting, and evaluating functions. No longer would semiautonomous boards be able to control their own monies. Accountability would be clearly lodged, and the capacity of any individual or agency undertaking independent action curtailed. In adopting a functional approach, the church moved away from the multidivisional idea and instead sought to manage the church more effectively through budgeting and planning processes at the center (GA, UPCUSA, 1971, pp. 458–465).

The contentious 1971 General Assembly was so preoccupied by controversy over a grant given to the Angela Davis legal defense fund that it passed the reorganization with little dissent. A commission, chaired by W. Sherman Skinner, a tall-steeple pastor who had served on numerous national committees and boards, was created to implement the plan. The Reverend Hugh Annett, who had studied management and organizational theory, served as consultant. Another commission member, S. David Stoner, later executive director of the General Assembly Council of the PC(USA), worked for a management consultant firm. Even with that expertise, the task was enormously unsettling. In an effort to symbolize the beginning of a new era, the entire national staff was asked to resign and then invited to reapply for positions. This was devastating to many longtime church employees. The reorganization involved changes in staffing patterns and relationships between newly created synods and General Assembly agencies. It soon became apparent the Assembly staff would decrease. To emphasize the unity of mission and to encourage ecumenical exchange, the church voted to centralize its agencies in the Interchurch Center in New York. Denominational editor Dennis Shoemaker complained the General Assembly had "not sufficiently taken into consideration the human cost" of restructuring.[40]

New faces were sought for the newly elected boards. Indeed, one executive estimates that only one third of the new personnel had previously served on a board. This lack of experience affected hiring process for staff, since the most creative people were sometimes not sought or were discouraged by the cumbersome procedures. "The church cannot afford creativity," opined one church manager during the scramble for jobs in 1973. More positively, the church had made a clear commitment to being more open in its hiring practices and consciously sought to give greater visibility to women and racial ethnic persons.[41]

The reorganization had involved three separate committees and had taken ten years. Once begun, it developed in some unexpected directions. A church structure was created whose agencies operated with different assumptions from the old boards. Especially apparent was the confidence in the capacity of organizational process and management techniques to create a more responsive and effective church. Indeed, Daniel Little, who served as executive director of the GAMC, suggests the framers were not aware how significantly they were influenced by "managerial fundamentalism." A critical element of the actual process was the cultural ethos of the late sixties and early seventies, with its suspicions of elites, its passion for rectifying injustices, its desire to strip away the old order, its enthusiasm for participatory process and decision making, and its confidence that problems could be solved by expert management.[42]

Reorganization in the Presbyterian Church in the U.S.

The particular factors that led to the reorganization of the Presbyterian Church in the U.S. in 1972 were different from those in the UPCUSA, and yet in significant ways the results were the same.

Among the underlying factors was the emergence of a group of people who wanted to create a more effective vehicle of mission. They saw the General Assembly as a countervailing force to a decentralized church structure, which they viewed as a theological version of a states' rights philosophy. A new cadre of board leadership who knew and trusted one another was chosen to lead the church out of its own regionalism. A number of officials had taken part in National Council of Churches seminars on church organization, which increased their awareness of trends in other denominations and provided a spark for undertaking reorganization.

The perception of organizational inefficiency, however, provided the catalyst for creating an Ad Interim Committee on Restructuring Boards and Agencies (hereafter CRBA). Since the 1949 restructuring, a proliferation of activities produced duplication of responsibilities. The General Council had proven ineffective as a coordinating body. There was a tendency for certain constituencies to identify with particular boards and for the boards themselves to compete for resources and support within the denomination.[43]

On the whole, the idea of reorganization was broadly supported within the church. Although there had been some ferment surrounding the initiatives in urban and racial justice ministry taken by John Anderson at the Board of Home Missions, there was little desire to curtail the power of the executives, as it existed in the UPCUSA. Nevertheless, issues of accountability and participatory decision making were part of the fabric of thinking which influenced the CRBA.

Synod executive William Fogleman chaired the committee. Significantly, not only were there no members who had a current relationship with one of the boards, but in contrast to the UPCUSA tradition Stated Clerk James Millard had no relationship with the committee. The politically balanced committee, representing the theological and geographic diversity within the church, considered the key question of who would control what became known as "the agentry."

Early in its discussions, the CRBA hired Robert Worley, a specialist in church organization from McCormick Theological Seminary. Worley was asked to develop models for consideration and provide analysis of their consequences for leadership and their adherence to Presbyterian polity. He also kept in touch with developments in the UPCUSA. This was an important consideration, since the same General Assembly that established the CRBA also created a committee to explore reunion. Fogleman's committee met several times with the Mason committee.[44]

The committee's goal was to create a structure that would be responsive to the church's priorities and provide an effective instrument to coordinate the church's work. No independent policies or programs could be established that were not reflective of the will of the whole church. In a time when theological verities were being challenged and social issues were stimulating new understandings of mission, there was an incredible confidence that effective management processes were the essential means to create a consensus (GA, PCUS, 1972, pp. 86–88).

At the heart of the proposed new structure was a General Executive Board responsible to the General Assembly for three systems. First was a priority-building system. Its stated intention was to shift decision-making power from the boards to the Assembly itself, thereby reflecting more closely the Thornwellian tradition of polity outlined earlier in the chapter. Second was a program system, which implemented the goals set by the General Assembly. The General Executive Board was divided into five functional divisions: National Mission, International Mission, Corporate and Social Mission, Professional Development, and

Central Support Services. These divisions were supposed to work collegially to implement their programs in light of the functions of the others. Third, there was a communication system, which provided for regional communication directors, called jointly by the GEB and the synods, to provide for two-way communication between the constituencies and the agentry (GA, PCUS, 1972, pp. 92–99).[45]

The systems were intended to create a structure that was open and responsive and where everyone had a stake in reaching a consensus regarding mission. Recognizing that all structures are subject to corruption and therefore need periodic review, the committee built in a self-renewing capacity. An independent Office of Review and Evaluation was to monitor the agentry and make suggestions about the effectiveness of structural forms at periodic intervals (GA, PCUS, 1972, p. 100).

There was a significant effort made to make the church agentry more inclusive and representative. At least one of the divisions of the GEB was to be headed by a woman. Terms were limited to two terms of four years each, institutionalizing the tradition of considering service in the bureaucracy a temporary calling. More than half the GEB were to be nominated by synods. Most of the rest were nominated at large, with the stipulation that "adequate representation of women, youth, Blacks, and Hispanic Americans" be assured. The days of domination by large-church pastors were over. The committee recognized that presbyteries and synods were developing their own mission and staff. It was quick to say its plan was intended not to capitulate to the spirit of regionalism, but rather to provide a way of trying the structures together (GA, PCUS, 1972, pp. 88, 94).

It was an ambitious approach. Fogleman acknowledged it asked a great deal of the church. The church at large, the presbytery and synod staffs, and the "agentry" executives had to be willing to work in a collaborative style and to seek to overcome their vested interests. According to the original design, there was to be a period of transition and training. Yet there was an eagerness to implement the plan, perhaps influenced by theological tensions at this 1972 Assembly moderated by noted conservative Nelson Bell. Despite Fogleman's warnings, the Assembly went ahead, and the nominating committee struggled all night to come up with a representative slate for the General Executive Board. Thus, the restructuring began with people selected for the GEB on the basis of political considerations, rather than beginning with the intended training period.[46]

What took the UPCUSA ten years to accomplish, the PCUS accomplished in three. A major shift in the ethos in which the church would undertake its mission was established. Hopes were high that the processes of inclusiveness and accountability would help overcome potential divisions and that management procedures would enable the church to develop unity in mission.

The Uncomfortable Adjustment

In both the UPCUSA and the PCUS the early years of reorganization were very difficult. In part that was due to the inherent nature of restructuring. But the difficulties were exacerbated by turbulent times in society and the church.

Reorganization was initiated in an era that assumed the ongoing expansion of the churches in membership and influence. Yet circumstances were changing. Membership peaked in the UPCUSA in 1967 and in the PCUS in 1968 and then began a steady decline. Moreover, in each tradition the restructuring took place at a time when traumatic events were causing division. In 1971, the Angela Davis controversy rocked the UPCUSA. Early in 1973, nearly three hundred PCUS congregations, angry at what they perceived as the abandonment of historic Presbyterian principles and fearful of the merger with the northern church, withdrew to form a new denomination—the Presbyterian Church in America. By 1975 monies for General Assembly mission were estimated to be only 50 percent of what they had been earlier (GA, PCUS, 1975, p. 117).

Each of the churches faced problems particular to its situation. In the UPCUSA the new organization was "so complex and confusing hardly anyone could understand it," as one journalist put it. It also seemed designed for faceless leaders, in contrast to the former strong, visible leaders who had been clearly identified with particular programs. This was compounded by personnel difficulties, especially in the crucial General Assembly Mission Council, where there were six executive directors in the first three years.[47]

The processes that were designed to be participatory and ensure accountability proved cumbersome. One of the operating assumptions of agencies as well as judicatories was that it was not individuals but groups who govern. Hence, there were incessant meetings. Frank Heinze, of the Support Agency, lamented how difficult it was to be creative, since he was "always in meetings . . . trying to protect the staff from red tape." Since a crucial component of the new design was to better coordinate the one mission of the church, the GAMC staff was constantly meeting with the staffs of the three agencies. Although they worked hard, the participants agreed the process was incredibly time-consuming and not altogether satisfactory.[48]

Some of the more elaborate plans to ensure that every decision would be seen in light of the whole never really worked. The matrix management model, which was to ensure that each problem would be seen multidimensionally, was given only lip service. Planning, budgeting, and evaluating (PBE as it was known), a management tool borrowed from General Motors, proved unworkable and was abandoned after a few years.[49]

Financial difficulties plagued the new structure. Not only had controversy reduced the General Assembly's resources, but the restructuring and the move to New York had been more costly than anticipated. Moreover, the Board of National Missions and COEMAR had spent their reserves before going out of existence, leaving the church almost no financial cushion. Consequently, the consultative, consensus-building process focused almost exclusively on allocating diminishing resources rather than on

revitalizing mission.[50] James McCord, for example, who
initially was on the evaluation segment of PBE, quickly
realized the power was in budgeting, where real decisions
about priorities and program were being made. In contrast
to the old boards, which had financial responsibility for
their work, the three agencies were dependent on the
GAMC to allocate resources. The allocation was a source
of some tension, particularly within the Program Agency,
which had the responsibility for the bulk of the program.
Moreover, it was very difficult for the GAMC to get a clear
picture of the financial state of the church. Richard Miller,
a lawyer who served on the GAMC, and Daniel Little, staff
member in charge of the budgeting section, began to make
sense of the financial picture by 1975. The budget situation
was critical, and some of the recently hired staff people,
especially women and racial ethnic persons recruited
through affirmative action, had to be dismissed.[51]

The openness that characterized the appointment of the
new boards and staff was not without problems. Board
members were eager to initiate their ideas, and in at least
several of the agencies there was a tendency for the boards
to be more involved in the management than the staff considered wise. In the opinion of one veteran church administrator the idea that "everyone has to have a crack at it"
influenced too many staffing appointments.[52]

Almost everyone who was involved with the restructuring acknowledges there were serious problems. Daniel
Little, executive director of the GAMC for most of its existence, admits that the GAMC, having no programmatic
substance, was trivialized by focusing on process.

Even so, after about five years, the system began to function more smoothly. Margaret Thomas, who became dep-
uty executive director of the GAMC in 1976, attributes
some of the difficulty simply to adjusting to a radically
different style of operating. Synod executives were uncom-
fortable with the idea of shared leadership instead of
clearly defined lines of hierarchy. Some of the turf battles,
in her view, had overtones of racism and sexism, as the
church adjusted to a more inclusive bureaucracy.

In part the job was made easier because of lowered expectations. There was a growing recognition that it was impossible to force everything into a single planning system. When one management consultant heard about presbytery-synod relationships, he commented to a veteran administrator, "But it won't work." The church is a highly complex network of relationships and rather impervious to comprehensive-type management solutions. Some individuals responded to their frustration with the practice of shared leadership by becoming overly conscious of drawing lines limiting their accountability, which made for efficiency, but often inhibited creativity.[53]

Despite the difficulties, the church did become more open, and those who had been marginalized were brought into leadership. New styles of leadership which were more collegial and inclusive emerged. Effective systems of budgetary and personnel oversight were developed. Yet overall, it was a confusing time. Despite the hopes that the participatory processes would enhance trust within the church, suspicion of the national bureaucracy only seemed to increase.

Within the PCUS, the turbulence surrounding reorganization was equally strong. The creation of a purposely different style of management was wrenching. At the first meeting of the General Executive Board, the old and new styles were in tangible conflict. Tension emerged over as seemingly trivial an issue as seating at the table. At that meeting a decision was made to try things in a new way, replacing a hierarchical style with the collegial model.[54]

The mixture of styles was apparent in the staff. A sign of the new was the presence of a woman and an African American to head divisions, but at the same time there was a desire to maintain continuity in staff selection. The concept of a management team to make decisions for each of the divisions was never fully understood or implemented. Corporate decision making proved difficult for some veteran administrators. The general staff director was to facilitate the process rather than assert executive authority. This meant there were incessant meetings, and some division heads lamented the plan's restriction on strong decision-making capacities at the center. Yet that was precisely the design's intent.

There were other problems. It was difficult to find information about the financial condition of the church. When they were finally obtained, the figures proved dismal. A number of staff people had to resign, undermining efforts to be inclusive. The different operating philosophies that had existed in the boards were incorporated into the divisions, also creating tensions. Moreover, the priority-development process never really worked, and the communication process ran in fits and starts as some synod staff people did not trust the communicators.

Moreover, the Office of Review and Evaluation (ORE), whose job was to reorganize the church from within, made the staff uneasy and defensive. Fogleman observed that the better it did its job, the worse it was perceived. Painful personnel decisions, such as the recommendation not to reelect National Missions head Evelyn Green, a longtime and much-loved leader in women's work, undermined confidence.[55]

By 1975 there was consensus that major revisions had to be undertaken. The General Assembly, "deeply concerned with an apparent laxity of sound business management and financial principles," stipulated that an in-depth evaluation of the agentry be made well in advance of the seventh-year review mandated by the Plan of Restructure. The ORE, under the leadership of former CRBA member Richard Hutcheson, presented an "Organizational Modification Study" the following year.

Substantial changes created clearer lines of authority. There was a backing away from the corporate leadership model and a return to the chief executive officer pattern. The name of the GEB became the General Assembly Mission Board in a symbolic effort to soften the uneasiness with the term "executive." The communications system was eliminated.

Patricia McClurg was called from the Division of Professional Development to become administrative director of the GAMB in 1977. Working within the revised framework of expectations, she helped build that collegial style which had been so elusive, even while exerting strong leadership and giving the division directors more latitude over their own program.[56]

Within a few years, as in the UPCUSA, the administrative kinks were ironed out and the system was working reasonably well. Morale had improved; the consolidation of all offices in Atlanta, from multiple cities, was accomplished; the commitment to approach mission globally was strengthened; women and racial ethnic persons were given heightened visibility in the church's bureaucracy; and the church's financial picture was clearer.

Reorganization and Social Transformation

Although neither reorganization worked out as its originators intended, each can be seen as part of a larger process that changed the ethos and style of the church's life. Daniel Little, former executive director of the UPCUSA's General Assembly Mission Council, suggests that the restructuring represented a tacit admission that the partnership of the mainstream mission boards with the destiny of an expanding American nation was at an end. The old boards were designed to serve an expanding church in an expanding nation. By the time the boards were restructured, that clarity of purpose had become blurred. More egalitarian forces called for increased openness and participation of those who had been on the edges of society. What James I. McCord called a "romanticism" was in the air, which was suspicious of expert leadership and convinced that everyone could contribute equally well.[57] Given the changes in society, it was almost inevitable that the church would be transformed in ways that would be turbulent and even traumatic. The organization would be held responsible for what was a broader societal change.

Yet, at the same time, there was an intentionality about the enthusiastic incorporation of managerial principles in church life. Restructuring was fueled by a confidence that process and organization themselves could be the crucial contribution to bring clarity and unity to the church. In retrospect, that seems to have been overly optimistic, tending to forget that organization is only a tool that cannot substitute for substantive vision. Activist and author John Fry has suggested that the reorganization was a deliberate attempt to muzzle the most creative and prophetic voices in the church. While that suggests too much of a conscious conspiracy, in fact reorganization did tend to reduce the visibility and creative capacities of leaders in a muddle of process.[58]

The significance of the reorganizations should also be seen in the context of other, countervailing pressures in the church. At the same time that both churches sought to have greater coordination at the General Assembly level, the size and significance of the staff at that level was diminishing. Mission was being decentralized at the presbytery and synod levels, and thus executive staff burgeoned in these middle governing bodies, providing yet another stage in the ongoing reshaping of the malleable Presbyterian tradition.

Reunion Brings Restructure: The 1980s

When the Presbyterian Church in the U.S. and The United Presbyterian Church in the U.S.A. finally united in 1983, another restructuring was necessary. The merger was possible in part because the two churches had developed similar commitments to mission and a comparable pattern of organization. Nevertheless, there were differences in tradition and style. And neither denomination was content with the organization it had created. The committee proposing a new structural design rejoiced that the church had "been given a rare opportunity to develop a new approach to mission."[59]

The new approach affirmed basic commitments to the open, inclusive, process-oriented style of decision making that had been established in the turbulent reorganizations of the 1970s. Enabling the presbyteries and synods to do mission continued as a goal, and with it the emphasis on providing executive staffing there.[60] The new approach to mission did not mean a return to larger General Assembly agencies.

Yet there was a determined effort to avoid some of the earlier mistakes. The Plan for Reunion stressed continuity. Members of the General Assembly Council (hereafter GAC), whose task it was to oversee the development of a new mission structure, were to serve for six years without change, other than to fill vacancies. The 1972 and 1973 reorganizations were marked by a deliberate commitment to secure new personnel as board members and staff, and the result was a turbulence created by a craving to innovate. Now the church opted for stability, at least in personnel. The Plan for Reunion stipulated, for example, that "care and sensitivity shall be shown employed personnel" if the General Assembly offices were relocated. That commitment was later honored when anyone who desired to move to the new headquarters in Louisville was guaranteed a position.

The Formation of the General Assembly Council

The Articles of Agreement of the Plan for Reunion provided continuity in the composition of the General Assembly Council. Twenty-four members would be nominated by the UPCUSA from the membership of the General Assembly Mission Council, and twenty-four by the PCUS, twenty-one of them from the General Assembly Mission Board. The GAC was to be half clergy, half laity. The euphoria of reunion did not eliminate suspicions as the new church considered specifics. The Southerners feared being swallowed up by their larger UPCUSA counterparts. The Northerners were unhappy with compromises that seemed to tip the political balance in favor of PCUS perspectives. Just prior to reunion the PCUS added twenty-two of its most experienced and competent people to its General Assembly Mission Board for a special one-year term; many of these were then nominated to serve on the GAC. The

UPCUSA could not do that constitutionally, and it was further constrained from naming its most experienced people to the GAC by requirements to secure representation from all the synods.[61]

These forty-eight persons, plus the new Moderator of the General Assembly and the Moderators of the two previous General Assemblies of each church, were given enormous responsibility to develop the new church. Their task of overseeing the ongoing mission while proposing a new structure was quite unlike that given to any previous elected council, board, or agency. The same people were to keep at this task for six years, until a new mission organization was created and staff secured. The commitment of time and energy was staggering, with the entire GAC meeting generally five times a year.

For some time elected persons had been assuming more direct involvement in program planning. This was a legacy of the long-standing attempt to curb the power of staff, which in itself reflected a cultural fabric of mistrust of authority and institutions. Even after Donald Black was hired as executive director, the GAC made it clear that his responsibilities were circumscribed. When decisions were made, it was a GAC member and not he as staff who made the announcements. There was also some reluctance to involve staff and representatives of ongoing boards, agencies, and governing bodies, until their roles were clearer. In the UPCUSA these relationships had been highly structured, while in the PCUS they had been informal.[62]

The GAC faced the initial challenge of developing working relationships among people from the two churches who did not know each other well, so that they could move beyond old issues and the tendency to perceive decisions as a success for the Northern or Southern perspective. At the first meeting Sara B. Moseley, a former Moderator of the PCUS, was elected Moderator of the Council, narrowly defeating Kenneth Hall from the UPCUSA stream. In response to a desire to be more responsive to the church's theological pluralism, the General Assembly added four advisory members from recognized conservative-evangelical circles. Working committees were established, including one on mission design, chaired by Josiah Beeman, a political consultant with extensive administrative expertise and lobbying skills, who had headed the General Assembly Committee on a Just Political Economy.[63]

Special committees were charged with exploring other aspects of church life, including the adjustment of synod and presbytery boundaries, the development of appropriate vehicles to address women's concerns, both lay and professional, and the location of General Assembly agencies.

Clarifying the role of the Stated Clerk received high priority. In the UPCUSA the Clerk had considerable authority, serving ex officio on most bodies and acting as an ecclesiastical check to administrative power. In the PCUS, the ecclesiastical stream was deliberately kept separate from the programmatic. The new position description recommended to the Assembly by the GAC reflected the church's ongoing desire to restrain powerful leadership. The Stated Clerk was not the chief executive officer of the denomination, but simply the "continuing officer of the General Assembly." There were clear limits on the Clerk's role in ecumenical relationships and as interpreter of General Assembly actions. Though the position was diminished, and tenure in office limited to three four-year terms, nevertheless, it was eagerly sought during a protracted election at the 1984 Assembly. James Andrews, who had been Clerk of the PCUS, was finally elected on the fourth ballot.[64]

True to its commitment to a participatory style of decision making, the Mission Design Committee developed "Today Into Tomorrow—A Year of Consultations" in order to "involve the entire denomination in rethinking its understanding of mission." Twenty-four percent of the congregations, 81 percent of the presbyteries, and 100 percent of the synods engaged in a priority-defining process. This data become the basis for a five-day meeting at Mo-Ranch in Texas, in February 1985, from which a "Life and Mission Statement" was written as the theological foundation for the development of new structures.

The priorities listed by the church at large were mostly personal: (1) leading others to a saving knowledge of Jesus Christ; (2) promoting peacemaking; (3) equipping and supporting laity in their witness; (4) revitalizing congregations; (5) enriching family life; and (6) emphasizing the primacy of scripture as a standard for our faith and practice. The General Assembly entities listed priorities somewhat different from those of the church, emphasizing public policy concerns, support of ministries relating to particular constituencies, and issues regarding mission funding.

Differences in how to assess the varying priorities led to the final statement's becoming "a treaty among tribes," with various interests getting some mention of their concerns. The Life and Mission Statement listed no priorities, but rather focused on style of mission. Its concluding section, "How We Live and Work Together," argued that the church was to be marked by inclusiveness, namely the "deliberate empowerment of people previously excluded from full participation," and partnership, that is, working "alongside one another in mutual assistance, avoiding patterns of domination or control." In elevating a particular style of management to a major element of witness, the church sent a clear signal there was to be no retreating from the commitments of the 1970s.[65]

The Structural Design for Mission

Because the Life and Mission Statement gave no clear priorities, the Mission Design Committee had considerable latitude as it designed structures. The committee investigated the theological basis for structure, principles of organization, the traditions of the two streams, and the experiences of reorganization in other denominations. They held hearings at the 1985 Assembly and consultations with racial ethnic leaders and theologians. By October a draft had been presented to synods, presbyteries, and General Assembly agencies. A month later, congregations received the draft for study and review.

Consultation was widespread, although conducted on a tight schedule. An early proposal suggesting that synods be replaced with no more than ten regional governing units met stern resistance from those who saw it both as a radical revision of Presbyterian polity and transcending the mandate to revise General Assembly–level agencies. The idea was abandoned. Response to the draft focused largely on the power of the General Assembly Council itself. Modifications were made in the plan, and it was presented to the 1986 General Assembly by Beeman, who had been a major architect and strong advocate of the plan. With some minor changes, it was adopted overwhelmingly.[66]

At the heart of the Design was the creation of nine ministry units: Church Vocations, Education and Congregational Nurture, Evangelism and Church Development, Global Mission, Racial Ethnic, Social Justice and Peacemaking, Stewardship and Communication Development, Theology and Worship, and Women's. Sixteen elected members comprised each unit, with nominations coming largely from synods and presbyteries. In reaction to criticism of the previous restructurings, the Design sought to create ministry units "with names that communicate to the church-at-large the work of each Unit" (GA, PC(USA), 1986, pp. 369–374).

Although the units were to be of varying size in budget and staff, the identifying of nine functional units raised the question of whether they would be seen as having equal priority. That dilemma was highlighted by bringing groups that had been advocacy-oriented or advisory into the mainstream of the structure as ministry units or related bodies. As Jack Rogers, formerly of the Theology and Worship Ministry Unit, pointed out, the structure does not appear to reflect the priorities set by the church in the year-long consultation. For example, four of the six priorities of the church at large were subsumed under one ministry unit—Education and Congregational Nurture.[67]

The Structural Design sought to demonstrate through mission structures the unity of the church, while affirming its diversity and inclusiveness. As in the uniting churches, partnership and collaboration were the key phrases. Clear patterns of accountability and review were developed. Building on the conviction that "no Unit can function completely alone, but will need to work with other Units in giving and receiving help and in supporting what is good for the whole," patterns of linkage were established to ensure effective coordination. First, the GAC itself placed members on ministry unit committees, and each ministry unit committee nominated a person to serve on the GAC. Secondly, each ministry unit was to use its annual planning and budget process to review linkages. Thirdly, the staff itself provided coordination through the Coordinating Cabinet of unit directors. Each ministry unit was to report annually to both the GAC and the Assembly and could submit recommendations for the Council to submit to the Assembly either with or without its endorsement. In another effort to correct perceived weaknesses of the previous reorganizations, the GAC was given considerable leverage for planning, coordinating, and budgeting, simply because the programmatic ministry units were *units* of the GAC (GA, PC(USA), 1986, pp. 374–375).

The partnership motif was followed through in the budgeting process, which was something of a hybrid of the patterns used in the previous churches. Guidance in the distribution of funds, including mission partnership funds, was developed through a process of consultation with the next more inclusive governing body (GA, PC(USA), 1986, pp. 394–395).

The Structural Design for Mission assumed a single location for the GAC and the ministry units. The 1987 General Assembly rejected all attempts to maintain multiple locations and settled on one location, albeit not the Assembly committee's choice. In one of the most spirited and controversial contests ever experienced at a General Assembly, the Assembly voted to make Louisville, Kentucky, its headquarters, largely because of stewardship considerations.

At the same meeting, the GAC reported the progress made at implementation. With a certain rhetorical flourish, it admitted that the "new mission design was not mission itself," but was "like a trellis on which the church's mission could grow, blossom, and flourish." Leadership was critical to that growth, and directors for each of the units were elected by the GAC and confirmed by the General Assembly. They were people who had demonstrated administrative experience in General Assembly agencies, though not necessarily in the field to which they were called. Management skill was more critical than expertise in particular fields. Five of the nine had experience in the former PCUS church, three were women, three were laypersons, and two were racial ethnic persons. Significantly, the executive director of the Council, whose primary task was to coordinate the work of the units, was an elder, S. David Stoner, whose professional life had been spent in management consulting.[68]

With the work of establishing the new structure complete, the GAC has had to clarify its ongoing task. According to the Form of Government (G-13.0200), the GAC is to engage in churchwide planning, be involved in budget development, and coordinate the work of General Assembly agencies. After being so involved in a direct way with overseeing the development of the new organization and managing the work of the church in the interim period, the challenge, according to several GAC members and General Assembly staff, is whether the GAC will be able to back off and release the staff to generate ideas and program. As the GAC members who have served since 1983 began to rotate off in 1989, the composition began reflecting the constitutional mandate of one-third clergy, one-third laymen, and one-third laywomen. This is a change from the tradition of parity of clergy and laity and reflects the increasingly visible role of the laity in the power structures of the church. Moreover, the GAC will maintain a goal of 20 percent racial ethnic members. This is a higher percentage than the racial ethnic membership of the church and is an indication of the denomination's desire to be a witness to the principle of inclusiveness in its institutional life.[69]

Still in the process of being worked out is the relationship between the Stated Clerk and the GAC. The Council has responsibility for reviewing the work of the Office of the General Assembly in consultation with the Stated Clerk. Changes in the Structural Design proposed by the GAC to the 1989 General Assembly evoked a stiff reaction from the Clerk, who felt they encroached on the Clerk's prerogatives and would upset the checks the Presbyterian system places on accumulating too much power in one place. The Assembly deferred any changes in the Design until the comprehensive review scheduled for 1991.[70]

If we use business historian Alfred Chandler's interpretation, we can say that the Presbyterian Church in the 1980s created a structure that fits its diffuse strategy. That the church is pluralistic and inclusive not only has been acknowledged, it is celebrated. Amidst a variety of options, the church has developed a structure that seeks to embrace them all. Despite the often-stated concern about power flowing to the GAC, the issue is not one of centralization or decentralization. In fact, the church has multiple centers of power. The Council and its units represent an effort toward centralized coordination, but the presence of nine distinct ministry units and several related bodies will certainly impede the accumulation of authority in just a few individuals. Moreover, the shift of focus to mission at the synod and presbytery levels over the past several decades has created the presence of a strong executive staff who tend to work as a countervailing force to the national structure. Presbyterian polity continues to be extraordinarily malleable. Moreover, it is apparent that the church has continued to create structures in which management and process skills are essential components. Given that fabric, the key issue is whether strong executive leaders can emerge who can create a vision for the church and implement it.[71]

One crucial task undertaken by the GAC was the creation of priorities for the church. Since 1983 the General Assembly had adopted a number of chief priorities, but it found difficulty in utilizing these to guide allocation of limited resources. Finally, the Bicentennial Assembly adopted two priority goals, evangelism and developing congregations, and doing justice, as well as sixteen nonprioritized continuing goals. The diverse goals of a highly pluralistic church were embraced, and although some guidance was offered, it remains to be seen how the vision statement and goals actually will affect the work of the ministry units and GAC.

The Current Challenge

During the twentieth century the church has been transformed by structural change that reflects the values of business organization and the science of management. The church has continued to affirm that organization is only a means by which it does mission and that the Holy Spirit, not organization, is the source of power for the church. But there has been an underlying conviction that with the right organization and effective processes for involving the church in decision making, the church can find its way and have a renewed and vital mission.

This trend has become pronounced during the last twenty-five years. As synod executive and GAC member William Fogleman put it, "The organizational revolution in America has seized the church by the neck and shaken it like a dog shaking a rat. Because we are so immersed in it, we do not realize it has happened." What was once done by personal, informal contact is now done by process and procedure. In part, of course, that has been positive and has resulted in the opening up of the decision making of the church to those who were formerly marginalized. But organization has not solved and cannot solve the dilemmas the church faces at the end of the twentieth century. As Kenneth Hall, Moderator of the 1988 General Assembly, often put it, "The church is ripe for the inbreaking of the Holy Spirit." The question is how do the structures allow for the genuine breaking in of the Holy Spirit?[72]

The Presbyterian denominations have paid inordinate attention to their internal needs and organizational well-being in the 1970s and 1980s. Despite the theological commitment to being a church in the world, the focus has often been on denominational concerns, creating an organization, ensuring participation within the power structures, and finding a way to secure adequate financing for the commitments we have desired to make. Historian Leonard I. Sweet draws a distinction between ecclesiastical establishments, which focus inward on stability, rules and regulations, and religious movements, which value change and innovation and look outward. Establishments tend to strive toward goals and talk more about our *church* than about our *Christ,* while religious movements inhabit a vision and do just the opposite. He suggests "old-line" churches need to be open to the movements of renewal within their denominations precisely because they will be a challenge to the establishment and press the denomination outward in mission that elevates Christ.[73]

In part, the organizational focus of recent years reflects an uncertainty regarding the church's role in a changing society. There has been a diminished confidence regarding the influence of the church in our society and the willingness of the culture to listen to the church. In adapting the values of the culture regarding organization and process, the church has sought to remedy its own uncertainty about its role. It has created a structure that embraces the pluralism of the church in a multitude of perspectives and programs.

Peter Drucker, one of the foremost management theorists of the twentieth century, argues forcefully that "the first question in discussing organizational structure must be: What is our business and what should it be?" This is precisely the question the contemporary church has difficulty answering. Sociologist Robert Wuthnow points out that there has been a major religious realignment in America and considerable division within denominations over what are the key issues of faith. Historically, Presbyterians have often sought to resolve their doctrinal differences by focusing on mission, but there is less clarity on what the fundamental mission of the church is. The consensus that the church was to spread the gospel so that people would become believers in Jesus Christ, establishing worshiping communities and building churches, has waned as the frontier has disappeared, both nationally and globally.[74]

Structure itself cannot define the task of the church. There can be an organizational myopia through which adjusting structure gives the illusion of activity while accomplishing little. The structure created in 1983–1988 provides an organizational way to keep the varying visions of the church in creative interplay with each other. The unanswered question is whether from that structure leaders will emerge to create a vision of mission that will engage and energize the church. It may hinge, as John Leith has put it, on rediscovering "what the church has to say that no one else can say."[75] It is easier to analyze the church than it is to find solutions for its dilemmas, of course. While it certainly has considerable investment in and responsibility for the outcome, the church must continually reaffirm its confession that Christ is Lord of the Presbyterian Church (U.S.A.) and that its future is ultimately in God's hands.

3

The American Presbytery
in the Twentieth Century

Lewis L. Wilkins, Jr.

The American presbytery in the twentieth century has been shaped by multiple forces past and present: the canon law legacy of Reformation polity; the rise of the evangelical denomination as a distinctive American form of the church; fascination with "frontiers" as objects of mission; mid-nineteenth-century arguments over how to reconcile the denominational form with traditional Presbyterian polity; and the shifting environments for mission.

Setting the Stage: The Origins

The "presbytery" has been a distinctive and important element in the polity structure of all churches that trace their lineage back to the Church of Scotland.[1] Churches that stand in the streams of the continental Reformation strongly influenced by the work of John Calvin also have bodies similar to presbyteries, but call them by other names.[2]

Roots in Canon Law

Reformed approaches to ordering and organizing the post-Reformation church were set firmly within the tradition and concepts of Western Catholic canon law in which many of the founders of Reformed churches were well schooled.[3] Their redefinition of medieval canon law concepts and reassignment of ecclesiastical powers formed the basis for rules for presbyteries in the Presbyterian forms of government.

The Reformed founders relocated the "particular church" from the diocese to the congregation, retaining the terms "particular church" and "bishop" but applying them to the congregation and to the pastor, who was authorized to preside over the congregation, to preach, and to celebrate the sacraments in it.[4] The Reformed founders vested "powers of jurisdiction" (legislation and government, reserved to a bishop in canon law) in groups of persons, an ordered hierarchy of "assemblies" or "judicatories"[5] composed of ministers and lay "governors" or "elders."[6]

They lodged the power to "make ministers" in the presbytery. This power has two aspects, one governmental and the other liturgical. The governmental decision about whether a particular candidate was qualified to be ordained belonged to the presbytery, and each minister and elder cast an equal vote. Until the nineteenth and twentieth centuries[7] the liturgical right to ordain by the laying on of hands with prayer was reserved to ministers; at least three ministers, the quorum of a presbytery, were required to perform the rite.[8]

As in the medieval church, ordination granted certain "powers of order" to an individual minister: power to celebrate the sacraments, to pronounce forgiveness of sins to a congregation, and to bless the people in God's name. Like their predecessors in the medieval church, Reformed ministers required additional authorization ("granting of faculties" in canon law) from a session or presbytery to exercise these powers in a particular place and at specified times.

Overseeing ministerial candidacy, ordaining and overseeing ministers, and seeing to the calling and installing of pastors in congregations are core responsibilities of every

American presbytery in the twentieth century. These responsibilities are erected on the basis of a revision and redefinition of the canon law of the Western church catholic.

Reform in Scotland

A fully developed polity with a clearly defined "presbytery" did not emerge in the sixteenth-century Scottish *Books of Discipline,* which set forth changes to be made and abuses to be corrected within the traditional Scottish framework of parishes, dioceses, and synods.[9] Presbyterian polity evolved in Scotland through acts of the General Assembly and Parliaments.[10]

Organizing the Diaspora

In 1645, a half century after the Scottish *Books,* the Westminster *Form of Presbyterial Church Government* was written to serve the needs of a church that existed as a relatively stable diaspora minority in England, not for a community living in pre-Reformation dioceses. For the diaspora, the Westminster *Form* sought to give Presbyterianism a recognizable identity distinct from Anglicans on the one hand and congregationalists on the other.[11] It was a more concise and "constitutional" document than the Scottish *Books.* Its language aimed for precision in definitions of key terms and concepts; its architecture is comprehensive. The Westminster *Form* marks the first appearance of the later "presbytery" as a body made up of ministers and lay representatives of congregations and charged with government and ordering ministry.

Transplanted to America

The presbytery that evolved in Scotland and England in the sixteenth and seventeenth centuries and was codified in the Westminster *Form of Presbyterial Church Government* was well suited for organizing a distinctive Presbyterian Church in America.

The Scotch-Irish and other Reformed immigrants who

began arriving in the middle colonies in large numbers in the first decade of the eighteenth century lived as a diaspora among already established English Anglicans and congregationalists, English Catholics in Maryland, and Dutch Reformed in New York. Their chief task for almost a hundred years was to receive, organize, and incorporate immigrants arriving from Ulster, Scotland, Germany, and France within the relatively close geographic confines of the lands east of the Appalachian Mountains. Their language reflected roots in the long-established European church: they "settled" pastors in congregations organized according to the only model they knew, the settled "parish" models of Europe and Britain.[12]

They used the 1645 Westminster *Form of Presbyterial Church Government* as their polity handbook for organizing the Presbytery of Philadelphia in 1706 and other presbyteries and synods that came under the jurisdiction of a new Form of Government (FG) in 1788 and a General Assembly in 1789. The functions and duties of a presbytery as set forth in FG 1788 have provided the constitutional core definition of the presbytery's role in all subsequent American Presbyterian constitutions:

> Cognizance of all things that regard the welfare of the particular churches within their bounds . . . receiving and issuing appeals from the sessions . . . examining, and licensing candidates for the gospel ministry . . . ordaining, settling, removing, or judging ministers . . . resolving questions of doctrine or discipline . . . condemning erroneous opinions . . . visiting particular churches . . . uniting or dividing Congregations . . . ordering whatever pertains to the spiritual concerns of the Churches under their care.[13]

The Challenge of the Frontier

Until the American Revolution and the opening of the Western frontier, two centuries of experience in reforming church life in stable European parish settings served Presbyterians well. They showed steady growth, especially on the western fringes of earlier colonial occupation.

The U.S. Constitution and the Northwest Ordinance created an environment in which the original settlements on the East Coast would not hold hegemony forever over the nation's values and destiny. Churches that drew on the settled conditions of Britain and Europe had to adapt their forms of life and governance to minister effectively to a population that became a rapidly westward-moving target.

As people streamed west, Easterners wanted to influence the destiny of the Westerners' eternal souls, as well as their temporal behavior. Although the West attracted people and their imaginations, it also inspired fear that the ignoble, rough-hewn ways of the pioneers would eventually take over the politics and culture of the country.[14]

From the rigorous perspective of New England, many of the eighteenth-century immigrants seemed to be lacking in any religion at all because they were less intensely Puritan than English Calvinists who had come to America in the seventeenth century. The already-settled saw a great need for "awakening" the newcomers to fervent faith. Predestination, a most useful and reassuring doctrine in Europe's communal context of social stability, was challenged by "New Light" evangelists, who preached an experiential and individualized gospel to stir up faith and good works among the new settlers.

"New" churches, especially the Baptists and the Methodists, oriented themselves quickly and wholeheartedly toward this moving population and the new evangelical theology. Their members had not arrived early enough or owned enough property on the seacoast to have deep roots in the East. They saw quickly that their fortunes, not only in a spiritual sense, were to be found among the newcomers moving West.

Presbyterian Schisms

Among Presbyterians, the dilemmas posed for a settled polity in a demographically unsettled situation appeared first and most sharply in the westernmost parts of the church beyond the mountains. The divisions that marked American Presbyterian history in the eighteenth and early nineteenth centuries directly involved issues of how to deal with the frontier and its challenges to Presbyterian polity and organization.

The division started in presbyteries around issues of their particular concern: resolving matters of doctrine and equipping congregations with educated, competent, and committed ministers. The Old Side–New Side division (1741–1758) "grew out of contextual, praxis concerns about Christian experience, precisely the points (liturgical and political) at which the new church had no constitutional standards."[15] The Cumberland Presbyterian Church was formed in 1810 when a presbytery in Tennessee seceded to free itself from constitutional constraints that prevented presbyteries with large needs for ministers from preparing them for ordination on the frontier, instead of sending them back across the mountains to Princeton. The Campbell-Stone movement began about the same time, when some Presbyterian ministers withdrew from Lexington Presbytery in Kentucky after a similar fight. The Old School–New School schism in 1837 involved questions about whether evangelization of the West should be done by Presbyterians alone or in concert with the Congregationalists, and whether it should be carried out by church judicatories, church boards, or independent lay boards.[16]

As a result of these controversies, Presbyterians were about forty years later than other denominations in committing themselves wholeheartedly to the task of churching the unchurched in the West.[17]

The Evangelical American Denomination

The frontier challenge of the western movement transformed all the major Protestant churches into versions of a uniquely American institution: the evangelical denomination. Whatever their formal polity, American churches took on a distinctive form quite different from the church in Europe.[18]

The engine that drove the Presbyterian and other American Protestant evangelical denominations in the nineteenth century and shaped presbyteries as they existed at the beginning of the twentieth century was a compelling call to mission defined as evangelizing and civilizing a nation, *especially its westward frontier regions,* in the name of the Lord Jesus Christ.

The evangelical denomination came to have two distinguishing characteristics: it organized itself for mission (evangelizing and churching the West), and it added "mission"[19] to its definition of the church.

Alternative Presbyterian Forms
of the Protestant Denomination

The Presbyterian churches (Old School and New School 1837–1870, northern and southern 1861–1983[20]) were full, if somewhat tardy, participants in the development of the American evangelical denomination, but that participation involved the church in decades of conflict. This conflict reflected the high value Presbyterians placed on church polity as an expression of the church's theological and ecclesiological commitments. Presbyterian disagreements over how to organize for mission were not just disputes over how to act in concert to achieve goals; they escalated quickly into conflicts over the nature of the church and its governing bodies.[21] This is especially clear in the debates between Charles Hodge and James Henley Thornwell, in Old School General Assemblies in the 1840s and 1850s, over the biblical legitimacy of "boards" for missions.[22]

Both Hodge and Thornwell subscribed to the manifest destiny consensus, common in evangelical Protestantism, that it was God's will for the Protestant denominations to evangelize and civilize the American frontier. They differed in their visions of how to do the work. Hodge, from Princeton Seminary in New Jersey, felt the best way for

Presbyterians to play their part in the historic task was through mission boards sponsored by the General Assembly but distinct from the governance structure inherited from the Reformation. Thornwell, from Columbia Seminary in South Carolina, opposed boards because he could find no basis for them in scripture. Instead, he proposed reconciling traditional Presbyterian polity with the evangelistic call of the frontier by turning the whole church, every judicatory from the session to the General Assembly, into a missionary society, and lodging implementing responsibilities in committees.[23]

This conflict had not been resolved when the Civil War ruptured the church in 1861. After the split, each side had a church of its own in which to act out its vision of the missionary church. The church in the North followed Hodge's line and developed an organization much like those of other American evangelical denominations. The church in the South developed as a mission experiment with the ecclesiological and missional structure envisioned by Thornwell; it also became an American evangelical denomination, but was a different species of the genus. The differences affected especially the development of presbyteries in the late nineteenth and twentieth centuries.

At the constituting General Assembly of the Presbyterian Church in the Confederate States of America, Thornwell outlined his alternative vision for the new evangelical denomination:[24]

> The ends which we propose to accomplish as a Church are the same as those which are proposed by every other Church. To proclaim God's truth as a witness to the nations; to gather his elect from the four corners of the earth, and through the Word, Ministries and Ordinances to train them for eternal life. . . . The only thing that will be at all peculiar to us is the manner in which we shall attempt to discharge our duty. . . . It is our purpose to rely upon the regular organs of our government, and executive agencies directly and immediately responsible to them. We wish to make the Church, not

merely a superintendent, but an agent. . . . From the Session to the Assembly we shall strive to enlist all our courts, *as courts,* in every department of Christian effort [italics added for emphasis].

Presbyteries and Mission: 1900–1945

In the twentieth century, Presbyterian mission and the American presbytery have been shaped by these two different Presbyterian responses to the frontier. In the Presbyterian Church in the U.S.A., mission was the work of national boards (consolidated in 1922 into a single Board of National Missions) and was carried out by a nationally appointed staff in synods and presbyteries, while presbyteries continued the functions they inherited from the Reformation—governance and ordering ministry. In the PCUS, mission was added to the list of a presbytery's responsibilities, and staff to implement all three functions came to be called and funded locally by presbyteries and synods.

The Shape of Mission

Differences between the two varieties of the Presbyterian evangelical denomination are evident in reports brought to the General Assemblies by the mission boards/committees. In both churches reports were organized by synods and included narratives supplied by persons responsible in "the field." The PCUSA reports assume that "the work" was being done by the board in these geographic areas. The PCUS reports tell what the synods and presbyteries did, and how the executive committee worked in partnership to support them. The difference is clearest in the reports on how mission funds were raised and dispensed.

The PCUSA reports limited the "mission" on which they reported to work supported by the board. From 1900 to 1960 the number of deployed mission personnel supported by the board at one time was about three thousand (numbers for 1900 to 1920 include personnel of all boards later merged into the Board of National Missions):

Year	Supported Personnel
1900	3021
1910	3629
1920	1819
1930	3768
1940	3375
1950	2952
1960	2971

In the narrative reports from the field, the need for national support is stressed. For example, the report on work in Kansas in 1900 was at pains to show by statistics on the size of churches (181 of 325 having fewer than fifty members) that "this Synod is pre-eminently home mission ground," while also demonstrating efficiency in "grouping" churches so that twenty were served by self-sustaining pastorates "so as to demand no help from the Board."[25]

The PCUS reports present a diverse picture. The report for 1900, for example, described in great detail the patterns of supporting and conducting mission in various parts of the church. In Alabama, Florida, and Georgia "each Presbytery cares for its own fields." The synods of Arkansas, Memphis, Missouri, South Carolina, Texas, and Virginia had synodical committees that raised funds by collection and subscription and employed "synodical evangelists" who were assigned to work in presbyteries, while the presbyteries also did their own work through their committees and treasuries. Three of four presbyteries in the Synod of Nashville worked together with a common mission treasury. Mississippi, Kentucky, and North Carolina had different combinations of synod and presbytery committees and treasuries, and different patterns of revenue sharing to ensure that people were deployed where needs were greatest.[26]

The Executive Committee of Home Missions and its

successors in the South sometimes reported to the General
Assembly on the number of mission personnel deployed:

Year	Supported Personnel
1900	137
1910	no report
1920	764 (whole or part support)
1930	650
1940–1960	no reports

From 1960 on, the reports to the PCUS Assembly included
money spent on missions in the United States by the national agency, by synods and presbyteries, and by congregations:

	(Millions of Dollars)		
	1960	1970	1980
GA Church Extension	$1.260	$1.275	$n/a[27]
Synods	6.446	8.129	4.960
Presbyteries	4.877	7.106	13.272
Congregations	1.045	1.462	12.318

Mission to the West

Mission understood primarily as an enterprise of
churching the unchurched in the West sets the dominant
tone in the reports of mission agencies to both General
Assemblies until World War II. Other forms of mission—
neighborhood houses to meet the needs of urban immigrant poor and evangelistic outreach to non-English-
speaking immigrant groups, for example—were carried
out and reported, but they appear in the reports more as
ancillary good works than as the real work of mission in
which the churches were engaged.

The westward movement was explicit in the 1900 Kansas narrative report to the PCUSA Assembly: "The Synod
of Kansas is scarce a generation old. . . . We are now in the
race for future greatness where Indiana, Illinois, and Iowa
were thirty years ago." The Michigan narrative reflected a
little defensively a belief that the frontier had passed

through its territory: "Only three churches have been organized during the year. This small number is not due to indifference, nor to indolence in extending the Church. It is due largely to the fact that church extension in the form of new organizations is practically at an end."[28] Later reports highlight progress of "the work" in the Southwest, California, and Alaska, and development of churches and schools for Native Americans on Western reservations.

In the South, the West was Texas, since the westward frontier was bounded by the borders of the Confederacy. Reports to the General Assembly show a constant preoccupation with mission in that state. The Assembly was alerted regularly to new movements of unchurched populations into Texas and the large needs for mission work this immigration created. Success in starting new missions and churches in Texas regularly came in for special praise. Although it had a smaller membership than other synods, the Synod of Texas consistently was reported as having a lion's share of presbytery Christian education staff (ten of a total twenty-nine in 1930, for example). These peripatetic educators played a significant role in supporting the development of strong small churches in the county seats of thinly populated areas of the state. They were supported by field staff deployed in synods by the PCUS Board of Christian Education, the only agency in the southern church that used the field staff model.

The Shape of Presbyteries

In both denominations, the development of presbyteries from 1900 to World War II was influenced more by the frontier and the denominations' sense of mission to the West than by any other single factor. Geographic boundary changes were predicated on assumptions about the numbers of churches and ministers a presbytery needed to be programmatically effective. Organizational structures, perceived staffing needs, and role definitions and job descriptions for staff persons who came to work in presbyteries and synods were developed in response to how the

churches saw presbytery leadership to be important to promote the mission cause in settled parts and in doing "the
work" in parts still being settled.

The statistical data in General Assembly records show
how presbyteries grew steadily in size while the churches
ordered themselves for effectiveness in mission.[29]

Among Presbyterians before the Civil War, the size and
shape of judicatories remained about the same despite divisions. During the Old School and New School schism,
the average presbytery had 1,300–1,800 members in 18
churches with 15 ministers. Synods were composed of five
or six presbyteries. In the period of the division, the Old
School membership increased by 131 percent and the New
School by 78 percent; U.S. population increased by 81.5
percent. In the Old School, the ratio of ministers to congregations increased from .69 to .87; in the New School, from
.87 to 1.13; the ratio of members to ministers ranged between 89 to 1 and 109 to 1. Presbyteries and congregations
were mostly small, and the excess of pulpits over ministers
exerted constant pressure to recruit candidates for ordination as well as providing many places of service for
unordained church workers.

By 1900, the impact of post–Civil War changes had left
its mark on the demographics of the presbyteries in the
PCUSA and the PCUS. Although the average number of
congregations per presbytery was similar, total membership and average congregational size differed considerably:

	PCUSA	PCUS
Churches	33	37
Members	4,401	2,859
Ministers	32	18
Members per minister	136	155
Members per church	132	76
Ratio ministers/churches	.97	.49

In the North and West, presbytery and synod staffing
developed from the beginning on a field staff model. Even
before the major reorganization of 1922, several boards

already had a system of field staff deployed directly or in concert with synods and presbyteries.[30] The 1922 reorganization[31] reduced the number of General Assembly boards from sixteen to four and further affected the development of presbyteries. It created a Board of National Missions equipped with a highly articulated, centralized "national staff" to do the work of mission in the United States in an efficient, nationally coordinated way. The elements of this "executive organization" were delineated in the plan of organization for the board presented to the 1923 General Assembly:

> a. The Synodical Organization, to which each Synod and Presbytery shall be related. Its duties are development of program, preparation of budget, distribution of budget, administration of budget, and cooperation with the Board.
>
> b. The Synodical Executive and Presbyterial Executive
>
> c. The National Staff, consisting of the Executive and Staff Councils of the Board, the Synodical Executives and the Executives of the specially designated Presbyteries. Its functions shall be to formulate and recommend to the Board general policies and methods, to prepare the annual budgets, the relating of the experience of Presbyteries and Synods to the work of the entire church, and the providing of specialized service for the use of Presbyteries and Synods.[32]

One of the administrative problems posed for a centralized, nationally administered mission bureaucracy that intended to use the church's synods and presbyteries as boundaries for its administrative units was inefficient disparity in presbyteries' and synods' sizes.[33] The administrative plan addressed the problem by recognizing certain large, urban "specially designated presbyteries" that were to be treated administratively as synods; that is, those presbyteries would have mission executives. Of the 293 presbyteries in the PCUSA in 1930, only thirteen were "specially designated" and allowed to have staff; in the other 280 presbyteries, mission executive services were provided by nineteen synod executives.

In the PCUS, an organizational base (presbytery and

synod committees responsible for supervising and carrying out mission) and a funding system (synodical and presbyterial treasuries and local fund-raising) was in place in 1900 for development of presbyteries as units of mission. This base provided for the employment of "evangelists" by the presbyteries with their own funds. They both organized churches and supervised other ministers who were organizing churches in the presbytery. The home mission superintendents in a few small presbyteries received salaries from General Assembly mission funds, but these were considered unusual and temporary situations.

Two models of presbytery organization can be identified in the period from 1900 to mid-century.[34]

The *Constitutional Presbytery*[35] was the organizational model described in Form of Government 1788 and subsequent American Presbyterian constitutions. Its responsibilities were the traditional tasks of ecclesiastical jurisdiction: government and ordering of ministry. Its only staff was an elected stated clerk, often the pastor of a small church who received supplementary compensation from the presbytery.

In the PCUSA and UPCUSA, the vast majority of presbyteries in the church continued to operate on this model until reorganization of the national boards in 1972–1973. The northern pattern of conducting mission through national boards left the Constitutional Presbytery in place as the church's normative organizational model, with some functions delegated to councils in larger presbyteries after 1922. For reasons of efficiency in organizing "the field" in which the national mission corporation did its work, most of that work was organized by synod boundaries. Organizing of new churches was done by the national board directly through synods or by large congregations with their presbytery's blessing and cooperation.

Although the Constitutional Presbytery continued to be the presbytery described in the constitution in the PCUS until 1983, the *Home Missions Presbytery*[36] began to develop in the PCUS before the turn of the century, when economic conditions began to improve after the Civil War.[37] The only constitutional change was introduction of

Commissions on Ministry in the 1920s. However, as a result of the decision to pursue mission on the basis of Thornwell's view of judicatories as missionary agencies, the PCUS added responsibility and structures for churching the unchurched to the tasks of a presbytery. This led to development of a new type of presbytery to carry out this responsibility. Mirroring the "executive committee" pattern used by the southern General Assembly, these presbyteries developed "home missions committees." The committees came to function in many places as powerful presbytery boards that raised and dispensed funds for evangelists' salaries, bought and sold property, and employed staff to administer and support the presbytery's program.[38]

Presbyteries and Mission: 1945–1989

After World War II, the West no longer appeared to be the compelling arena of mission to which God was calling. The denominational bureaucracies, which had been potent agents of mission for almost a century, looked for new frontiers to challenge the heart, imagination, and support of American Presbyterians. The reports to General Assemblies after World War II have a very different tone and reflect a sharply changed focus of activity for the churches' mission enterprise. While the old frontier rhetoric of urgency in meeting mission needs continued, the location of the frontier changed.

The Surrogate Frontiers

Suburbia: the 1950s. In the 1950s, the movement of population from rural towns and villages to the burgeoning suburbs around American cities became an institutional surrogate for the old frontier. People who needed churches were in the West, but they were also in new housing developments surrounding the older cities.

This change in focus is evident in the 1951 reorganization of the PCUS, when the name of the Executive Committee of Home Missions was changed to the Board of Church Extension. "Home missions" had served since the 1860s to describe frontier-driven missionary outreach to the West in distinction to the "foreign missions" of the church overseas. When the focus shifted after World War II to "extension" of the church into the booming world of new South suburbia, the agency responsible for the work was given a new name. In the years after this change in mission focus, the PCUS grew by 79 percent, from 532,000 members in 1940 to 953,000 in 1970. The number of congregations grew by 12 percent, peaking at 4,067 in 1980.[39]

The reports of the Board of National Missions in the PCUSA in the 1950s show that its mission, too, was targeted on suburban new church development. In the 1940–1970 period, the church's membership grew by 50 percent from 2 million to 3 million members.[40] The number of congregations, however, grew by only 1 percent, or 80, even though this period included the union with the United Presbyterian Church of North America. The number of PCUSA/UPCUSA Presbyterian congregations had peaked at 10,051 in 1910.

The inner city: the 1960s. In the 1960s, a second institutional surrogate frontier was presented to the church as an engine for the mission enterprise: urban and inner-city mission.

Several factors played a role in this change. Urban riots and Martin Luther King, Jr.'s, assassination made the churches aware of a "crisis in the cities" to which they tried to respond. "New Frontier" and "Great Society" legislation in the Kennedy and Johnson administrations opened the door for churches to use federal funds to develop new forms of urban ministry, sponsoring Head Start programs and constructing residential and care facilities for the elderly.

To mark the shift in focus, the PCUS again gave the General Assembly's mission agency a new name—the Board of National Ministries. In the North, Board of National Missions devoted many of its staff resources to urban ministries.

Few new congregations were started in the 1960s. Furthermore, many congregations launched with high hopes after World War II had by the 1960s turned into long-term sustentation drains on presbytery and national resources instead of generating new resources for mission.

Racial ethnic concerns: the 1970s and 1980s. The third institutional frontier surrogate for Presbyterian mission became racial ethnic America in the 1970s and 1980s. The priority of this mission commitment is seen in rules for "inclusiveness" applied in naming members to boards and committees; in policies by which limited national funds for new church development and redevelopment of existing congregations have been disbursed since the early 1970s; and in publication of denominational materials in Korean and Spanish.

Reorganization: The Response to the Loss of the Frontier

By the end of the 1960s, the mission enterprise in both churches had paid a price for its institutional failure to find a frontier surrogate capable of generating support equal to its cost of doing mission.[41] Behind other factors that triggered the General Assembly reorganizations in both churches in the early 1970s was stark economic reality: the General Assembly boards had drawn heavily on their reserves in the 1960s.

Reorganization in both the UPCUSA (1972) and the PCUS (1973) responded to this reality by encouraging an enlarged role for synods and presbyteries in the mission enterprise. They did so by forming multistate regional synods and increasing the geographic and membership size of presbyteries. Simultaneously they redesigned national board structures and reduced the size of national board bureaucracies.[42]

Even before the General Assemblies instituted regional

synods and encouraged formation of enlarged presbyteries, presbytery demographic patterns in the North and South had converged toward common norms. In 1970, the average presbyteries looked like this:

	UPCUSA	PCUS
Churches	47	53
Members	16,244	12,881
Ministers	73	59
Members per minister	224	217
Members per church	343	243
Ratio ministers/churches	1.53	1.12

By 1980, after the boundary changes of the 1970s had taken effect, the average presbyteries were even more similar:

	UPCUSA	PCUS
Churches	58	69
Members	16,013	14,453
Ministers	95	91
Members per minister	168	160
Members per church	276	210
Ratio ministers/churches	1.64	1.31

In most places in the PCUS, growth in membership and presbytery mergers provided the economic base necessary for presbyteries to equip themselves with the staff they deemed necessary for mission after World War II. When the mission frontier was redefined as "church extension" to new South suburbia, many presbyteries had only to refocus the activity of an existing, effective organization. They did not have to develop new structures for new responsibilities.

Restructure in the UPCUSA was more abrupt. Until the 1972 reorganization, the pattern established in the nineteenth century of determining staffing needs at the national level and denying staff to the majority of presbyteries continued. The 1972 restructure gave all synods and all presbyteries responsibilities as units of mission "in light of" mission goals and priorities set by the next higher judicatory. However, it also continued the 1922 national staff structure and a "circulating funds" pattern of funding synod and presbytery staffing in whole or in part from the national treasury. A Council on Administrative Services was created to inherit the Board of National Missions management role in relation to the national staff. Denominational resources for synod and presbytery staff funding dwindled steadily between 1972 and the 1980s, and lower judicatories' share in paying the costs of their own staffing increased accordingly.

Controversy arose over relationships and role definitions between presbyteries, newly responsible for planning and implementing mission program, and synods, which traditionally had borne primary responsibility for those activities. Resistance focused especially on a churchwide planning, budgeting, evaluating (PBE) system intended to link the newly defined presbyteries into a holistic, rational system for deploying the church's resources in mission at all levels. The PBE system did not long survive, and the denomination did little after 1972 to actively assist presbyteries in their evolution toward new norms set by the reorganization.

The Shape of Presbyteries

Two new presbytery forms developed, especially after World War II, in response to the changed circumstances of mission in the Presbyterian churches.

The *Comprehensive Program Presbytery*[43] developed in the PCUSA/UPCUSA in the "specially designated" presbyteries and in the PCUS in presbyteries with large memberships concentrated in urban areas. This presbytery was organized as a multiple-staff presbytery with a manager-executive, an elaborate structure of program divisions and committees, and one or more program specialists for mission, Christian education, and stewardship.

This type of presbytery began to develop in urban presbyteries in the PCUSA/UPCUSA especially after World War II as a part of a gradual diversification of mission activities supported by the Board of National Missions.

In the PCUS, specialized presbytery staffing for Christian education was well established by the 1920s on the church's Western frontier in Texas.[44] Rapid growth of large, multiservice suburban churches in the 1950s and introduction of a new and more demanding church school curriculum in the 1960s raised expectations that presbyteries should provide diversified staff support and programs. In both churches this development was accelerated when presbyteries became involved in specialized urban ministries in the 1960s.

This Comprehensive Program Presbytery was the normative presbytery model on which the changes in presbytery size and role were based in the reorganizations of the early 1970s. The reorganizers expected that all presbyteries would conform themselves to this type. Two things are noteworthy about the view of this model as normative. First, though they had traveled different paths since 1860, by the 1970s both Presbyterian denominations had come to see the mission role of presbyteries in similar ways. Second, there were large differences in the presbytery contexts in which the changes of the 1970s were introduced. In the PCUS, those changes amounted to an organizationally evolutionary step. In the UPCUSA, the Comprehensive Program Presbytery was received in many presbyteries as a radical departure from their idea of what a presbytery should be. Presbyteries that had never had any staff except an elected stated clerk (the Constitutional Presbyteries) were suddenly expected by the reorganization to have an executive presbyter and to fill other, specialized staff positions.[45]

The *Congregational Mission Support Presbytery*[46] began to develop in the late 1960s and early 1970s in response to local issues and needs, rather than the denominational mission definitions and understandings that had shaped presbyteries until then. Many presbyteries were beginning to recognize that all was not well in relationships between congregations and the denomination. Since presbyteries relate directly to congregations, they became the front line for thinking about how to deal with issues of mistrust and threats of schism.[47]

The union presbyteries, formed after 1969 as full members of both Presbyterian churches and governed by mandatory provisions in both church constitutions, found themselves in a situation that forced them to rethink basic questions of meaning and purpose that presbyteries in only one system did not have to face.

Also contributing to the emergence of this presbytery type were the translation and application of new concepts, techniques, and leadership models from organizational development and conflict theories into language and forms usable in Presbyterian judicatories. Robert Worley and Hugh Halverstadt of McCormick Seminary were central figures in this theological appropriation of social science into presbyteries, and the middle judicatory executive track in the McCormick doctor of ministry program was a means by which this knowledge was disseminated into the presbyteries of both Presbyterian churches.

The identifying characteristic of this presbytery type is a focus on enabling congregations to be healthy and effective in mission. This focus leads the Congregational Mission Support Presbytery to take its own members and churches seriously as sources of wisdom about God's purposes and the principles that will guide their work together in the presbytery. It does not assume that purposes and principles are given to it from without or that its only task is to conform its structure and mission to denominational norms. Distinctive patterns of presbytery life are built on the foundation of this perspective. These presbyteries began, for example, to make regular periodic visitations to sessions. They placed high priority on the work of their committee on ministry as an important center of innovation, trust-building, and problem-solving in the presbytery's relationships with congregations.[48]

A Presbytery for the Twenty-first Century:
The Presbytery as Parish and Particular Church?

The era of the American evangelical denomination as a connected, coherent, and potent mission enterprise is over.[49] The central element that made that enterprise powerful was its underlying consensual foundation: a strong and widely held belief that mission defined as churching the unchurched in the West was what God was calling the denominations and their members to do. That consensus made it possible for presbyteries, as parts of larger denominational systems, to play clearly defined roles that contributed positively to the overall enterprise. While the roles were defined differently by the two Presbyterian churches after the Civil War, clarity more than content of definitions seems to have been the factor that enabled their positive contribution to the whole.

A generation of efforts since World War II to find surrogate frontiers to pull the denominational mission wagon has failed. Church membership has declined; mission giving has stagnated. The target populations for mission in the past two decades are no exception: apart from new Korean immigrant churches, racial ethnic membership has not grown; membership among groups traditionally served by Presbyterian mission (Blacks, Hispanics, Native Americans) has not increased significantly overall and may actually have declined in the last two decades.

Churchwide denominational understandings and visions for mission long were the most important single factor that shaped the evolution of presbyteries. While General Assemblies did not have coercive hierarchical power to force presbyteries to play assigned roles in mission, the mission frontiers they defined made sense to presbyteries as targets for concerted denominational effort.

Since about 1960, presbyteries have not been pulled by a convincing denominational vision and have been left to their own devices to decide what role they will play in the mission of the Presbyterian Church. The reality of presbyteries today is diverse, even chaotic. A typology of the presbytery structures that have developed in response to mission demands in the twentieth century has been used in this essay to sort, categorize, and interpret the diversity. Yet these presbytery types offer little guidance for the future.

Perhaps it is time to give up the illusion that any new mission frontier is going to restore the power that has slipped away from the American denominational church. That need not be an act of institutional resignation or suicide. It could be a clue to the institutional vocation and direction a church guided by the principle "reformed yet always to be reformed" is called to move at the threshold of the twenty-first century.

American Presbyterians have been an evangelical denominational mission enterprise since the 1840s, but before that they understood themselves in the terms they brought to America from the Reformation in Europe: *as a church,* settled and rooted in particular places, secure in an identity grounded in the elective love of God and answering a call to discern and seek God's will for the good of all who lived in each place. Their "mission" was not something the church did to or for people who lived somewhere else. It was living a life of responsibility before God in a disciplined, worshiping community of persons certain of the love of God (that is, of their election), free from anxieties about their eternal destiny and free to embody as best they could, for themselves and their fellow citizens, God's will as they understood it from scripture for the place where they were put. Embodying God's will meant for them a disciplined piety, passion for education and learning, compassion and generosity toward neighbors in need, and freedom to organize and advocate politically on behalf of the public good when circumstances warranted.

The American Presbyterian Church did not organize congregations formally on the European parish principle. There membership in a congregation is assigned on the basis of where one lives in relationship to geographic parish boundaries. Presbyterians long practiced, however, a parish, communitarian assumption that one should belong to the church in the place where one lived and worship with whoever else shared one's persuasion and lived in that place.

A geographic, "parish" principle was applied in the definition of presbyteries, however. All Presbyterian constitutions in America have defined presbyteries as ministers and congregations within particular geographic boundaries. When the Old School and New School were dividing, one argument was whether ministers and churches could pick and choose presbyteries on the basis of elective theological affinity; in their reunion, geography won.

In looking for new language to give clarity in defining the role of presbyteries in a fresh and coherent way that is not dependent on the concept of a denominational "mission," perhaps the church can recover and reformulate a metaphor akin to the "settled church" imagery that Presbyterians used to define their corporate identity before the westward movement began.

Geographic parish language, applied to one particular place, might sound something like this:

> Palo Duro Presbytery is a parish of 14,000 Presbyterians in a territory a little larger than the state of Pennsylvania. These Presbyterians worship in 65 places and are served by a team of 75–80 ministers of Word and sacrament.

> This parish seeks to build its purposes and principles on an assumption that all its members have experienced the love of God and therefore have valid perceptions of God's will, not just for themselves but for all humankind.

> It shapes and directs its ongoing life by celebrating what God is doing in this time and place and by listening with respect to what all of us discern in our life together as God's calling to care for and support one another, to love and serve the communities and region where we live, and to extend God's love as far as our imagination can reach.

> The members of the presbytery and the team of ministers are led by a presbytery pastor, or general presbyter. The presbytery pastor leads worship, preaches, teaches, visits, cares for people in need, administers affairs of the parish, and helps us

work together to focus on what God is doing and on the opportunities God is providing us.

This parish understands itself to be a full partner in a larger system called the Presbyterian Church and with sisters and brothers in other churches who share our responsibility for the temporal and spiritual well-being of the place where we are.

We believe that our experience of God is real and valuable, and we are eager to speak and listen to other presbyteries, to our synod, to the General Assembly, to other fellow-Christians and people of good will.

This description of the Parish Presbytery recaptures an old Christian and Presbyterian notion that the "particular church," the smallest unit that can be viewed as bearing the "marks of the church" in the fullest sense (worship, sacraments, order, as well as mission and racial ethnic diversity) could be the presbytery, not the congregation. It affirms a presbytery's being "particular," uniquely rooted in God's love for a place with its history and its culture, without competing with, or asserting prerogatives at the expense of, other less or more inclusive parts of the church. It allows and requires describing the work of presbytery staff as ministry in the same language Presbyterians use to describe the work of ministers who serve congregations. It lies in the trajectory of the Congregational Mission Support Presbytery and frames core elements of that type in language borrowed from presbytery experience before the frontier transformation began. Consistent with *reformata semper reformanda,* it can claim both continuity with the past and promise for the future.

The Parish Presbytery is a presbytery with boundaries, but no frontiers.

4

A Financial History
of American Presbyterian
Giving, 1923–1983

Scott Brunger and Robin Klay

Economic Factors in Presbyterian Giving

This essay compares contributions to the two major branches of American Presbyterianism from the reorganizations in 1923 until their merger in 1983. These two denominations are the Presbyterian Church in the U.S.A. (PCUSA) and its successor, The United Presbyterian Church in the U.S.A. (UPCUSA), and the Presbyterian Church in the U.S. (PCUS). This essay employs the statistical technique of linear regression to explain changes in contributions for each church. The results of these studies show the importance to church contributions of secular economic influences, such as personal income and inflation, as well as ecclesiastical variables, such as membership and per capita apportionments approved by the General Assemblies to support their expenses. By explaining the influence of economic factors on church giving, this essay focuses on secular influences rather than theological reasons for contributions.

Presbyterian emphasis on giving is based on the theological importance of stewardship. Declines in church giving are often attributed to controversies. For instance, the fundamentalist controversy in the late 1920s may have discouraged giving to the church. In addition, the decrease in 1972 in the northern branch of the Presbyterian Church is sometimes blamed on a proposal to donate funds to the legal defense of Angela Davis, even though no General Assembly funds were ever spent for this purpose.

The effect of theological controversies might be gauged by looking at the following graphs of total contributions to the PCUSA/UPCUSA and the PCUS. As can be seen in figure 4.1, by 1930 both churches saw contributions drop, falling noticeably after 1928 in the PCUSA and in the PCUS after 1929. Is this the effect of theological controversy over fundamentalist issues or the onset of the Great Depression? In 1972 in the UPCUSA, giving slows its increase, though it rises again in 1973. In the PCUS the increase in giving slows in 1973 and rises faster again in

Figure 4.1 Contributions at Current Prices

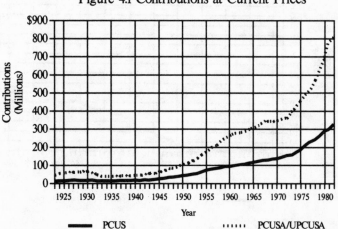

1974. Are these changes the effect of theological controversy over social action or the beginning of the great inflation following the 1973 oil crisis?

Figure 4.2 removes the effects of falling prices during the Great Depression and rising ones during inflation by adjusting the contributions by the Consumer Price Index. In this graph the effect of economic change on church contributions is seen more sharply as they plummet during the 1930s and reach a plateau during the 1970s. In this graph, while PCUS inflation-adjusted contributions fell in 1928, they remained steady in the PCUSA until 1931. Both recovered slightly in 1937 and dipped during World War II. Inflation-adjusted contributions in both churches reached their highest points in 1967. Then they flattened in the PCUS. In the PCUSA they dropped sharply thereafter and then flattened in the 1970s. During the Angela Davis controversy in 1972, inflation-adjusted contributions fell slightly in

Figure 4.2 Contributions Adjusted for Inflation

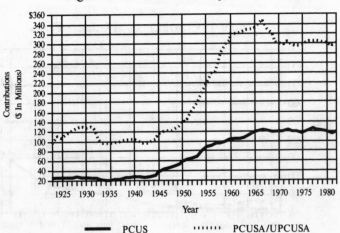

the UPCUSA and rose slightly in the PCUS, which never considered giving money to legal defense of Angela Davis.

Since one form of protest in theological controversies is the withdrawal of individual members or local congregations from the denomination, figure 4.3 adjusts for departures by showing "contributions per member." In this graph PCUS church members are seen to have consistently given more than their PCUSA/UPCUSA counterparts. During the Great Depression, per member giving adjusted for inflation dropped sharply from 1933 to 1934, then leveled off until 1937 in both churches. In the PCUSA/UPCUSA, membership reached a high point in 1965 and showed a slow decline thereafter. Per member inflation-adjusted giving followed a slow upward trend. No drop occurred in 1972 among members remaining in the denomination. In the PCUS inflation-adjusted giving has followed an upward trend since World War II.

Figure 4.3 Contributions per Member
Adjusted for Inflation

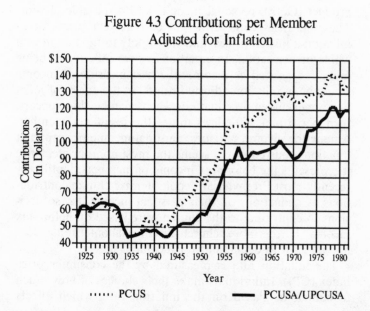

Explanation of Data

To explain the variation in total contributions to each church over the period 1923 to 1983, the following variables were tested: income, inflation, business cycles, number of members, national church requests, and trends over time. First, the theoretical justification will be given for the choice of these variables.[1] Then the statistical results will show their effects on contributions.

The total contributions would normally depend on members' incomes, which are not readily observable for the whole period. However, the income trends for the U.S. population as a whole are available from government sources.[2] Compared to the general population, Presbyterians have above-average incomes over the sixty-year period, but their incomes would normally vary in relation to national trends. However, which type of government income data should be used?

The choice of income statistics includes gross national product (GNP), personal income, and disposable income. These statistics come either in current year prices or in inflation-adjusted prices, and they apply to the nation as a whole or per capita. In equations where inflation is being measured as well as income, the best measure of income would be in inflation-adjusted prices, so the effects of inflation are excluded. In equations where membership appears, then per capita statistics capture the result per member. Among the income statistics, personal income per capita at inflation-adjusted prices seems the most appropriate, since it represents the before-tax income of members. Until very recently most Presbyterians could itemize church contributions as deductions on their personal income tax, so decisions to contribute to the church were based on before-tax income. Furthermore, church teaching about tithing does not adjust it to deductions for income taxes.

The inflation rate is measured by the consumer price index (CPI). Individuals make their choices of how much to contribute based on the inflation rate, which affects them directly. Since the largest part of church expenditures is salaries, the CPI provides a measure of changes in price of church programs. Presbyterians often pledge their contributions during the preceding year, so the former-year inflation rate may be more relevant to total contributions than the current-year inflation.

The business cycle can be represented either by changes in GNP or by the unemployment rate. Changes in GNP would reflect differences in income received by church members and should rise and fall with contributions. The unemployment rate indicates likelihood of a member's being laid off, so it would negatively affect decisions to contribute to the church too. The two measures are closely related, so only one can be used at a time. Neither of these measures appears to affect Presbyterian giving, even though the sample covers the period of the Great Depression.

The trend over time indicates whether giving habits change over the years independently of all the other influences. Several other variables are highly associated with time, such as personal income, General Assembly per capita assessments, and membership, so it is statistically difficult to measure the independent effects of changes in giving habits.

Results of Statistical Test

In this study six variables each were estimated for the PCUSA/UPCUSA and the PCUS over the period 1923–1983.[3] The influence of the causal variables is as expected.

Growth in personal income per capita at constant prices does have a positive effect on church giving. In both churches, for each additional dollar of personal income received, each member contributes between one and two cents to the church. The amount of effect on the total contributions in the PCUS ranges from $7,000 to $15,000 for each dollar change in per capita personal income, depending on which other variables are considered as well. In the

PCUSA/UPCUSA, which had three times as many members, the effect ranges from $28,000 to $34,000, approximately three times as much.

Inflation has a negative effect on church giving. Each percent increase in inflation deducts from total contributions between $368,000 and $372,000 in the PCUS and between $893,000 and $1,009,000 in the PCUSA/UPCUSA, depending on what other influences are important. Again, the effects per member are very similar in the two churches, since the PCUSA/UPCUSA had three times the membership of the PCUS.

The business cycle, represented by the unemployment rate and yearly change in gross national product at constant prices, is never significant in Presbyterian giving. The time trend is positive in one of the equations used, though it cannot be measured in the other ones.

The other variables are internal to the churches. The addition of new members adds a realistic amount of $73 to $85 per member in the PCUSA/UPCUSA and $168 per member in the PCUS to total contributions.

The General Assembly per capita apportionment in the PCUSA/UPCUSA may serve to add about $698,000 for each penny increase. However, this estimate implies that the average church member gives thirty cents to the total church when asked for an additional penny for the General Assembly's budget. Such a response is unlikely, since fund-raisers would quickly discover such a potent incentive for donations. Perhaps the fund-raisers ask for money only when they are sure that other influences will permit high levels of church giving. The likely economic influences considered by fund-raisers are already analyzed in the above equations. The remaining economic influence would be the business cycle, but no statistical relationship can be found between the business cycle and church contributions. The other explanation is that the statistical estimate is probably biased too high.

Despite statistical problems in estimating the equations, the results are generally satisfactory in both branches of American Presbyterianism.

Conclusion

The foregoing study indicates that almost all of the total church contributions can be explained using economic statistics and time trends as well as church statistics on membership and on per capita apportionments for the budgets of the national church. The effects of theological controversies can be seen in the way actual statistics deviate from the predicted levels.

In figure 4.4, inflation-adjusted contributions are compared to contributions predicted from the two equations used.* Obviously the predictions follow the actual contributions very closely, except at the beginning of the Great Depression and during World War II when contributions were lower than predicted and in the early 1970s when they were higher than predicted. The fundamentalist con-

Figure 4.4 PCUS Contributions
in U.S. Dollars Adjusted for Inflation

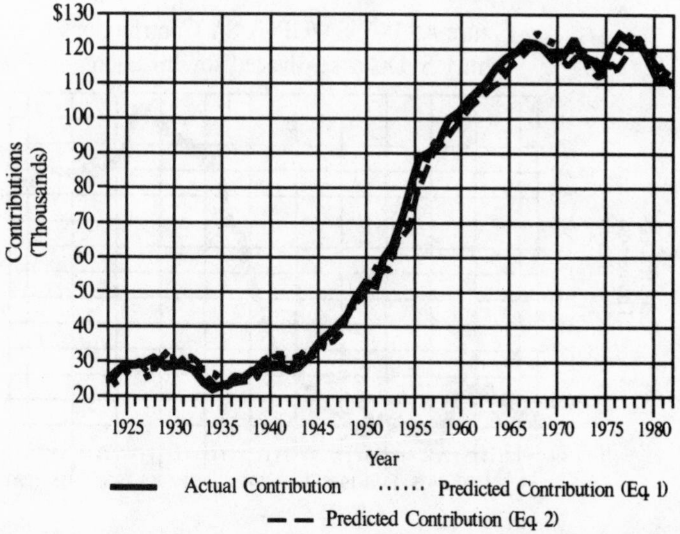

---

*For information on the way in which equations in figures 4.4 and 4.5 were formulated, please contact the authors.

troversy of 1927–1931 occurred at the beginning of the Great Depression. Only in 1929 and after 1931 are predicted contributions higher than actual ones, so apparently the controversy did not affect total contributions to the church. During World War II, forced savings for government bonds meant that income appeared higher than the amount available for giving to the church. During the period of social action controversy in 1968–1970 contributions were below predictions; after that they were higher than predicted.

In figure 4.5, the inflation-adjusted contributions are again similar to predictions from two other equations. Contributions fell faster than predicted at the beginning of the Great Depression. However, they did not start their fall until 1932, after the controversy. Again, they were lower than predicted during World War II. In the 1950s they were higher than predicted. From 1968 to 1970 they were lower than predicted, perhaps a reflection of social

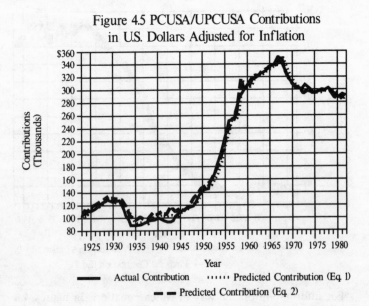

Figure 4.5 PCUSA/UPCUSA Contributions
in U.S. Dollars Adjusted for Inflation

action controversy. Though they were slightly lower than predicted in 1972—the date of the Angela Davis issue—they more than made up for it in 1973.

This essay suggests that economic variables, such as church members' incomes and inflation rates, weigh heavily in their contributions to both the PCUSA/UPCUSA and the PCUS branches of the church. Though in the years 1968–1970 theological controversy may have lowered giving in both denominations, at other times it has not had much effect. It remains to be seen whether the principal effect of theological controversy is the reorientation of funds away from national church control or the loss of church membership.[4] This study also demonstrates the possibility of using linear regression to explain the effect of economic and ecclesiastical variables on contributions to the church. An economic regression model, by separating out key economic influences on charitable giving and generating predicted levels of giving, permits a clear focus on the independent effects of ecclesiastical variables. In this way, a two-stage analysis of economic variables and, subsequently, ecclesiastical variables, may provide helpful long-term church policy planning. Furthermore, by controlling predictions for the effect of economic variables on contributions, the potential effect of theological controversies on church finances can better be analyzed.

5

Changing Priorities:
Allocation of Giving
in the Presbyterian Church
in the U.S.

Robin Klay

This essay presents major twentieth-century trends in
the allocation of members' contributions to churches
in the Presbyterian Church in the U.S. (PCUS). It seeks to
explain changes that occurred, especially in the shares of
contributions that were sent from the local congregation to
the national denomination.[1]

The first section describes trends in expenses (as a share
of all contributions) and shifts in the allocation of benevolences among the church judicatories, or governing bodies
(the levels of church government: presbyteries, synods, and
the General Assembly) for the period 1956–1982.[2] When
possible, the data are presented in graphs and tables, showing contributions as far back as 1923. Most analysis, however, focuses on the post-1950 period. The second section
examines possible explanations for the General Assembly's
great loss of financial importance. Special attention is
given to dissension that arose over changes made in the
process for handling benevolences. In section three, the
financial history of the southern Presbyterian Church in
this century is interpreted in the larger context of economic growth. This interpretation presents a real challenge
to the now-united Presbyterian Church (U.S.A.).

Two major themes emerge from the study. First, for a long time Presbyterians have gradually increased the share of their giving devoted to their local congregations' needs at the expense of benevolences. Second, they have increasingly substituted giving to local and non-Presbyterian causes for giving to denominational causes. This trend was aggravated initially by unpopular measures the PCUS General Assembly took toward centralized budget-making, as we shall see. Pressures of falling membership on overall finances also contributed toward "localism," the desire to make decisions about finances at the congregational level, where consensus about priorities was more likely than at the denominational level.

Trends in Finances with Emphasis
on the Period 1956–1982

Though the focus of this section is on changing financial trends since 1956, a few words about the preceding three decades will provide a useful backdrop for interpreting the shifts of recent years. During the Great Depression, real total contributions per member fell by 36 percent (see fig. 5.1). Benevolences bore the greater brunt of lower Presbyterian giving, shrinking by 49 percent, compared to a drop of only 29 percent in local congregational expenses. This is what we would expect because local expenses—consisting almost entirely of ministers' salaries—were regarded as necessities. Because local expenses loomed large (about two-thirds of total contributions for the period from 1928 through 1939), protecting ministers' salaries from severe collapse necessitated a dramatic drop in allocations of contributions toward benevolences. Figure 5.2 shows how the composition of spending on local expenses also shifted dramatically. Building expenses fell by half, from 32 percent of local expenses in 1928 to 16 percent in 1934.

Since real personal income per capita had recovered nationally by 1940, it is perhaps surprising that real benevolences per member did not return to their pre-Depression level until 1955 (while total contributions per member sur-

Figure 5.1 PCUS Real Contributions per Member
in Constant 1967 Dollars

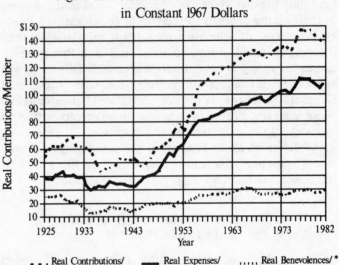

* . . Real Contributions/   ——— Real Expenses/   . . . . . Real Benevolences/*
    Member   Member   Member

* Over the 1925–1955 period, the data for these three categories are not
mutually consistent. It appears that some portion of the total contributions is not fully accounted for in the data on benevolences and
expenses.

passed their pre-Depression level in 1950). Undoubtedly,
World War II interrupted many peacetime spending, saving, and giving patterns for various reasons, including successful war bond appeals. The war itself also disrupted
foreign mission and other mission efforts. However, it is
noteworthy that per capita benevolences as a share of per
capita contributions never did recover from the Depression. They fell from 35 percent in 1928 to 25 percent (from
1950 to 1967) and down to 20 percent by the 1980s. This
can be seen, in part, by the dramatic drop in giving for
foreign and home mission as shares of total contributions
(see fig. 5.3). Even as shares of total benevolences, foreign
mission giving dropped until 1953, recovering only slightly
in the next two years (see figure 5.4). Home missions' share

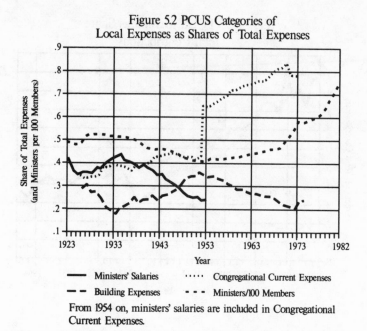

Figure 5.2 PCUS Categories of
Local Expenses as Shares of Total Expenses

From 1954 on, ministers' salaries are included in Congregational
Current Expenses.

of benevolences—less than half that of foreign missions in 1923—was boosted a bit by Depression needs but then also fell until the early 1950s, when it stabilized before continuing its decline in the late 1950s.

Thus, the trends of the more recent period analyzed in this paper—the displacement of benevolences by more spending on local expenses and rising localism in the use of benevolences—were anticipated by developments from the 1920s to the 1950s.

During the quarter century preceding the 1983 union of the southern and northern Presbyterian churches, total giving per member in real terms increased fairly steadily, with a notable bulge between 1976 and 1980[3] (see fig. 5.1). Over the period 1956–1982, real contributions per member rose a total of 31 percent. These contributions per member can be divided into congregational expenses and benevolences. While expenses per member rose a total of

Figure 5.3 PCUS Mission as Share of
Total Contributions

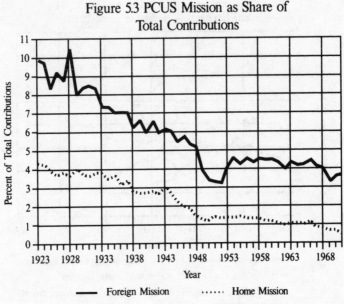

— Foreign Mission   ······ Home Mission

34 percent, benevolences per member rose only 21 percent. Although separate data are not available throughout this period for per member current expenses and building expenses, they do exist for the years 1956–1974. During this time, real per capita expenses in total rose 28 percent. But that part representing current expenses rose by 51 percent, while real per capita building expenses actually fell by 14 percent. Hence, for the quarter century preceding union, the faster growth of total expenses per member compared to benevolence per member can be attributed to growth in current expenses rather than to any increase in real expenditures on buildings.

As can be seen in figure 5.2, the parallel trends since 1953 for ministers per 100 members and congregational current expenses (as a share of total congregational expenses) suggest that increased staff size is the principal reason that growth in per member local expenses vastly outstripped growth in per member benevolences. Data on

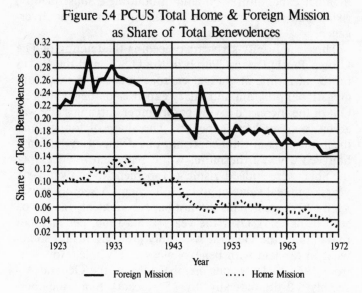

Figure 5.4 PCUS Total Home & Foreign Mission as Share of Total Benevolences

NOTE: This graph differs from figure 5.3 in that mission giving is calculated as a share of all benevolences (that is, contributions minus all local congregation expenses).

nonministerial staff are not readily available, but their numbers also clearly increased. Thus, Presbyterians have dedicated offerings out of their increased affluence more and more toward meeting expanded conceptions of local congregational "needs" (counseling, music directors, and so on). This is ironic given biblical teaching about proper responses to poverty and the obvious needs of Christian churches in such regions as rapidly evangelizing Africa. However, it is not surprising to economists, who find that as incomes rise people typically spend an increasing share of their incomes on luxuries. Apparently, services performed by local church staff are such a "luxury." The divergence between growth rates in per member benevolences and current expenses started even before the Depression (see fig. 5.1). Between 1945 and 1952, the divergence appears to be related to a rapid rise in per member expenditures on church buildings. Subsequently, rising staff size seems to be the explanation for the divergence.

Thus, the twenty-six years preceding the reunion of The United Presbyterian Church in the U.S.A. and the PCUS represent a time of gradual encroachment of current congregational program and salary expenses on benevolences. Out of the increased giving per member, a rising share was going to cover local expenses. The share of foreign and local missions in total contributions dropped by half in a half century. Furthermore, while real benevolences per member were indeed rising (21 percent over twenty-six years), the real value of giving to General Assembly causes *fell* by 20 percent. This did not happen suddenly (as can be seen in fig. 5.4). Over the years 1956–1966, per member real gifts to the General Assembly grew gradually, somewhat in tandem with benevolences as a whole. However, from 1966 to 1974, per member gifts to the General Assembly fell dramatically (by 45 percent). Since membership began to decline in 1969, the total effect on real monies available to the General Assembly was a decline of nearly 50 percent between 1966 and 1974 (see fig. 5.5). After 1974, per capita gifts to the General Assembly recovered somewhat, to a level about 20 percent below their 1966 peak.

The downward trend in giving to the General Assembly can be looked at through another lens—the distribution of the benevolence dollar among the various governing bodies and the local congregation. Figure 5.6 illustrates the changing relationships (see also figs. 5.7 and 5.8). At the beginning of this period, 1956, benevolences were spread out among the levels of church government according to their rank in geographic size:

- the General Assembly received the largest share, 36%
- the second largest share, 31%, went to synods
- the third largest share, 20%, went to presbyteries
- the smallest share, 14%, went to congregational missions and miscellaneous benevolences

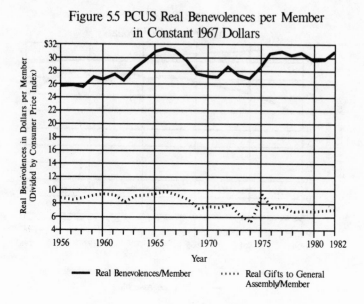

Figure 5.5 PCUS Real Benevolences per Member
in Constant 1967 Dollars

Real Benevolences in Dollars per Member
(Divided by Consumer Price Index)

Year

—— Real Benevolences/Member   ····· Real Gifts to General
                                                    Assembly/Member

From 1956 to 1967, this ranking was not disturbed, but
the presbyteries' share was growing gradually, while that of
the synods was shrinking. (Their combined share remained
relatively stable. Thus, as can be seen in figure 5.6, any
yearly movement of the presbyteries' share tended to be
offset by an opposite change in the synods' share.) Any ups
or downs in their combined share (see figs. 5.7 and 5.8)
were mirrored by opposite movements in the share of benevolence going to the General Assembly.

The big changes in relative size came in the period
1968–1974, during which time the General Assembly (previously on top) and congregational benevolences (including miscellaneous) actually traded ranks. The latter rose to
a peak in 1974, accounting for 25 percent of total benevolences in that year. The General Assembly's share fell to a
low of 23 percent. (Synods and presbyteries also lost some
ground, but not nearly so dramatically as did the General
Assembly.) Since 1974, the slide in General Assembly's

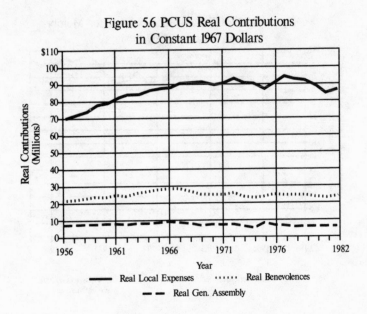

Figure 5.6 PCUS Real Contributions
in Constant 1967 Dollars

share has been halted, remaining relatively stable at about 24 percent.

Over the quarter century preceding the unification of the UPCUSA and PCUS, PCUS Presbyterians were not only devoting an increasing share of their total giving to local expenses, but also directing their benevolence giving dramatically away from the General Assembly to the local congregational level. Upon closer examination of the data for congregational missions and "miscellaneous," it appears that initially (from 1956 to 1966) miscellaneous contributions grew gradually (about 7 percent per year in nominal terms), while congregational missions was essentially constant. However, from 1967–1968 to 1974, both categories experienced rapid growth. Congregational missions almost tripled (in nominal dollars), while the larger category of miscellaneous contributions more than doubled in the same period. This accounts for their combined

Figure 5.7 PCUS Distributions of the Benevolence Dollar,
Without Special Campaign, 1956-1982

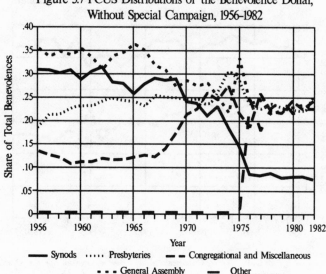

NOTE: Due to changes in reporting of data, 1975 is not comparable
with previous or later dates. And 1976–1982 is not directly
comparable with 1956–1974. In particular, after 1975,
nonbudgeted gifts to synods and presbyteries are pulled out
of the synod and presbytery categories and lumped together
with "other." It's not clear what "other" includes, however,
since it is a category of contributions reported by churches
(not receipts by agencies or units). These monies reflect giving according to local member and church priorities.

share in all benevolences rising from 11–13 percent in
1956–1968 to 25 percent by 1974.

Congregational missions are, of course, mission projects
undertaken by congregations primarily at their local level.
"Miscellaneous," on the other hand, represents giving by
Presbyterian congregations to causes that are not officially
sponsored by the Presbyterian Church. Thus, the dramatic
news of the decade of the late 1960s and early 1970s is

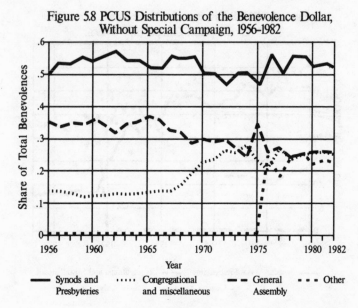

Figure 5.8 PCUS Distributions of the Benevolence Dollar, Without Special Campaign, 1956–1982

⎯⎯ Synods and Presbyteries	····· Congregational and miscellaneous	⎯ ⎯ General Assembly	▪ ▪ ▪ Other

NOTE: This graph is a variation of figure 5.7. First, gifts to synods and presbyteries are combined. Second, in this graph the "other" category is treated as something above and beyond the regular benevolence dollar; hence, the total of all shares, including "other," exceeds 100 percent after 1975.

that southern Presbyterians chose increasingly to shift their giving toward local and non-Presbyterian causes and away from their national denomination's causes. Why?

Explaining the General Assembly's Loss of Financial Prominence

Two types of explanations are usually offered for the decrease in giving to General Assembly. First, it is asserted that members of the PCUS, like all Americans, became alienated from large and remote bureaucracies. They increasingly preferred to do their giving (as well as pay their

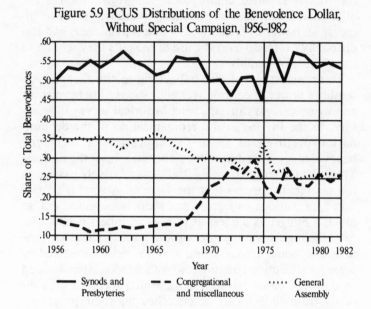

Figure 5.9 PCUS Distributions of the Benevolence Dollar,
Without Special Campaign, 1956-1982

NOTE: This graph is a variation on figure 5.7. First, gifts to synods
and presbyteries are combined. Second, "other" is omitted
from total benevolences.

taxes) at the local level, where they had a chance to exercise the greatest control over allocation. At the time of the 1973 reorganization of the PCUS, this trend was officially endorsed by the denomination with the objective to have mission take place at the "lowest practical level."

Another type of explanation is also to be considered—one that is complementary to the first but tied more closely to particular circumstances in the PCUS. The rather abrupt shift from national to local emphasis in giving was likely an expression of disapproval of the directions being chosen for the church at the General Assembly level. On the one hand, the General Assembly had been allocating a decreasing share of its funds (falling from 53 percent in 1956 to 22 percent in 1972) to international missions—a traditional favorite among local congregations. On the other hand, the General Assembly was attempting to increase its power over the choices that parishioners had traditionally exercised over the use of the gifts they sent on to the General Assembly.

To appreciate what was happening to the General Assembly's power of control over allocations of benevolences among its various causes, a brief historical survey is necessary. In the PCUS, until a reorganization of the denomination occurred in 1950, the allocation of members' benevolences was decided by the members themselves. Thus, the General Assembly itself was relatively passive in the matter. It appears that the General Assembly's "askings" for various causes before 1950 represented not so much a budget as a guess as to how members would allocate their gifts among the various causes. International missions, home missions, and so on, were administered by separate executive committees (with headquarters located in different cities of the South), which received gifts directly from individuals or churches for their programs. There was no central treasury that would have power to shuffle funds received among the causes. Instead, if any executive committee was seriously short of funds while another received gifts in excess of its needs, the only mechanism for dealing with the problem was voluntary negotiation among administrators of the executive committees.

This arrangement changed with the reorganization of 1950. An Equalization Fund was introduced, whereby each board (previously executive committee) of the denomination was "taxed" 5 percent of its receipts from living donors (except for receipts from donors who chose to designate their gifts for special programs). These "taxes" were received by the General Assembly's treasurer, who then used the funds to assist those causes which had fallen farthest behind their share of the General Assembly budget (the "askings" for each cause). During the existence of the Equalization Fund, its net effect was to shuffle some gifts away from the Board of World Missions toward other General Assembly causes. The greatest beneficiary of these reshuffled funds was the General Fund, a bundle of smaller causes; but the Board of Church Extension (home missions) was also an important recipient of Equalization funds.

During the entire life of the Equalization Fund (1950–1965), there were many complaints, with overtures for its elimination appearing in the General Assembly as early as 1952 (GA, PCUS, 1952, p. 31). The reasons given were that the reshuffling of benevolences could lead to decreased giving to the church, and that the system drained funds away from foreign missions. As a result of members' dissatisfaction with the system, the Equalization Fund was ended in 1965. At the same time, a Central Treasury was created; from this point on, both designated and undesignated gifts were to be received by the General Assembly's treasurer. He then allocated all *un*designated gifts so that the total of designated and undesignated funds directed to each cause would match the General Assembly's priorities as revealed in the "askings" budget. A "Basic Program" and "Advance Program" were introduced. In the Basic Program, each General Assembly cause was supposed to receive gifts minimally sufficient for maintenance of its programs, plus an annual increase of 4 percent to cover rising costs. Any receipts up to $500,000 in excess of the Basic Program would be allocated to the most urgent items on an Advance Program list, which was generated with input from all the General Assembly causes. Any gifts above this $500,000 were to be split equally between world and home mission.

Following these changes, complaints continued to appear in the General Assembly *Minutes* about "equalization" even after the Equalization Fund itself was eliminated. It seems that annual "supplemental offerings" were used to meet the budgets of certain causes. (For instance, the February Witness Season Offering was used for foreign and domestic missions.) But whenever such offerings yielded receipts in excess of budget, the excess was used for other causes. In periods of crisis, occasionally a "supplemental offering" was converted to "special offering" status, so that *all* gifts (even above budget) would go only to the designated cause. In 1971, for instance, the General Assembly's General Council recommended that 1972's and 1973's Witness Season gifts be treated this way, due to the adverse impact of worldwide inflation on the Board of World Missions' work. In this form, these offerings were sometimes referred to as gifts "not-to-be-equalized."

The data on giving over the period 1966–1972 suggest that opposition to what was still perceived as equalization found two increasing outlets. On the one hand, non-budgeted receipts such as special offerings for world mission increased as a share of total benevolences received by the Central Treasurer (from 2.3 percent in 1966 to 8.6 percent in 1972). Simultaneously, a rising share of benevolences to General Assembly causes was sent directly to the boards, rather than being funneled through the Central Treasurer—up from about 14 percent in 1966 to 22 percent in 1972. (Such direct gifts, though perhaps symptoms of opposition to equalization, did not prevent the Central Treasurer from using all undesignated gifts to ensure that the General Assembly's Basic Program budget was met.)

Thus, a reasonable explanation of the drastic decrease in the General Assembly's share of total benevolences—especially in the period 1966–1974—is that members of the PCUS were sufficiently frustrated by the General Assembly's attempt to impose its own priorities on giving[4] (through equalization in various forms) that they decided to retain a greater share of their benevolences for congregational missions and miscellaneous non-Presbyterian missions. This is a theme articulated by many PCUS leaders who remember these times.[5]

Apparently bowing to such pressures, the denomination declared that in the future mission should be undertaken at the lowest practical level. It appears that with the 1973 reorganization, member preferences concerning the use of their benevolences were once again to be determinative. The vehicles by which members could be assured that their donations would be used as specified included Second Mile Missionary Support, Major Mission Fund, and the Project Book. Total receipts in these *nonbudget* channels grew until, by the early 1980s, they were 85 percent of the level set for the entire General Assembly basic benevolence budget.

Since General Assembly's share of total benevolence giving stabilized after 1976, we may be able to conclude that PCUS Presbyterians were much happier with the new system, which they believed respected their own preferences about use of benevolences.

Part of the frustration members expressed with the various equalization attempts between 1950 and 1966 was their belief that equalization took funds away from mission, especially foreign mission. We have already noted that the Equalization Fund itself did reroute some funds from foreign missions to other causes. Consequently, it is perhaps surprising to note that over the entire period 1923–1972, the *only* time during which missions as a percent of all member contributions failed to drop was the Equalization Fund era (see fig. 5.3)! In fact, during the long period 1923–1949, when benevolences were essentially allocated as determined by members, not by the General Assembly, the share of benevolences going to foreign and home missions fell by about 50 percent. Thus, it is not at all clear that the General Assembly in the era of the Equalization Fund imposed on the denomination an antimissions pattern of benevolence spending that was dramatically at odds with the wishes of members. Their commitment to missions, as judged by *member* giving decisions, had been declining over the previous thirty years. (Because data are not available about the breakdown of benevolences among General Assembly causes by the same categories—that is, foreign and national missions—it is not possible to see what relationship the reorganization of 1973, giving greater member control over benevolence allocations, had on any subsequent mission emphasis.)

In the late 1960s and early 1970s, complaints were often heard about the decreased value (in real terms) of PCUS members' support for the General Assembly's causes. As we have noted above, the decline was substantial in total value (see fig. 5.5), and especially in per member terms (see

fig. 5.4). During the period 1966–1974, there was a pronounced reversal of financial status between the General
Assembly benevolences and benevolences controlled by
congregations (for their local missions and for miscellaneous non-Presbyterian causes). Ironically, this was an era
when the most rapid rise of total congregational expenses
had ceased (see fig. 5.5). (As a share of total contributions,
expenses had risen from 35 percent in 1923 to 80 percent
by 1973.) One might have thought this would result in the
subsequent release of funds for benevolences. However,
real benevolences *fell* (in total and per member terms).
This comes hauntingly close to verifying predictions made
by the earliest opponents to "equalization," namely, that it
would result in decreased giving. So the combination of
lower benevolence (owing to falling membership after
1968 as well as to falling benevolences per member) *and*
the shift away from commitment to General Assembly
causes hit the General Assembly with a double whammy.

One might wonder why Presbyterians, with a representative denominational government,[6] so effectively balked at
the General Assembly's 1950–1972 attempt to exercise
more control over the use of gifts made to it. After all,
members' wishes were annually conveyed in the General
Assembly meetings, and it does not appear that during
these years the General Assembly imposed on members
any unprecedented decrease in support for world missions.
(Members might have preferred to take advantage of the
lull in congregational expense growth to improve support
for world and home mission. If so, this did happen during
the era of greater General Assembly direction and control,
because foreign mission as a percent of total benevolences
ceased its nearly thirty-year decline—remaining practically constant from 1953 to 1968.) So why the apparent
"no vote of confidence" for the General Assembly in the
era during which it exercised more financial power?

I suspect the reason is linked to the culture of the South,
in which PCUS Presbyterians lived. The South's attach-
ment to states' rights is well known. Furthermore, the largest Christian denomination in the region, the Southern

Baptists, enjoy local control over financial and other decisions. Though the PCUS government was representative,
the pattern in the denomination was for the lower courts
and congregations to control nearly two thirds of all benevolences, and for presbyteries plus synods to manage benevolences more than one-and-a-half times the total for
General Assembly causes. (This contrasts markedly with
The United Presbyterian Church in the U.S.A., in which
the General Assembly received benevolences in the early
1960s nearly *three times* the total received by synods and
presbyteries together; see table 5.1.) With such a long history of financial prominence of the lower courts and congregations, and with an equally long history of direct
member control over the use of any gifts made to the General Assembly, PCUS Presbyterians apparently would not
accept any substantial interference in their benevolence
decisions, even by a representative General Assembly.

In the years between the 1973 reorganization and the
1983 reunion of the two major American Presbyterian denominations, real benevolences per member and real per
member gifts toward General Assembly causes recovered a
bit from their preceding decline and stabilized (see fig.
5.4). The relative shares of benevolences going to the various courts, or governing bodies, appeared to stabilize
also—with 25 percent each going to General Assembly and
local congregational use, and the remaining 50 percent to
synods and presbyteries (see fig. 5.7). After 1973, the financial crunch felt by the General Assembly increasingly resulted from the impact of membership declines on total
gifts. Apparently, the General Assembly's return to members of substantial control over the allocation of its benevolence receipts restored confidence and prevented any
further erosion of financial commitment to it.

Perhaps the General Assembly could even have enjoyed
some restoration of its previous position *if,* in addition to
restoring control to members, it had also been more clear
about its redefinition of mission with the 1973 reorganization. One overarching mission agency was created (an end
to the boards' independence), and several complex changes

Table 5.1 United Presbyterian Church, U.S.A., Giving to Synod and Presbytery General Mission, General Assembly General Mission, 1963–1983 (Thousands)

	Synod and Presbytery G.M.	General Assembly G.M.
1963	10,925	29,957
1964	11,834	30,562
1965	11,448	31,000
1966	11,519	30,946
1967	11,761	31,246
1968	11,626	29,945
1969	11,929	29,078
1970	11,953	27,250
1971	12,525	24,624
1972	13,201	22,597
1973	14,523	20,351
1974	14,385	21,327
1975	16,562	20,487
1976	18,427	20,946
1977	19,260	20,338
1978	22,408	20,499
1979	24,121	20,688
1980	26,765	20,866
1981	29,383	22,183
1982	33,456	23,843
1983	36,461	24,773

Source: The Research Unit and the Mission Treasury Service of the Support Agency, UPCUSA. June 26, 1984, publication; Appendix A.

were made in the way priorities were determined for allocation of General Assembly funds. Subsequently, it was certainly much more difficult for ordinary Presbyterians to understand to what extent their gifts to the General Assembly were being used in ways they might favor, for example, for international missions and evangelism.

By extension, one may wonder whether the reunion of the two branches of American Presbyterianism will bode well for total benevolence giving in the South and giving to General Assembly causes in particular. Obviously, this union created changes in benevolence structures and categories only a decade after the PCUS had to get used to its own reorganization and to major changes in the General Assembly's budgeting process. Furthermore, given the fact that the lower courts had greater prominence in PCUS benevolences than in UPCUSA benevolences (although the UPCUSA did experience a dramatic reversal of importance between General Assembly's share and lower courts' share of benevolences between 1963 and 1983; see table 5.1), Presbyterians in the South might be tempted to react against the lesser prominence of lower courts in the united denomination. For the united denomination this could compound financial problems resulting from their continued drop in total membership since union.

Interpreting Financial Trends: The Importance of Growth

This financial history of the PCUS denomination lends itself to interpretation beyond the confines of the data. Economists since Adam Smith have typically been partisans of economic growth. In the late 1960s and the decade of the 1970s, however, some Western economists began to doubt the prospects and even the advisability of further growth. Politically, there was a shift from concerns about growth to concerns about distributive justice. Yet today, many economists again strongly advise policies that favor growth.

Michael Novak has argued that economic growth is both essential to the survival of the democratic capitalist system and consistent with the Christian understanding of history as an unfolding story, in which the vocation of all people is to be distinctively different and to be cocreators with God. He says that "democratic capitalism depends for its legitimacy not so much upon equality of results as upon a belief among even the least well-off that things will get better for them."[7] This is only possible when the size of the economic pie is growing so as to accommodate newcomers baking in the kitchen and dining at the table. With growth, people need not feel forever trapped in their present circumstances. Furthermore, with growth, a spirit of mutual respect and accommodation among groups of differing values is more likely. The resources any group would use to fund activities reflecting its values can come from expanding the pie, rather than by exercising power to raid another group's share.

The financial history of the PCUS nicely illustrates these points. In 1968, when membership growth ended, the growth of real contributions also ceased (see fig. 5.5). The only factor that kept total real contributions from falling at first was increased giving per member. But over the period of stagnating per capita income growth in the U.S. during the 1970s, the consequent lower per member giving combined with membership losses to bring a downward trend in real contributions from 1977 to 1981.

It seems not at all surprising that increasing financial stringency since the mid-1960s aggravated dissension over the distribution of resources among the courts and among the various causes sponsored by the General Assembly. It was inevitable that those activities closest to the members and local congregations (physically or in terms of their values) were most likely to be maintained, while those farther removed were not. It was also inevitable that without growth in real contributions, the diverse interests and values represented in the denomination would increasingly be in conflict—giving rise to a lower confidence in the General Assembly's ability to fairly represent the interests of all.

This interpretation of trends does not offer great hope for the reunited denomination to achieve financial stability for the General Assembly's work or internal harmony within the denomination. The difference between the PCUS's history of greater local control of benevolences and UPCUSA's history of greater prominence and control by the General Assembly is one more source of friction, on top of those already existing, not favoring harmony or adequate financial backing for the ongoing work of the united church's General Assembly.

If per capita income growth in the United States continues, per member giving will likely respond. But this may not be enough to make up for membership losses. (Previous campaigns to increase giving per member in the PCUS do not appear to have made a lasting positive impact.) Without an increase in total contributions, dissension over how the stagnant or dwindling real contributions are allocated will likely continue—and must adversely affect the General Assembly's budget.

If the Presbyterian Church is to survive as a denomination, rather than as a loosely knit association of congregations, it will have to make every effort to focus increasing attention and resources on membership growth. Without it, the multiplicity of causes that members say they want the national denomination to sponsor will not be adequately funded. But if the Lord's injunction to make disciples is taken seriously, then the resources to respond to Christ's leadings in ministry will likely become available.

6

Global and Local Mission: Allocation of Giving in the Presbyterian Church in the U.S.A. and The United Presbyterian Church in the U.S.A., 1923–1982

Scott Brunger

Presbyterian giving to the two major branches of American Presbyterianism during the past sixty years is remarkably similar. In the 1920s both denominations tended to allocate a significant portion of their funds for the missions of the denomination at the General Assembly level. However, throughout the twentieth century Presbyterians have allocated a decreasing portion of their funds for General Assembly mission and instead increased support for local mission. Robin Klay argues that the long-term downward trend for General Assembly mission in the Presbyterian Church in the U.S. (PCUS) is due to a belief in local autonomy,[1] but this explanation does not account for the changes in the allocation of funds in the Presbyterian Church in the U.S.A. (PCUSA) and its successor, The United Presbyterian Church in the U.S.A. (UPCUSA). A number of alternative explanations are evaluated in this essay:

1. Inflation-adjusted contributions to special receipts destined for church building and investments stopped growing in the mid-1950s. Shortly thereafter, membership stopped growing.

2. The percentage of contributions going to the General

Assembly has fallen after denominational reorganizations, and the percentage retained by the congregations has risen. Theological controversies have had smaller effects.

3. Denominational priorities may not have been popular with the membership. Emphasis on foreign missions has been popular, even when the proportion spent on them declined. Costs of administration of the church bureaucracy have not been popular.

4. Church membership losses reduced the proportion of giving available to national missions programs. But the remaining members showed an upward trend in giving even when other economic influences, such as income and inflation, are taken into account.

5. Increasing heating costs after the early 1970s necessitated more spending by congregations, leaving less for the denomination.

Unlike the PCUS, the PCUSA and the UPCUSA had a well-established tradition of unified budgets. At each level of the church, the financial committee proposed a budget for vote. After it was approved, the judicatory solicited unrestricted funds for its budget. A strong system of organization for a planned education program and Every-Member Canvasses raised more funds through local initiative.[2]

In recent years the emphasis on "locating mission [and the dollars to accomplish mission] at the level nearest the congregation where it is feasible to do so" has ratified this trend toward decreasing support of General Assembly mission.[3] As will be seen in what follows, the trend preceded the emphasis on localizing mission, so the emphasis should not be seen as causing the trend.

The PCUSA and UPCUSA accounts can be divided into two periods—1923–1972 and 1973–1982. The 1923 reorganization of regional mission boards and women's mission boards left a streamlined structure that included the following: the Board of National Missions, the Board of Foreign Missions, the Board of Christian Education, the Board of Ministerial Relief and Sustentation (later renamed the Board of Pensions), and the Board of Theological Education. In addition, the church funded ecumenical

agencies—the American Bible Society and the Federal
Council of Churches (GA, PCUSA, 1923, p. 260). The
merger of the PCUSA and the United Presbyterian Church
of North America to form the UPCUSA did not change
the administrative structure, except in the case of the old
Board of Foreign Missions, which became COEMAR
(Commission on Ecumenical Mission and Relations). This
merger did not alter the format of the accounts presented
to the General Assembly.

After 1973 this system was reorganized using theories of
business management. What emerged were the Program
Agency, the Vocation Agency, the Support Agency, the
Board of Pensions, the Council on Theological Education,
the Council on Administrative Services, and the Presbyterian Foundation.[4] This model had more sophisticated internal accounting controls that are difficult to adapt to the
previous categories.

A noteworthy feature of the Presbyterian Church reorganizations in 1923, 1972, and 1983 is the way they follow
contemporaneous trends in the business world.[5] Alfred
Dupont Chandler, Jr., an eminent management theorist,
discussed how in the early 1920s America's leading corporations consolidated their multiple production, marketing,
buying, and research organizations into centralized divisions concentrating on related products.[6] Similarly in the
Presbyterian Church, fourteen independent mission
boards consolidated into five specialized ones. Following
Chandler, other theorists have proposed that churches organize as multinational corporations after the 1950s.[7] For
example, the creation of COEMAR in 1958 corresponds to
the creation of international divisions in multinational
corporations. Furthermore, the 1972 reorganization introduced more sophisticated management by objectives into
the church, and the 1983 merger of the PCUS and
UPCUSA followed a merger trend in business.

The first section of this essay charts the changes in contributions to the different levels of the PCUSA and the
UPCUSA from 1923 to 1983. This will include contributions in actual dollars to each level, then will show these

contributions removing the effects of inflation and percentages of total contributions. The second part indicates
the effects of changes in budget and spending priorities at
the national church level on the proportion of contributions allocated to the denomination. The third part explores whether the rise in utility costs in the 1970s can
account for the increase in the proportion of contributions
retained by congregations for their own use.

Contributions to PCUSA/UPCUSA
Judicatories

In American Presbyterianism there are four levels of organization, often called "judicatories," "governing bodies," or "courts":

1. The General Assembly, composed of representatives
of the entire national church
2. Synods, composed of representatives from a large geographical area consisting of a state or several states
3. Presbyteries, composed of representatives from a
small geographical area
4. Sessions, which govern each congregation

In the higher judicatories above the session level an equal
number of clergy and lay delegates represent the church. In
theory church policy, including financial policy, is decided
in concert by clergy and laity.

While stewardship is seen as the main motivation for
Presbyterians to contribute to their church, the General Assembly, synods, and presbyteries have the power to set "per
capita apportionments," which are fixed contributions assessed per church member. Originally the apportionments
were designed to help with only travel costs to General Assembly meetings. Since the reorganization of the PCUSA in
1923, these apportionments have covered both mileage
costs for representatives to attend meetings and also some
administrative expenses. These apportionments were even
seen as "taxes" from 1923 to 1929, until their voluntary
nature was clarified by the General Assembly.[8]

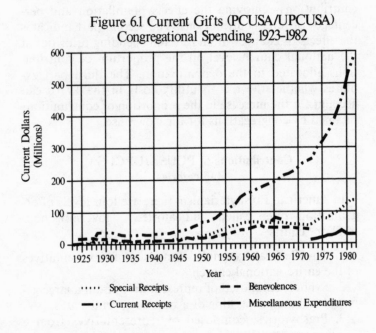

Figure 6.1 Current Gifts (PCUSA/UPCUSA)
Congregational Spending, 1923–1982

At the level of the local congregation, figure 6.1 indicates actual dollar expenditures for the period 1923 to 1982. The general trend in current dollar expenditures rose throughout the period 1923 to 1982. As would be expected, the period of the Great Depression in the 1930s caused a fall in church contributions. From 1929 to 1934, as congregations struggled to maintain their essential programs, special receipts and benevolences fell faster than current receipts. Special receipts are used for investments and buildings, which provide for new members. Postwar reconstruction led to a rapid increase in the 1950s along with membership growth. Special receipts leveled off by the mid-1950s, after which membership lagged too. Again, after the oil crisis in 1973 contributions rose quickly in current dollars, though inflation eroded the value of those dollars.

In figure 6.2, gifts are calculated as percentages of total

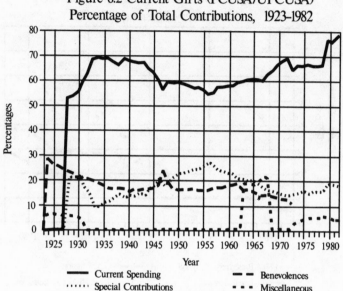

Figure 6.2 Current Gifts (PCUSA/UPCUSA)
Percentage of Total Contributions, 1923–1982

Presbyterian contributions. The percentage of current congregational spending rose from 53 percent in 1928 to a
high of almost 70 percent during the 1930s, fell back to 55
percent in the mid-1950s, and then rose to over 78 percent
by 1982. The percentage of special contributions fell from
21 percent in 1928 to under 10 percent during the Great
Depression, rose to over 27 percent in the mid-1950s and
then returned to 18 percent in the 1980s. The percentage
of benevolences fell from 29 percent in 1924 to 5 percent
by 1973.

Figure 6.3 compares spending by different judicatories.
Local mission by congregations is a small but rising
amount for the years 1958–1969 and 1980–1982 when
data are available. Presbytery and synod causes correspond proportionally with total contributions. They are
combined during the period 1958–1968 and then separate
1969–1982. The jump that occurs in 1973 is associated

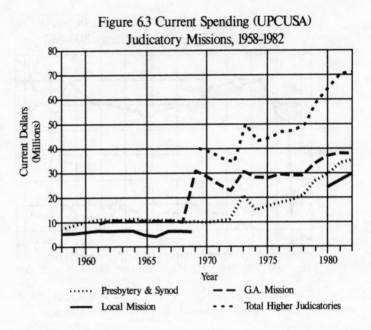

Figure 6.3 Current Spending (UPCUSA)
Judicatory Missions, 1958–1982

with the expenses of church reorganization. General Assembly expenditures are available from 1961 to 1972 and from 1973 to 1982, though the bookkeeping systems may not be entirely comparable. They also rise sharply in 1968 without explanation. Again in 1973 a jump shows the expenses of church reorganization. The higher judicatories above the level of the congregation rise in the same pattern as the components, with a jump in 1973. During the Great Depression, the higher judicatories had not lowered their expenditures until 1930, and even then the decrease in expenditures was small. Proportionately the decrease was more than the drop in current contributions to congregations, but much less than the fall in special contributions.

In figure 6.4 judicatory expenditures represent only a small percentage of church contributions. Each judicatory shows a different pattern. Local mission has expanded

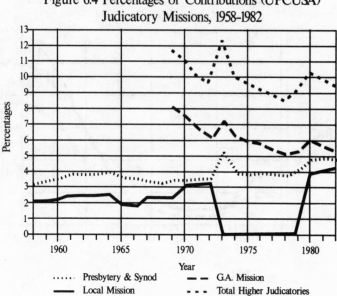

Figure 6.4 Percentages of Contributions (UPCUSA) Judicatory Missions, 1958-1982

..... Presbytery & Synod   — — G.A. Mission
—— Local Mission   - - - Total Higher Judicatories

from 2 to 4 percent of the total contributions. Presbytery and synod causes increased slightly to above 3 percent until 1972. After the reorganization in 1973, the combined presbytery and synod causes drifted down from 5 to 4.5 percent by 1982. General Assembly expenditures decreased from 7 to 5 percent. Total higher judicatories' expenditures dropped from 12 to 9 percent.

Figure 6.5 compares gifts for mission work of the whole church. Benevolence giving at the congregational level fell during the Great Depression and then rose quickly after World War II until the 1960s. Most of it was passed on to denominational programs, though from 1923 through 1930 the difference between the two was recorded as miscellaneous giving. Denominational giving, including gifts from women's programs and the Sunday schools, reached a plateau in the 1960s. Much of it was spent by the boards and agencies of the Presbyterian Church, though some was

Figure 6.5 Current Spending (PCUSA/UPCUSA)
Missions Spending, 1924–1968

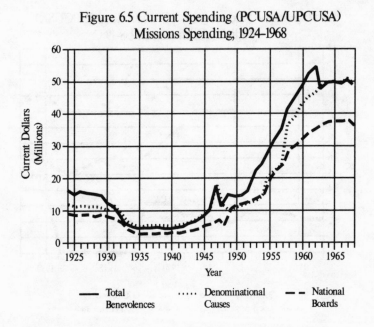

designated for ecumenical projects and agencies. Receipts
of the national mission boards and agencies of the church
began to fall by the mid-1960s.

In figure 6.6 similar results appear. Total benevolences
fell from 29 percent of total giving in 1924 to 11 percent by
1973. Presbyterian mission boards saw their share reduced
from 17.5 percent in 1924 to 10 percent by 1968.

When one examines the proportion of funds retained as
current giving by congregations, one finds they rise after
denominational reorganizations. After the 1922 reorganization that created centralized mission boards, the proportion of total contributions retained by congregations rose
by 3.5 percent while denominational giving fell by 4.2 percent between 1923 and 1928 (see figs. 6.2 and 6.6). After
the 1968 reorganization congregational current spending
rose by 7 percent while higher judicatories spending fell.

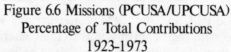

Figure 6.6 Missions (PCUSA/UPCUSA)
Percentage of Total Contributions
1923-1973

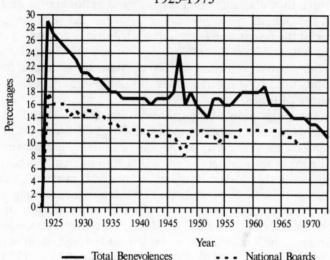

Year
—— Total Benevolences   • • • National Boards

As expected after the 1973 reorganization explicitly gave more responsibilities to lower judicatories, congregational spending again rose significantly. Apparently the turmoil of reorganization at the national level disorganized the networks of trust and flow of contributions. This resulted in a smaller proportion of funds available to the national church.

Figures 6.1 to 6.6, then, show major changes in the PCUSA/UPCUSA from 1923 to 1982. The proportion of contributions to the denomination diminished in favor of local church programs. Miscellaneous expenses, which would include giving to "non-Presbyterian causes" outside the denomination, did not rise in proportion to total contributions.[9] The proportion of benevolence giving fell. Spending on new church development diminished in importance and membership losses occurred.

Allocation of General Assembly Funds

In the PCUSA after 1923, congregations were encouraged to send their contributions to the General Assembly, which then allocated them according to national priorities. In the General Assembly budget, priorities may have influenced the proportion of church contributions controlled at the national level. In the PCUS, although the General Assembly budget priorities formed the basis for an appeal for funds from congregations, they did not determine the allocation of funds.

The proportion of contributions going to General Assembly mission causes in the PCUSA/UPCUSA might depend on the popularity of the programs being undertaken. The hypothesis explored here is that church members have favored either foreign missions or national missions, and they did not favor expenditures on administrative budgets and social action programs. Administrative budgets are not available in the PCUSA/UPCUSA *General Assembly Minutes* until after 1973, when the budgeting system was completely reorganized. During the period 1923 to 1973, General Assembly expenses represent a proxy measure of administrative overhead.

As for social action indicators, there is no good index for statistical purposes. Benton Johnson argues that the old social action agenda emphasizing temperance and Sabbath observance has been replaced by a new one involving broad societal issues. Today the old social action agenda would belong to a conservative political program, while the new one would be considered liberal. In "Presbyterians and Sabbath Observance," Johnson also points out that a change occurred in the 1950s and 1960s, when the church dropped its emphasis on the ritual observance of the Lord's Day and witnessed a decline in fervor and financial support.[10] Because the social action agendas change over time, their influence cannot be computed from statistics on spending or pages in the *Minutes*.

At the General Assembly level there is a difference between the budget and disbursements that was very large until after the Depression. Although the national budget was published by 1923, the first years of consolidation of the various church boards were devoted to removing board deficits that had been accumulated and to centralizing their endowments. The accounting arrangements for disbursements were not in place until 1934. For many of the early years, budgets differed greatly from disbursements, so calculations based on budgets differ from those based on disbursements. Since the General Assembly accounting system changed drastically in the 1973 church reorganization, the expenses after that date are no longer comparable.

First equations are calculated for the budget from 1923 to 1973 and then for the disbursements from 1934 to 1970. The results are quite comparable in both cases.

Foreign mission. A 1 percent increase in foreign mission's proportion of PCUSA/UPCUSA mission is associated with an increase in contributions to General Assembly mission programs of 30 to 33 cents per member for the budget and $7 to $10 per member for disbursements. Foreign missions are popular with Presbyterian contributors.

National mission. A 1 percent increase in national mission's proportion of the budget is associated with no predictable increase in contributions. A 1 percent increase in national mission disbursements is associated with an increase of $7 per member. National missions are not as popular, especially since the $7 figure does not have a high level of statistical probability associated with it.

Percentage of General Assembly cost in total contributions. A rise of .1 percent devoted to the budget of General Assembly meetings and bodies reduces the mission budget between $83 and $94 per member. The same rise of General Assembly costs reduces the mission disbursements by $47. It should be noted that these rises are drastic, since historically the General Assembly cost has varied between .3 and .7 percent of total contributions in the northern church. Apparently meetings that cost for each delegate approximately the yearly contribution of three church members have repercussions on giving, though the means by which church members learn of the cost of church bureaucracy are unclear.

Real per capita apportionment.   A rise of one penny per member in the apportionment raises 6 cents for the mission budget or expenditures. Apparently the General Assembly does not request higher apportionments unless the contributions are already forthcoming.

Membership.   A decline of one million members reduces the national mission budget by $9 per member and disbursements between $2 and $8 per member.

Time.   Giving habits change over time. After other influences have been accounted for, the question arises whether stewardship education has had an effect in raising contributions. The time trend for the budget is ambiguous, and for disbursements it rises between 13 and 24 cents per member per year. Stewardship education may have had a positive effect in raising yearly contributions.

The similarity in the results of the different ways of explaining the amount of contributions to the General Assembly mission programs in the PCUSA/UPCUSA gives good reason to believe the underlying hypotheses. Foreign missions are popular within the Presbyterian Church. National missions can be carried out by lower judicatories in place of the national church. Costs of bureaucracy are not popular. General Assembly apportionments ratify trends in giving that are already under way. The loss of denominational membership leads to a small loss in resources for General Assembly mission programs. The effects of the time trend may be positive, indicating successful stewardship education.

Use of Funds by Local Congregations for Energy Costs

The PCUSA/UPCUSA, unlike the PCUS, did not publish a breakdown of local congregation current expenses according to categories, so the use of current funds cannot directly be identified. Samples of local congregation budgets would reveal whether: (1) staff compensation has been rising as more professional services are demanded, (2) equipment has increased, or (3) increased utility costs after the oil crisis have drained local church budgets. The above discussion indicates that local mission causes have not benefited from the rise of local budgets.

Staff compensation in local congregations may show a rise because financial accounts do not include the important contributions of lay volunteers in the church. If paid staff have replaced volunteers as church secretaries, cooks, librarians, youth workers, and hospital visitors, then local church budgets may have grown even though the ministry performed has only switched from volunteer to professional labor. In that case, rising budgets may reflect a diminished commitment by church members rather than the contrary.

Local church equipment budgets have risen dramatically over time too. Today churches own choir bells, videocassette recorders, and copiers, which were not common two decades ago. In part the equipment is an efficiency-raising measure, designed to save paid labor from work that volunteers used to do manually. However, the comfort sought by middle-class churches disturbs a conscience that recognizes the material poverty of churches in poor regions.

Both equipment and staff represent long-run time trends in the equations below.

Utility costs for local congregations represent a partially uncontrollable expense. The architecture of a building with high-ceilinged sanctuary and drafty hallways may not lend itself to energy efficiency. In that case a rise in utility costs would lead local congregations to divert their money to local expenses.

The hypothesis to be tested here is that increased heating oil prices caused an increase either in local real current expenses or in the percentage of local current expenses to total contributions. Though utility costs are available back to 1935, the years after 1960 are chosen, since before then some churches may have been heated with coal.

Two different methods of estimation indicate that heating oil prices have a significant influence on congregational current spending. One method estimates congregational current spending and the other the percentage of congregational current spending out of total contributions. In each, the changes in the consumer price index for heating costs and time trends are used to explain changes in congregational current spending.

Time. Each year total congregational current spending rises by between $6 and $10 million, the former if heating costs are included in the explanation as well. Each year the proportion of congregational current spending changes between a fall of −.02 and a rise of .47 percent, the former if heating costs are included. These results indicate that staff compensation and equipment might influence the allocation of Presbyterian finances to local churches, though this is not definite.

Heating oil costs. A one-point increase in the index of heating costs raises current spending by between half a million and one million dollars, depending on whether time is included as well. A one-point increase in the index raises the proportion of current spending between .7 and 3 percent, depending on the presence of time in the calculation. Apparently heating costs do influence the allocation of finance to local church budgets.

Conclusion—Corporate v. Congregational Resource Allocation

In the early part of the twentieth century, the modern American denomination emerged. In 1923 the PCUSA reorganization was modeled after a business corporation, as a hierarchical bureaucracy capable of delivering goods and services to congregations and mobilizing resources for carrying on mission in this country and around the world. However, beginning in the late 1950s and early 1960s, this denomination began to lose financial support as well as clear direction in its mission and theology. Membership fell, and resources were redirected to the local congregation. This trend was exacerbated by the reorganization of 1973.

A facile conclusion to this study would be to summarize the policy changes that would help to orient more contributions to church mission programs. They are: more emphasis on church development, more emphasis on foreign missions, less spending on church bureaucracy, and continuation of stewardship education programs, since individual giving habits are increasing over time.

Such management tinkering, though, may be a source of problems rather than a solution. As the former head of the All-Africa Conference of Churches, who presided over the fastest-growing churches in the world, once said: "The Holy Spirit works in confusion!"[11] The purpose of management is to structure an organization efficiently to reach its goals. The purpose of a church is to liberate believers to serve God in Jesus Christ. Often the two approaches are not compatible, despite the efforts of church management theorists to make them so. Evidence in figure 6.6 showed that massive church reorganizations resulted in smaller proportions of giving to the denomination, even when their purpose was to enhance giving. As would be expected, the ties of trust to former personnel were broken during the reorganizations, while new personnel struggled to learn their responsibilities and establish new relationships.

Theological controversies, which are often blamed for causing congregational disaffection with the denomination, do not appear to have had effects as strong as reorganizations in changing giving priorities toward congregations and away from the denomination. The fundamentalist controversy during the early 1930s corresponded with the Great

Depression, which would normally result in budget retrenchment. Between 1930 and 1934, proportions of congregational current giving rose dramatically, but the General Assemblies of both denominations received a greater proportion of total contributions than before, not less. During the period of intense civil rights activity, denominational and board accounts run only until 1968. From 1960 to 1968 the proportions of congregational current giving rose 4 percent and denomination and boards fell 1.5 percent. Both the rise and the fall are smaller than the results of the reorganization that occurred afterward.

The Presbyterian Church is called to mission both to the local neighbor in need and to the ends of the earth. The response to this mission call, both in its amount and in its relative size, is to be determined by the activity of the Holy Spirit. Compared to the incomes available in the 1920s, this response was much greater then than today. The proportion going to global mission was also much greater. While those Presbyterians who have served in mission programs can point to cases in the past when resources devoted to mission were overwhelming rather than liberating, few would disagree today that our church is devoting inadequate resources to mission programs. In the case of church development and stewardship information programs, these inadequacies probably diminished the long-run growth and commitment of the church, so the problem was exacerbated. Still, as Christians the priority is not to build an efficient church organization but rather to follow Christ's call to mission, both global and local.

7

A Financial History
of Presbyterian Congregations
Since World War II

D. Scott Cormode

Some Presbyterian congregations thrive financially while others starve, even though each year almost half of all philanthropic donations are made to religious causes. The purpose of this essay is to explore the evolving picture of Presbyterian congregational finances from 1950 to 1985, both by describing the patterns of change in receipts and expenditures and by suggesting explanations for these patterns.

The first half of the essay uses statistical evidence to analyze these trends while the second looks to social scientific scholarship to explain some of the ways in which a religious institution can facilitate its financial growth. In looking at receipts and expenditures during the period of study, the emphasis will be on discerning the underlying reasons for the trends.[1]

The Path of Benevolent Giving

Congregational receipts[2] followed a stepped path from 1950 to 1985 (fig. 7.1),[3] rising from 1950 before leveling in

The author was assisted in the production of this paper by regional studies provided by William L. Fisk, Harold M. Parker, Stephen R. Weisz, and James B. Wirth.

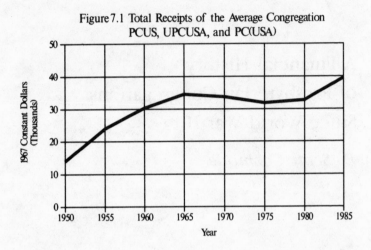

Figure 7.1 Total Receipts of the Average Congregation
PCUS, UPCUSA, and PC(USA)

1965, only to rise again after 1980.[4] The average Presbyterian congregation had more than twice the purchasing
power in 1965 that it had fifteen years earlier. Total receipts then remained almost unchanged until 1980, when
expansion occurred again at a rate comparable to that
prior to 1965. The path followed by congregational giving
from 1950 to 1985 shows two periods of significant growth
separated by a plateau from 1965 to 1980.

Accounting for the contour of this path requires that
attention be given to the changes in congregational membership and in the character of personal contributions.
When the membership of a local church changes, the
amount of its total receipts is affected because the number
of contributors changes. In like manner, if each of the congregation's members donates a little less money, the total
received will be significantly reduced. The path of congre-

gational receipts is shaped by trends in congregational membership and personal contributions.

The rise and fall of membership in the Presbyterian Church caused the level of total contributions to rise and fall correspondingly. Prior to 1965, local churches experienced unprecedented growth (fig. 7.2).[5] The subsequent decline in membership was just as noteworthy. Thus, during the fifties and early sixties, the number of contributors in the average local church increased each year; over the next fifteen years, that same church had fewer people each year to help to meet the budget. Membership trends boosted receipts prior to 1965 but have dragged them down since that time.

While membership trends have intermittently helped and limited congregational receipts, personal contributions have grown steadily (fig. 7.3). Personal contributions,

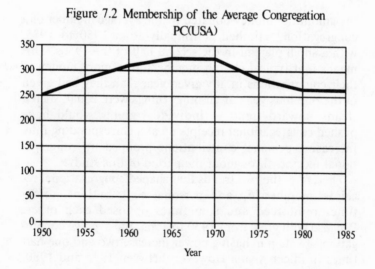

Figure 7.2 Membership of the Average Congregation PC(USA)

Figure 7.3 Personal Contributions
PC(USA)

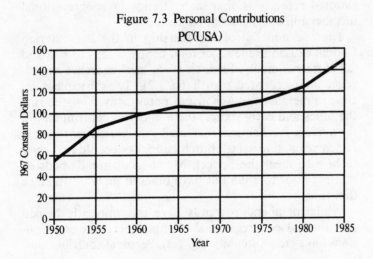

the amount of money donated by the average member of a
congregation,[6] climbed continually from 1950 to 1985,
with a small plateau in the second half of the 1960s. This
means that typical church members gave more money to
their congregations in any given year than they had given
in the previous year. If all other things were equal, such a
steady upward trend in individual giving would have
pushed congregational receipts up at a corresponding rate.
Increasing personal contributions propped up congregational receipts throughout the period of this study.

Therefore, the two trends that shaped congregational receipts, membership and personal contributions, sometimes reinforced and sometimes opposed each other.
Because both grew from 1950 to 1965, the average congregation saw its purchasing power increase two and one-half
times in fifteen years. However, between 1965 and 1980,
as many people left their churches but those who stayed
donated increasing amounts, total receipts neither in-

creased nor decreased much. Finally, the decline in membership slowed following 1980, which allowed personal contributions to propel congregational accounts higher again. The income of the typical local church, therefore, grew or dwindled over the last forty years depending on the interaction of its membership size and the donations of its typical member.

The question remains as to why membership and personal contributions followed the changing paths we have observed. Factors influencing membership have been addressed elsewhere and will not be rehearsed in this essay. New light can be shed, however, on personal contributions. In order for individuals to contribute more money to the church, they must donate a higher percentage of their income or donate a similar proportion of an increased income.

It is unlikely that personal contributions rose because individuals gave an increasing percentage of their earnings, because the percentage grew only during the 1950s and 1980s (fig. 7.4).[7] The church actually received a decreasing proportion of its members' incomes during the sixties. Only a portion of the ascending path of personal contributions can be explained by members' giving a greater share of their yearly incomes to their congregations.

Although members did not increase the proportion of their incomes that they donated to the church, their personal income did rise substantially throughout the period of this study—even when adjusted for inflation (fig. 7.5).[8]

This continual growth outstripped even the decline in percent giving, except in the last half of the 1960s. Congregations received more money each year even if individuals did not increase the share of their income that they donated.

Data on philanthropic giving in general reinforces the relationship of congregational receipts and increased per-

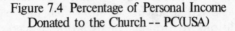

Figure 7.4 Percentage of Personal Income
Donated to the Church -- PC(USA)

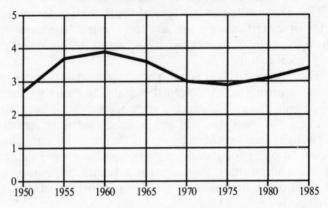

sonal income. If the reason for the increase in giving to
Presbyterian congregations was related to a societal phenomenon like the rise in personal income, then other entities that were unrelated to ecclesiastical pressures but
still dependent on the donations of Americans would
have been affected in similar ways. Philanthropic giving
increased steadily before 1968 and after 1975, with a plateau in the period between these years (fig. 7.6).[9] This
pattern is very similar to the one followed by congregational receipts, which showed substantial growth both
before and after a plateau between 1965 and 1980. Furthermore, the paths followed by philanthropic giving to
religious bodies and philanthropic giving to nonreligious
organizations are almost parallel (fig. 7.6), suggesting that
broad cultural influences affected both categories. The
idea that the growth of personal income in the society at
large stimulated the rise in congregational receipts is sup-

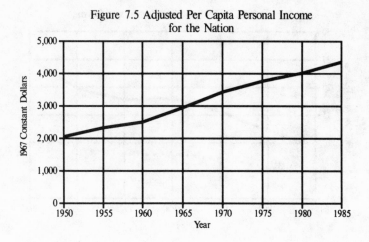

Figure 7.5 Adjusted Per Capita Personal Income
for the Nation

ported by a corresponding pattern in donations to all philanthropic enterprises.[10]

Therefore, it has been shown that the path followed by congregational receipts resulted from the interplay of membership growth and decline on the one hand and a steadily increasing level of personal contributions on the other. In the fifteen years prior to 1965, when both congregational size and personal contributions soared, the purchasing power of the average congregation increased two and one-half times (fig. 7.1). In the decade and a half after 1965, the purchasing power of the average congregation changed little, because membership and personal contributions negated each other, with membership declining while personal contributions continued to rise. The reason people donated increasing amounts of money to their local churches was the steady increase in their own personal income.

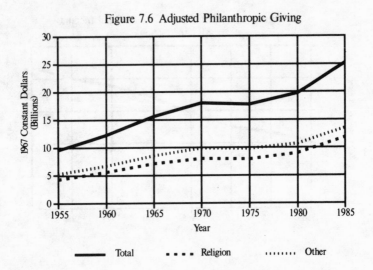

Figure 7.6 Adjusted Philanthropic Giving

The Path of Congregational Expenditures

Although congregational decision makers must continually decide how to apportion local and nonlocal spending priorities, over the period in which congregational expenditures were studied (1973–1985) the great majority of the typical United Presbyterian[11] congregation's resources was expended on local priorities. During the same period, as local emphasis increased, nonlocal expenditures played a diminishing role in congregational priorities, principally because of a declining commitment to denominational mission.

The average UPCUSA congregation in 1981 is indicative of the spending priorities of congregations during the period of study (see below).

Local spending, which can be further divided into local program, local mission, capital expense, and investments, constituted roughly 84 percent of the total budget.

Local Spending		*Nonlocal Spending*	
Local Program	63.3%	Per Capita	1.8%
Local Mission	3.6%	G.A. Mission	2.8%
Capital	11.5%	Synod Mission	2.0%
Investments	5.2%	Presbytery Mission	1.7%
Total	83.6%	Other Mission	3.8%
		Women's Organizations & Special Offerings	2.0%
		Total	14.1%

Local program, encompassing all the categories that involve the normal activity that takes places within the walls of the local church, including pastoral compensation as well as utilities and administrative costs, accounted for 63 percent of the 1981 budget. Local mission, on the other hand, which refers to activity beyond the walls of the church but focused in its immediate vicinity, including such activities as homeless shelters and crisis counseling centers, comprised 3.6 percent. Together, local program and local mission encompassed two thirds of the total expenditures of the average congregation.

Capital expense, which measures the cost of improvements and repairs to the physical plant, accounted for the second largest portion of the typical congregation's budget. This can be deceiving, however, because capital expense may be fairly low for a number of years. Then a major purchase will be made or a large project undertaken that will often command not only a significant portion of that year's budget but draw on past and/or future receipts. Thus, when averaged over a large number of congregations which are in various stages of development and redevelopment, capital expense subsumed over one tenth of total expenditures.

The final category to describe how congregations use their money locally is investments. In 1981, about one dollar in twenty was either saved or invested by the average congregation.

The portion of the representative budget devoted to local expenditures grew slowly from 1973 to 1985. The total of local spending increased from 80 percent of purchases in 1973 to 86 percent in 1985. Overall, local spending encompassed at least four times as much of the average congregational budget as did nonlocal spending.

Nonlocal spending, which refers to money contributed to entities outside of the local setting, can be divided into per capita apportionment, "other mission," special offerings, contributions from women's organizations, and presbytery, synod, and General Assembly general mission giving.

About one dollar in fifty donated to a congregation in 1981 and throughout the period of study was divided among the various governing bodies as the per capita apportionment. Another 3.8 percent was devoted to "other mission." Unfortunately, conclusions cannot be drawn using this "other mission" category because its ambiguity produced different interpretations by the various congregational treasurers who completed the forms on which the statistics were based.[12]

More specific conclusions can be drawn about the remaining nonlocal spending categories because detailed statistical information is available on general mission giving (fig. 7.7).[13] The total portion of expenditures devoted to special offerings, contributions from women's organizations, and presbytery and synod general mission remained constant from 1957 to 1981.[14] While the average 1957 congregation allocated 3 percent of its budget to presbytery and synod mission, by 1981 the sum of these two categories was still less than 4 percent of the average budget. Special offerings and giving through women's organizations such as United Presbyterian Women (together labeled "Special" on the graph) accounted for between 2 and 3 percent of churches' budgets. The sum of expenditures for presbytery mission, synod mission, special offerings, and contributions from women's organizations (the lower three levels of fig. 7.7) comprised an almost constant 6 percent of the average congregational budget from 1957 to 1981.

Spending on General Assembly General Mission (GAGM), on the other hand, was not as constant. After rising in 1963 to a high of one tenth of congregational expenditures, moneys allocated to GAGM declined sharply. Ten years after this high-water mark, the proportion had been cut in half, to 5 percent, and, by 1981, had plummeted to 2.8 percent, about one fourth its prominence twenty years earlier.

The percentages must, in this case, be seen in light of dollar values. While the real or adjusted[15] dollar amounts contributed to General Assembly mission dropped close to

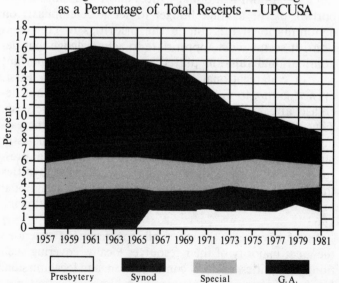

Figure 7.7 Total General Mission Giving
as a Percentage of Total Receipts -- UPCUSA

one quarter of their 1965 value by 1981, the slide begins abruptly in 1973 even if no adjustment is made. This is significant, because to the average congregation it would appear that because they were giving the same amount of money each year, a consistent level of support was being maintained. It may be possible that congregations did not know that they were de-emphasizing General Assembly mission after 1973.

Over the same period, giving to presbytery and synod mission grew little in real dollars (adjusted for inflation) but soared in terms of nominal (nonadjusted) dollars. Thus, the perceived financial commitment by congregations to presbytery and synod mission may have increased significantly.

The relationship of congregations and denominational mission can be interpreted by focusing on the nominal-dollar (nonadjusted) figures so that no significant de-emphasis of General Assembly mission is seen. Or, one can look at both real dollar figures and the declining proportion of the average budget to see a de-emphasis on denominational mission in the priorities of congregations. It seems most appropriate to acknowledge that denominational mission played a decreasingly important role in congregational budgets, for two reasons. First, even if giving to GAGM in nominal dollars did not decrease after 1973, every other category did increase. Thus, it was not valued enough to be allocated an increasing piece of the growing pie. Second, this de-emphasis in budgetary priorities is consistent with broad cultural pressures which were loosening the institutional loyalties throughout our society.[16] The priority of denominational mission in congregational budgets plummeted following 1963.

As we have seen, then, overall, congregations expended the great majority of their resources locally, covering such things as utilities, pastoral compensation, and local mission. Nonlocal expenditures remained an almost constant portion of congregational budgets, with the exception of the declining support for General Assembly mission.

Shaping the Path of Expenditures

The two trends noted for expenditures, slightly increased local spending and decreased funding of denominational mission, are related. An increase in local allocation must, by definition, lead to a decrease in the portion of the budget allocated to nonlocal expenses. The problem comes in explaining the reasons for these trends.

Three causes have been adduced in various quarters of the Presbyterian Church to explain the trends. None seems to do an adequate job of explaining the local increase and nonlocal decrease.

1. Angela Davis. Many in the denomination, particularly conservative elders, would point to what they see as the UPCUSA's contributions to the Angela Davis Legal Defense Fund as a turning point where many members began to feel that the denomination no longer deserved congregational support. They would argue that the Angela Davis affair prompted congregations to keep money in the local area that was formerly allocated to national mission.[17]

Sociologist Dean Hoge, who studied the effect of the Angela Davis controversy on commitment within the UPCUSA, found that "despite the threats, in action there was little connection between the anger and the level of individual giving" to the congregation. He adds, however, that the question of whether an effect of this controversy was to move "allocation of benevolences away from national and to local programs" was beyond the scope of the study.[18]

An examination of the data collected in the present study suggests that the 1971 controversy was not the cause of the downward trend in giving to GAGM. The percentage of total receipts allocated by the average congregation to GAGM fell 2 percent in both the two years before and the two years after the controversy. Furthermore, in the eight years before and after 1971, similar results appear. The Angela Davis controversy did not affect the allocation of congregational resources.

2. Overture H.   Overture H was the conscious decision of the General Assembly in the early 1970s to place mission activities under the jurisdiction of the most local governing bodies that could feasibly coordinate their accomplishment. Many denominational leaders interpret this overture as a sign that support for mission was not de-emphasized, but redistributed. They point to the fact that the number of nominal dollars (nonadjusted) contributed to synod and presbytery mission doubled following 1971, while nominal dollar contributions to General Assembly mission remained stable.

There are two problems with calling congregational expenditure patterns a planned redistribution. First, focusing only on nominal dollar values does not account for the change in the percentage distribution of the average congregational budget (fig. 7.7). When congregational receipts increased with inflation, the funds allotted to presbytery and synod mission increased proportionately, remaining about 3 percent of the typical budget. Therefore, congregational commitment to regional mission did not increase.

Second, as noted with the Angela Davis case, the decline of GAGM support began in 1963 and continued at the same pace into the 1980s. The descent continued despite Overture H, which neither aggravated nor alleviated it. Neither the Angela Davis case nor Overture H is sufficient to explain changes in the spending patterns of Presbyterian congregations.

3. Pastoral compensation.   One possible reason why congregations are spending more money locally might be increased expenditures on pastoral staff, either because pastoral salaries have increased or because the average congregation is employing more staff members. To find out, we will have to answer the following questions: (1) Did the typical pastoral salary increase? (2) Did the pastoral staff of the average congregation grow? and (3) Did the percent of the average congregational budget devoted to pastoral compensation increase?

a. Pastoral Salaries[19]

Although the typical United Presbyterian pastor's adjusted compensation package grew prior to 1970, in 1985 it was 2 percent lower than it had been twenty years before (fig. 7.8).[20] Over similar periods, the adjusted salary of the typical clergy fell 4 percent for other denominations (1962–1983),[21] and per capita personal income for the nation leaped 48 percent (1965–1985). Thus, it is clear that an increase in the average pastor's salary did not trigger the enhanced local spending by congregations.

b. Staff Size

Showing that the typical pastor's salary did not rise appreciably from 1965 to 1985 is not enough to prove that congregations were not allocating a higher portion of their

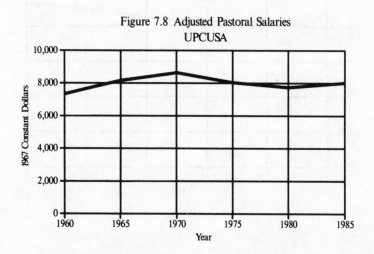

Figure 7.8 Adjusted Pastoral Salaries
UPCUSA

expenditures to pastoral compensation. If a greater number of clergy had been employed per congregation, then the total expenditure of a congregation for pastoral staff would increase, even if each of the pastors' salaries remained constant.

The number of parish clergy per congregation and the total parish clergy among the whole nonretired clergy population changed little in the period prior to 1985. The size of the average staff increased slowly throughout the period of study, with the number of parish clergy per congregation increasing 8.3 percent, from .836 clergy per congregation in 1965 to .905 in 1985 (fig. 7.9).[22] The distribution of parish clergy changed little, moving from 66.9 percent of all nonretired clergy in 1966 to 67.3 percent in 1986. While the proportion of supply pastors grew over that period, rising from 3.0 percent of the nonretired clergy

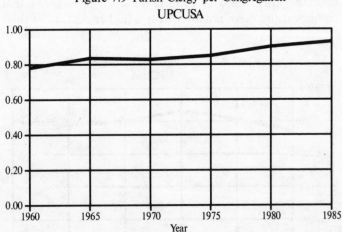

Figure 7.9 Parish Clergy per Congregation
UPCUSA

population to 6.7 percent, the proportion of pastors and associates actually shrank, with pastors accounting for 52.7 percent of nonretired clergy in 1966 and 50.3 percent in 1986 and associates representing 11.2 percent in 1966 and 10.6 percent in 1986. Thus, neither the distribution of parish clergy nor the size of the typical congregational staff changed appreciably in the two decades prior to 1985.

c. Pastoral Expense

The data gathered on typical pastoral salaries can be combined with the number of clergy employed by the average congregation to yield an approximation of the yearly expense that this average congregation incurred for pastoral compensation (fig. 7.10).[23] Congregations spent 6.3 percent more for pastoral ministry in 1985 than they did in 1965, but almost all of that expansion was in the last

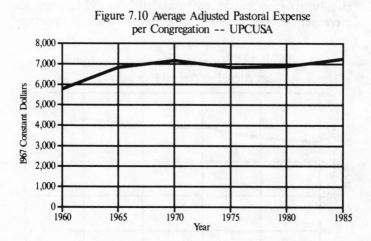

Figure 7.10 Average Adjusted Pastoral Expense
per Congregation -- UPCUSA

half of the 1960s. In the decade and a half following 1970, the total expenditures by congregations for pastoral compensation rose 1.2 percent when adjusted for inflation. Thus, it does not seem likely that the expense of pastoral ministry itself would be the reason congregations would keep money in the local setting rather than contributing to nonlocal programs such as General Assembly mission.

Nevertheless, if pastoral expense remained fairly constant while congregational budgets were shrinking, then there could conceivably be pressure to restrict nonlocal spending. For example, despite the fact that adjusted pastoral expense grew only 1.0 percent from 1965 to 1980 (fig. 7.10), the percentage of the average congregational budget allotted to pastoral expense actually rose 2.9 percent, from 18.4 percent of receipts to 21.3 percent (fig. 7.11), because the adjusted total receipts of the average UPC congregation fell 12.8 percent[24] during that time. The inverse can also be true, as happened from 1980 to 1985, when an increased pastoral expense accounted for a smaller portion

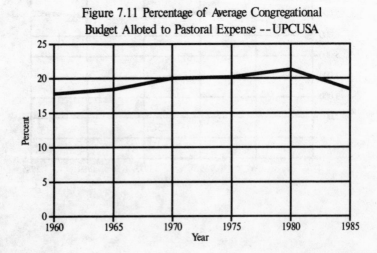

Figure 7.11 Percentage of Average Congregational
Budget Alloted to Pastoral Expense -- UPCUSA

of the congregational budget (fig. 7.11) because receipts increased. Overall, pastoral expense added 2.9 percent to the congregational budget between 1965 and 1980, which does not seem to be significant enough to trigger either an increase in local spending or a substantial decrease in non-local or denominational expenditures.

None of these three explanations can explain the changes in congregational expenditures. The Angela Davis conflict occurred after the changes had begun and did not perceptibly affect any of the data examined. In similar manner, the redistribution of resources precipitated by Overture H neither increased the portion of congregational budgets allocated to regional bodies nor accentuated the downward trend in denominational expenditures. Finally, the change in pastoral expense, both in constant dollars and as a proportion of receipts, was too small to have exerted significant pressure on congregations to reorganize their expenditure priorities. The reasons must be found elsewhere to explain why congregations have increased local spending to over 86 percent of expenditures while deemphasizing denominational mission's portion from over 10 percent to less than 2.8 percent of total receipts.

How Local Ecclesiastical Factors Shape Contributions

Congregational receipts and mission expenditures can be related to each other by seeing each as a contribution. Receipts are normally the contributions of individuals to the local church, while expenditures can be seen as contributions by the local church to mission activity.[25] Why do individuals and congregations choose to donate their money to one organization and not another? Or, asked another way, which religious institutions—congregations, denominational structures, or para-church mission agencies—are likely to be funded?

Although generalizations must be balanced by the idea that every congregation is shaped by its own particular local factors, we will show how "ownership" is the key concept for understanding congregational and mission funding. People feel ownership for causes rather than for institutions. The particular *causes* that people own are those which correspond to their understanding of the mission of the church, while people feel ownership for an *institution* when they identify with its agenda. An organization can influence the degree to which it is financially supported by establishing a shared identity between its agenda and its potential contributors.

Local Factors

Because contributors respond to local ecclesiastical factors, church leaders can influence the level of support their bodies receive. This should not be seen as contradicting those studies which argue that specific ecclesiastical factors, such as denominational policy decisions, do not significantly affect the average congregation's monetary support or total membership.[26] Local forces are masked when an average is computed using aggregated data; and the negative influence of some local decisions is balanced by the positive effect of choices made by other leaders. Because the cumulative effect of these local forces on the national average tends to be constant over time, dramatic national shifts are precipitated only by broad cultural or economic factors, such as the growth of personal income, but are felt at the local level as they are refracted through the lens of the local situation. Every congregation is affected by its own unique set of local factors.

Local factors can be contextual.[27] Local contextual factors are the overriding reason that the Hanmi Presbytery, a nongeographic presbytery composed of Korean-American congregations in the Synod of Southern California and Hawaii, is the national leader in per member giving. There is a strong sense of family among Korean immigrants due to the "uniquely non-assimilating character of the Korean people."[28] Because "the Korean churches are the only social organs in their community that furnish relatedness with oneself, neighbors and God,"[29] "one of the main functions of the Korean churches is to provide church members with a 'family atmosphere.' "[30] The result is a tremendous sense of ownership for the Korean congregations, which is manifest in financial giving.

Hanmi Presbytery ranked first in 1985 among presbyteries in per member giving, with a per member total 85 percent higher than the national average.[31] This is particularly striking considering that most of the immigrants who populate the churches "own and/or operate small businesses, shops and restaurants,"[32] leaving them with a median income far below that of many suburban presbyteries. Members of Hanmi congregations maintain a high degree of ownership for their churches because of the role the church plays in the Korean community, and give liberally to support their work. Congregational giving patterns in the Hanmi Presbytery are the result of local contextual factors.[33]

Local contextual factors include far more than ethnocultural concerns, encompassing any local influence beyond the realm of the church. For example, in the 1960s a national corporation moved a manufacturing plant to a rural Ohio county, bringing an influx of jobs and executives imported to manage the plant. Because the local economy thrived and many of the transplanted professionals joined the Presbyterian church, the local congregation saw its receipts soar. The congregation was helpless, however, to prevent a significant loss of income when the plant was closed in the early 1980s, taking not only jobs but many Presbyterian members who were company professionals. Local contextual forces exert tremendous influence on the congregations in their area.

By contrast, local institutional factors have roots in the local church. The clearest example of the effects of these forces is found in R. Stephen Warner's study of the transformation of Mendocino Presbyterian Church, *New Wine in Old Wineskins: Evangelicals and Liberals in a Small-*

Town Church. Although he looked for evidence that contextual factors shaped the congregation, he concludes,
"The trajectory of Mendocino Presbyterian Church does
stand out as remarkable [among the congregations in its
social setting], and [the pastor's] role was essential."[34] Institutional factors set in motion by the pastor caused the
church's membership to double, the budget to quadruple
(*after* adjusting for inflation), the portion of that budget
spent on local program to be reduced by 25 percent, and
the portion allotted to denominational support to double.[35] Congregations are shaped by the unique set of local
factors within which they live.[36]

Ownership

But how do local institutional forces shape the finances
of religious organizations—be they congregations, denominational structures, or para-church agencies? An important specific ecclesiastical factor is the degree of ownership
felt by potential contributors—both individuals and
groups. Ownership occurs when a personal tie is established between a group or individual and the mission activity or organization that is being supported. After such a
bond is established, giving occurs not because of obliga-
tion or a vague sense of duty but because donors see their
dollars having an effect. For example, a congregation has
established a formal support relationship with a man
named Bill, who grew up in that church and presently
works under the auspices of the Presbyterian Church, with
his family, in Tijuana, Mexico. Many of the older members, remembering when Bill was in the youth group, feel
ownership for Bill himself, while many of the younger
adults, who never knew Bill but are excited about the goals
of the project that he and his family are doing, feel an
ownership for the work that happens to be headed by a
former member of the congregation.

The question remains how ownership may be established for a particular Presbyterian body. First of all, peo-

ple feel ownership for causes rather than for institutions. The reasons for this are bound up in the very nature of the American religious experience since the 1960s. Causes[37] have become of primary importance because American religion, being voluntary, is by nature activist. At the same time, institutional loyalty has diminished because, in the wake of the 1960s, institutions are less capable of exercising authority.

American religion is voluntary; "individuals are free to choose their religious beliefs and associations without political, ecclesiastical or communal coercion."[38] Voluntary religion is so prevalent in American society that many Presbyterians assume that voluntarism is intrinsic to the gospel—that all churches in all times were meant to be voluntary. In fact, it "is so obvious a principle . . . that its significance is overlooked, but it is one of the revolutionary principles adopted by modern ecclesiastical organizations."[39]

Voluntary religion is activist, placing much more emphasis on doing things than on "proper belief or credal assent."[40] Christian debates now take place over mission activities and "moral concerns," rather than the identifying elements of an ecclesiastical institution such as "religious dogma or articles of faith."[41] Therefore, emphasis is placed on the actions one takes and the causes one supports rather than on the particular organization with which one allies to accomplish those tasks.

While devotion to particular causes is increasing, two separate sociological studies of modern denominations, including the PCUS and the UPCUSA, have concluded that loyalty to religious institutions is waning. Robert Wuthnow of Princeton has described what he calls "the declining significance of denominationalism,"[42] showing that "as the boundaries separating denominations have been lowered . . . many parishioners feel closer to people in other denominations than they do toward people at the other end of the theological spectrum" who make up a large part of their own denomination.[43] The result is that loyalty is directed toward causes represented by special purpose groups rather than to denominational structures as a whole.[44]

Wade Clark Roof and William McKinney come to similar conclusions. They point to historian Sidney Mead's description of a "denominational institution" as "a voluntary association of like-hearted and like-minded individuals, who are united on the basis of common beliefs *for the purpose of accomplishing tangible and defined objectives.*"[45] They write, "Typical Americans view religious congregations as gatherings of individuals who have chosen to be together, in institutions of their own making and over which they hold control."[46] This leads Roof and McKinney to conclude that the effects of the 1960s "gave rise to greater autonomy of the individual and reinforced the view that religious institutions should serve individuals and not vice versa."[47] Such a breakdown of "ascriptive loyalties" has diminished the allegiance held by individuals and groups for the denominational institution.[48]

The particular causes that individuals will own vary because people identify with causes that correspond to their understanding of the mission of the church.[49] Since there is no one understanding of the church's mission shared by all Presbyterians, members "display [such] a large amount of diversity on most social issues" that "denominational affiliation alone helps little in predicting how people will stand on current social issues."[50] Since the denomination, as well as many congregations, lacks the kind of corporate identity that would breed consensus,[51] the various activities that embody different concepts of church mission compete for the mission dollar as products in a marketplace.[52] When individuals feel a tie between a particular cause and their own understanding of what the church "should" be doing, they will be willing to share financial responsibility for that cause.

While the particular *causes* that people own are those which correspond to their understanding of the mission of the church, people feel ownership for an *institution* when they identify with its agenda. This agenda becomes the bridge which allows an individual to participate in an institution as if it were a cause. If a congregation has made plain its intention to support peace and justice, then a woman who sees peace and justice to be a primary concern of the church will see that congregation as a worthy recipient of her contributions. The agenda an institution follows is often the primary criterion upon which mission support decisions are made.

Therefore, the primary way in which church leaders can encourage ownership and financial support is by communicating the organization's agenda effectively to potential contributors. To translate an agenda effectively to an audience the communication must first incorporate the components of shared identity, which are a common history and a common language; and second, it must make the agenda portable.

At the core of ownership is a shared identity, which Robert Bellah and his associates have shown to be the result of a commonly claimed history and commonly used language.[53] All groups have events which they remember as formative or instructive. These serve as examples, both positive and negative, for the community as a whole. In the same way, a peculiar language, or at least a peculiar set of definitions, arises which allows the members to express their shared identity succinctly and clearly. For example, those who see the mission of the church as primarily evangelism feel affinity with those who can express their goals, their agenda, in terms of the Great Commission and look back with pride on examples such as William Carey or Billy Graham. Those who understand the church's mission as socially oriented might speak of doing something "to one of the least of these" and remember fondly the examples of the good Samaritan or the prophets of Israel. Because each group's identity is carved out of the history it chooses to recall and the language it has developed to communicate its meaning, an agenda that seeks to share that identity must emerge from that history and speak the language, not as an alien but as a native.

The agenda must also be portable. It must be communicated in a way that people can take it with them and make it their own. To do this, the agenda must be accessible, reasonable, distinctly Christian, and clearly embodied.

Robert Wuthnow has maintained that one of the effects of ecclesiastical bureaucracies is that the membership can become cut off from the vision and spontaneity of mission because they are not given "the operative knowledge on which decisions are made."[54] For example, a congregation or denominational agency may have very good reasons for choosing to support one project, say well-digging in Ethiopia, over another, perhaps an outreach project among the Kurds. But if those reasons are not communicated clearly, then those people who were already inclined to support programs like the Kurds' project will not feel any tie to the agenda or the institution. The underlying reasons behind agenda decision must be made clear to potential contributors for them to be able to carry that agenda as if it were their own.

Not only must an agenda be well reasoned, it should be distinctly Christian. Noted sociologist Phillip Hammond has shown that the urgency that was once present for foreign mission dissipated over the course of the century because "the American mainline denominations had lost their convictions that *as Christians* they had much to offer"[55] that was unique, different from what the society offered. When the agenda of a Christian organization is blurred or becomes indistinguishable from that of a secular one, it becomes difficult for people to see that agenda as intrinsic to the mission of the church. This does not mean that the church should not be engaged in some of the same activities as secular agencies. Homelessness is a problem of both spiritual and social concern. But it does mean that the church must have more to offer than is possible from a secular source. An effective mission agenda must embody, in the words of John Leith, "what the Church has to say that no one else can say."[56] For people to carry an ecclesiastical agenda with them as their own, it must be distinct from what might be the agenda of a secular organization.

Finally, hearers must be provided with many examples.

While the reasoning behind policy decisions is very important to some, many people who have neither the time nor the inclination to remember the details of an agenda will carry the agenda with them by remembering stories. When hearers (or readers) can be put in a position where they can vicariously see ministry occurring around them, whether down the street or across the world, they are likely to feel the kind of tie that brings ownership. People who have examples of a clearly reasoned and distinctly Christian agenda are inclined to say to themselves, "That is what the church should be doing." When men and women feel that kind of tie, they will support the institution whose agenda they own. Establishing a shared identity between an agenda and potential contributors involves a commonly claimed history and a mutually understood idiom. It should be reasonable and accessible, with many examples drawn from life. Most of all it should be discernibly Christian.

Conclusion

This study has attempted to combine lessons from the past with application for the future, as the statistical conclusions regarding congregational receipts and expenditures formed the background for the explanatory discussion of how local factors may be used to shape contributions.

The path followed by congregational receipts resulted from the interaction of membership growth and decline with a steadily increasing level of personal contributions, as can be seen by looking at data for fifteen years before and after 1965. While the purchasing power of the average congregation increased two and one-half times during the first period as congregational size and personal contributions worked together, the purchasing power of that same average church changed little in the second period because size and contributions negated each other. Personal contributions rose throughout the period of this study because personal incomes were constantly rising.

Congregational spending priorities changed less than

congregational receipts, with local expenditures commanding the great majority of congregational budgets. The only significant change was the de-emphasis of mission spending caused by the declining commitment of congregations to denominational mission. When the reasons for this trend were explored, none of three explanations commonly heard in ecclesiastical circles could adequately explain the phenomenon. Just as the Angela Davis affair occurred after the changes had begun and did not perceptibly affect any of the trends, the redistribution of resources precipitated by Overture H neither increased the portion of congregational budgets allotted to regional bodies nor accentuated the downward trend in denominational expenditures. Although some change was discovered in the expense incurred by congregations for pastoral compensation, it was deemed too small to have reorganized congregational priorities.

Finally, we have suggested guidelines for ways church leaders can influence the degree of financial support for their institutions. People feel ownership for causes rather than for institutions. While people own the particular causes that correspond to their understanding of the mission of the church, they feel personal ties to an institution when they own its agenda. The agenda of the religious body, whether congregation or denomination, provides the bridge that allows people to feel ownership for it as if it were a cause that they were supporting. People will support the activities, projects, and institutions for which they feel ownership.

8

Money and Power:
Presbyterian Women's Organizations
in the Twentieth Century

Joan C. LaFollette

Over the years, Presbyterian women's organizations have served as the means by which many committed churchwomen have made remarkable contributions to the life of the church. Working through local circles, as well as regional and national organizations, women have succeeded in making a major impact on the twentieth-century church.[1] Their well-organized programs of fund-raising for mission, Bible study and education, leadership training, communication, and support have helped inspire generations of women to become active in the church's work.

Women's Work in the Presbyterian Tradition

As early as the turn of the century, the successes of women's groups in a variety of endeavors raised fears that women's organizations were evolving into a separate and powerful "women's church." Some denominational leaders publicly applauded women and encouraged them in their work, but many others wanted to control and supervise women's activities. Women involved in all-female church groups never intended to be in competition with the regular programs of the church, but their exclusion from official leadership roles in the denomination in effect forced them into such alternative organizations.

In the early years of organized women's work, all-female church organizations were often a welcome refuge for progressive women who wanted to be active in church life. Their groups sometimes served as unofficial forums for discussions about women's lack of status in the church. Later in the century, however, when the feminist movement gained momentum, women's organizations often shied away from and even resisted open involvement in the work for women's rights. As other groups evolved in the church to take on the feminist cause, traditional women's groups were often unfairly viewed as outdated.

In recent years there has been a heightened concern in Presbyterian women's organizations over the lack of participation by younger women. Some in the church have even predicted the eventual demise of traditional women's groups in the church. Concern over younger women's apparent lack of interest is not a new phenomenon, however. As early as the 1920s, reports from the Presbyterian Church in the U.S.A. (PCUSA) indicated concern over the lack of participation by younger women.[2] Katherine McAfee Parker, a prominent leader among PCUSA women for many years, recalls first hearing complaints about this in 1929; after that, she says, she never worried about it. She remembered that, as young women, she and her friends were "very snooty" about not wanting to do women's work in the church, but eventually they came around to the fold.[3] Even so, the problem of attracting young women to the women's organizations of the church continued to be a concern into the 1950s in both the PCUSA and the Presbyterian Church in the U.S. (PCUS).[4]

There may be more reasons now than in previous decades to take note of the lack of interest on the part of younger women. Mainline Protestant churches are experiencing declining memberships and aging constituencies. Failure in the last thirty years to attract or hold young people has resulted in a noticeable increase in the average age of church members.[5] It is interesting to note that while the attendance of 5,617 at the July 1988 Gathering of Presbyterian Women at Purdue University was the largest ever for a national Presbyterian women's meeting, the percentage of attendees fifty-one years and over—62 percent—was significantly higher than the denominational membership percentage of 49 percent in 1987 for those age fifty-five and over.[6]

Other significant changes in church and society have also affected participation in women's church organizations. Economic necessity and opportunity have broadened women's involvement outside the home and restricted the time available for volunteer work. Opportunities within the official leadership of the church have been opened to women as well. In the PCUSA, women's ordination to the office of deacon was opened in 1923; to the office of ruling elder, in 1930; to the office of minister, in 1956. In the PCUS, women's ordination to all church offices—deacon, ruling elder, and minister—was opened in 1964. The lifting of restrictions on women's participation in the official leadership of the church has meant that women's organizations are no longer the sole formal channel for women's energy in the church.

In the face of these changes, how have traditional Presbyterian women's organizations fared? Are they in decline, or simply adjusting to the changing environments of church and society?

Membership Statistics

Measuring the health and status of an organization is a difficult task at best. Membership statistics would help substantiate or disprove impressions of growth or decline. Annual statistics, however, are not available for the PCUSA and The United Presbyterian Church in the U.S.A. (UPCUSA) women's groups. Traditionally, all female members of any local Presbyterian congregation were considered to be members of the local women's organization, whether or not they were ever active participants in the women's organization. This tradition meant that

PCUSA and UPCUSA women felt no necessity to collect membership statistics. PCUS women did, however, collect national membership statistics for active women. Those membership statistics for PCUS women's groups do seem to give the appearance of decline, but only since the mid-1960s. The figures also suggest a fairly steady increase in membership from 1912 until the 1950s, followed by little growth through 1972, after which statistics are no longer available. Peak membership occurred in the mid-1960s, followed by decline into the 1970s (table 8.1). It is important to note, however, that the rise and fall of the total membership of PCUS women's organizations roughly parallels in magnitude the growth and decline of the denomination as a whole.

Financial Statistics

Financial statistics, particularly of the benevolence contributions of Presbyterian women's organizations, are available and provide an interesting overview of women's work in the church. The contributions of PCUSA women peaked in the mid-1930s as a percentage of total denominational benevolence giving and have been decreasing ever since (Table 8.2). The percentage of PCUS benevolence giving contributed by women also peaked in the mid-1930s and has decreased in the following years (Table 8.3). If, indeed, money is power in denominations, Presbyterian women's organizations have had decreasing claims to both in the decades since World War II.

A History of Money and Power

The twentieth-century history of Presbyterian women's organizations is a rich and varied one, and it is a history that has been well documented by women themselves. There are stories of prayer groups and sewing circles, building programs and annual conferences, campaigns for the dignity of minority women and friendships with missionaries from around the world. There are reports of women being uplifted, educated, and freed from isolation through the Presbyterian women's organization network of mutual support and caring. The accounts are varied and colorful, but their common thread is the core commitment to the mission of the church—a commitment that, for many women, continues to this day. The title of "missionary women" has long fallen into disuse, but the concern for reaching beyond the bounds of the local church remains.

One of the many stories of Presbyterian women's organizations involves that core commitment to mission. It is an account that is less well documented and perhaps unfamiliar to many women active in church work. It is the story of how concerns for women's mission giving often played a determinative role in the relationship of women's organizations to their respective denominations.

The history of Presbyterian women's organizations is, in many ways, a financial history—a story of "second mile" giving to support mission projects. Both the PCUSA and PCUS women's organizations began as groups to raise money for mission causes, and those financial campaigns gave energy and a sense of unique purpose to disenfranchised women in the church. Money also gave women's organizations political power, for all too often denominational officials tolerated women's activities simply because they needed the funds women were so skillful in raising. But that toleration of women's power had its limits. What emerges is one story of Presbyterian women's work—a story of women's struggle for self-determination in their mission work. It is a story of money and power earned and money and power taken away.

Early Missionary Societies

Even though their success at fund-raising eventually gave women access to power in denominational circles, power had never been their first goal. The founders of the first female "cent societies" and charitable groups in the late eighteenth and nineteenth centuries were motivated by a great need to help others in the name of the gospel. They zealously worked to raise money for missions and

Table 8.1 Membership Statistics for PCUS Women's Organizations (1912–1940)

	1912 [a]	1915	1920	1925	1930	1935	1940
Number of Local Groups	2,606	2,684	1,802	2,132	2,359	2,472	2,553
Women's Groups Membership	66,684	67,643	59,061	110,257	147,365	163,589	186,048
Total PCUS Membership	300,771	332,339	376,517	457,093	457,855	477,467	532,177
Women's Groups % of PCUS Membership	22%	20%	16%	24%	32%	34%	35%
Sources	GAM[b] 1913, 70d, no pp.	GAM, 1915, 277, 291	GAM 1920, 307, no pp. (WA)	GAM 1925, 284, 26 (WA)	GAM 1930, 272, 30 (DWW)	GAM 1935, 226, 30 (CWW)	GAM 1940, 288, 42 (CWW)

[a] The PCUS Woman's Auxiliary was founded on May 20, 1912.

[b] *General Assembly Minutes* (GAM).

Table 8.1 (continued) Membership Statistics for PCUS Women's Organizations (1945-1972)

	1945	1950	1955	1960	1965	1970	1972[c]
Number of Local Groups	2,606	2,904	3,308	3,484	3,518	3,287	4,000
Women's Groups Membership	207,775	276,143	339,198	339,180	352,954	332,772	338,981
Total PCUS Membership	580,369	675,489	807,624	899,116	945,975	953,600	946,536
Women's Groups % of PCUS Membership	36%	41%	42%	38%	37%	35%	36%
Sources	GAM 1945, 313; III:41 (CWW)	GAM 1950, 292; III:40 (BWW)	GAM 1956, II:54; GAM 1955, III:49 (BWW)	GAM 1961, II:58; GAM 1960, III:43 (BWW)	GAM 1966, II:58; GAM 1960, III:45 (BWW)	GAM 1971, II:44; GAM 1970, III:31 (BWW)	GAM 1973, II:152; III:134 (BWW)

[c] The PCUS Board of Women's Work was discontinued as of December 1, 1973, when all operations were taken over by the General Executive Board as a result of PCUS reorganization. Membership statistics on PCUS women's organizations are not available after 1972.

Table 8.2 General Assembly Benevolence Contributions of PCUSA, UPCUSA, and PC(USA) Women's Organizations [a] (1900–1940)

	1900	1905 [b]	1910 [c]	1915 [d]	1920 [e]	1925	1930	1935	1940
Women's Giving to G.A.	$673,459	$545,461	$797,641	$864,259	$1,365,810	$2,387,320	$2,546,311	$1,673,892	$1,585,639
G.A. Receipts or Living Donations	$2,490,619	$3,305,027	$5,754,373	$8,615,016	$12,500,487	$9,722,529	$8,451,901	$4,895,879	$5,045,936
Women's Percent of Total	27%	17%	14%	10%	11%	25%	30%	34%	31%
Women's % of Home/Natl. Missions	40%	24%	30%	19%	29%	37%	40%	50%	47%
Women's % of Foreign Missions	36%	28%	32%	24%	21%	31%	34%	42%	39%
Women's % of Christian Education	—	—	—	—	—	—	—	—	—
Sources	GAM 1900, 307	GAM 1905, 305, 318, 382	GAM 1910, 121, 428, 374, 367; GAM 1909, 340	GAM 1915, 393, 394, 402, 448	GAM 1920, 351, 357, 422, 347	GAM 1925, 917, 329 (NM), 318 (FM)	GAM 1930, 1913; II:218 (NM), II:225 (FM)	GAM 1935, 1855; II:158 (NM), II:153 (FM)	GAM 1940, 1857; II:166 (NM), II:160 (FM)

Table 8.2

ᵃ In this table, given in actual dollars, women's giving to General Assembly mission is compared to either total receipts of the General Assembly Boards (1900–1920) or contributions to the General Assembly by living donors (1925–1985). Statistics are for contributions to General Assembly mission, *excluding* giving to local, presbytery, and synod mission. Comparing financial data over an eighty-five-year period is difficult because of periodic changes in reporting methods. Statistics are given for the purpose of rough comparison.

ᵇ In 1905, women's giving to the Woman's Board of Home Missions was $200,812; to the Board of Home Missions $7,451; to the Board of Foreign Missions $337,198. Total income of the Woman's Board of Home Missions, including contributions of Young People's Societies, was $475,043. Total income of the Board of Home Missions *including* the Woman's Board was $867,017.

ᶜ In 1910, women's giving to the Woman's Board of Home Missions was not given as a separate figure, although one report seems to indicate that it was $328,392. Women's giving directly to the Board of Home Missions was $1,519. Total income of the Woman's Board of Home Missions appears to be $602,000. Total income of the Board of Home Missions *including* the Woman's Board was $1,108,344. Women's giving to the Board of Foreign Missions was not reported; however, it was indicated that the total for 1910 exceeded 1909 giving by $7000, which gives a total of $467,730.

ᵈ In 1915, women's giving to the Woman's Board of Home Missions was $277,492; to the Board of Home Missions $1,162; to the Board of Foreign Missions $585,605. Total income of the Woman's Board of Home Missions, including contributions of Young People's Societies, was $449,321. Total income of the Board of Home Missions *including* the Woman's Board was $1,441,428.

ᵉ In 1920, women's giving to the Woman's Board of Home Missions was $582,603; to the Board of Home Missions $776; to the Board of Foreign Missions $782,431. Total income of the Woman's Board of Home Missions, including contributions of Young People's Societies, was $806,421. Total income of the Board of Home Missions *excluding* the Woman's Board of Home Missions was $1,219,223.

Table 8.2 (continued) General Assembly Benevolence Contributions of PCUSA, UPCUSA, and PC(USA) Women's Organizations (1945-1985)

	1945	1950	1955	1960	1965	1970	1975 [f]	1980	1985
Women's Giving to G.A.	$1,818,146	$2,631,652	$3,609,703	$5,043,266	$5,425,708	$5,145,348	$5,173,404	$5,715,314	$6,256,974
G.A. Living Donations	$7,103,633	$13,196,184	$20,361,707	$31,666,031	$36,717,504	$32,774,119	$24,345,508	$24,834,891	$29,811,168
Women's Percent of Total	26%	20%	18%	16%	15%	16%	15% [g]	15% [h]	13% [i]
Women's % of National Missions	38%	30%	29%	19%	16%	19%	—	—	—
Women's % of For. Miss. (COEMAR)	32%	24%	23%	22%	21%	22%	—	—	—
Women's % of Christian Education	5.4%	13%	17%	18%	17%	19%	—	—	—
Sources	GAM 1945, I:1013; II:120 (NM), II:140 (FM), II:73 (CE)	GAM 1951, I:947 I29; II:116 (NM), II:176 (FM), II:106 (CE)	GAM 1956, I:55; III:50 I; II:216 (NM), II:158 (FM), II:136 (CE)	GAM 1960, III:51 I; GAM 1961, I:256-7; II:158 (NM)	GAM 1965, III:51 I; GAM 1966, I:94-5; II:152 (NM)	GAM 1970, III:628; GAM 1971, I:172	GAM 1976, I:610, I:288	GAM 1981, I:409, I:229	GAM 1986, I:665, I:307

Table 8.2 (continued)

f In 1972, the UPCUSA was reorganized. The Board of National Missions, and the Commission on Ecumenical Mission and Relations (the former Board of Foreign Missions) were combined in the new Program Agency. Women's undesignated contributions were subsequently given to the Program Agency.

g In 1975, the General Assembly Mission Council reported only the undesignated giving by women ($3,711,546) as a portion of the $24,345,508 given by living donors to overall General Assembly mission. These are the figures used to calculate the percentage of women's giving at 15%.

h In 1980, the General Assembly Mission Council reported only the undesignated giving by women, less the UPW program budget, a total of $3,827,296, as a portion of the $24,834,891 given by living donors to General Assembly mission. These figures are used to calculate the percentage of women's giving at 15%.

i In 1985, the General Assembly Council reported only the undesignated giving by women, less the UPW program budget, a total of $4,022,284, as a portion of the $29,811,168 given by living donors to the General Assembly general mission program. These figures are used to calculate the percentage of women's giving at 13%. (As of 1985, the former UPCUSA and PCUS budgets had not been consolidated.)

Table 8.3

a In this table, statistics on total women's giving and churchwide donations (living donors only, 1945–1985) are for contributions to all mission *including* congregational, presbytery, synod, and General Assembly causes. Comparing financial data over a seventy-year period is difficult because of periodic changes in reporting methods. Statistics are given for the purpose of rough comparison.

b By 1945, the Committee on Woman's Work was no longer publishing detailed statistics on women's benevolence giving.

c As of 1957, local women's organizations were no longer required by the Board of Women's Work to report all benevolence contributions. Statistics were solicited only for the Birthday Offering (*PCUS GAM* 1958, Board of Women's Work, II:37).

Table 8.3 Local, Regional, and General Assembly Benevolence Contributions of PCUS Women's Organizations[a] (1915–1950)

	1915	1920	1925	1930	1935	1940	1945[b]	1950
Total Women's Giving	$442,982	$717,863	$1,432,549	$1,578,773	$1,076,958	$1,268,755	$1,772,788	$2,730,209
Women's Birthday Offering	—	—	$23,388	$52,289	$51,891	$50,242	$86,252	$142,040
Churchwide Living Donations	$4,792,860	$9,236,836	$14,935,170	$14,307,835	$9,086,068	$11,762,503	$18,633,788	$38,088,733
Women's Percent of Total	9.2%	7.8%	9.6%	11%	11.9%	10.8%	9.5%	7.2%
Women's % of G.A. Home Missions	13%	12%	15%	21%	26%	30%	—	—
Women's % of G.A. Foreign Missions	19%	17%	21%	27%	27%	36%	—	—
Sources	GAM 1915, 277, 291	GAM 1920, 307, no pp. (WA)	GAM 1925, 284, 26–27 (WA)	GAM 1930, 272, 30–31 (DWW)	GAM 1935, 226, 30–31 (CWW)	GAM 1940, 288, 42–43 (CWW)	GAM 1945, 313; III:41 (CWW)	GAM 1950, 292

Table 8.3 (continued) Local, Regional, and General Assembly Benevolence Contributions of PCUS Women's Organizations (1955-1985)

	1955	1960 [c]	1965	1970	1975	1980	1985
Total Women's Giving	$3,534,833	—	—	—	—	—	—
Women's Birthday Offering	$200,000	$182,372	$521,886	$309,189	$424,000	$474,532	$509,368
Churchwide Living Donations	$66,033,260	$91,596,114	$112,666,442	$138,621,628	$185,275,224	$290,480,811	Total Not Given
Women's % of Total	5.4%	—	—	—	—	—	—
Women's % of G.A. Home Missions	—	—	—	—	—	—	—
Women's % of G.A. Foreign Missions	—	—	—	—	—	—	—
Sources	GAM 1956, II:154; GAM 1955, III:149 (BWW)	GAM 1961, II:158; GAM 1960, III:133 (BWW)	GAM 1966, II:132; GAM 1965, III:137 (BWW)	GAM 1971, II:141; GAM 1970, III:137 (BWW)	GAM 1976, II:176; I:417	GAM 1981, II:479; I:513	GAM 1986, I:305

theological education, as well as to sew clothing for missionaries and seminary students. They were rallied not only by their shared compassion, but with the cry that it was the unique duty of women to help—especially to help other women and their children. Inspiring one another with the urgent need of "woman's work for woman," those early visionaries sparked the fire of a great women's movement for mission. That movement was indeed a financial campaign, and a very successful one at that.

PCUSA and UPCUSA National Women's Organizations

The Woman's Executive Committee of Home Missions, the first national Presbyterian women's organization, came into being in New York City on December 12, 1878. Building on the work of those early local and regional societies, the national Executive Committee oversaw great and continued successes by the women of the church. In its first decade, the Executive Committee was responsible for a hundred schools and 274 teachers in the U.S. mission field. In 1889 and 1890, receipts by the Woman's Executive Committee equaled more than the total contributions of all churches nationwide to the General Assembly Board of Home Missions. The *Minutes* of the General Assembly make a special note of the contributions of women in those years:

> The Annual Report of the Woman's Executive Committee is the marvel of business clearness, but the success of their work is of chief interest. In 1889, the churches gave $266,395.20. In the same year the women gave $278,940.93, an excess on the part of the women of $12,645.73. In 1890, the one gave $246,580.49, the other $286,627.51, an excess on the part of the women of $40,047.02. That is to say, the women of the Church raised last year $12,645.73 more than the combined offerings of all the Churches, and this year $40,047.02 more.[7]

As might be presumed, the women received requests

from a variety of constituencies in the church for monetary aid. In the late 1890s, the women were even asked to help pay the debt of the denomination's Board of Home Missions. The treasurer of the Woman's Executive Committee commented on this incident with a note of sarcasm: "Man-like, in their generosity they suggested that the women help pay the debt of the Board."[8]

The Woman's Executive Committee, renamed in 1897 to be the Woman's Board of Home Missions, was indeed a powerful organization in the church. By 1910, some women had raised the issue of incorporation of the board; by doing so, they created a controversy that would last five years. In particular, the women were concerned that their board was not legally entitled to legacies if it were not incorporated. They also felt that more control over their own funds and mission projects was essential for the success of their work. In their arguments, the women were not afraid to point out that the Woman's Board was self-supporting in all its expenses, including administration and mission work, and at times had come to the aid of the Board of Home Missions. The controversy ended when, despite concerns that the Woman's Board was competing with the denomination's board, incorporation was accomplished in 1915. Incorporation meant that the women had gained total control over their own income, administration, mission personnel, and properties; they were responsible only to the General Assembly.[9] This was indeed the high-water mark of independent women's work in the PCUSA, but it would last only eight years.

In the 1920s, the Woman's Board of Home Missions was merged with the seven regional women's organizations for foreign missions work. The newly consolidated Woman's Board oversaw the work of 6,000 local societies that contributed $3,000,000 annually to home and foreign missions work.[10] In 1923, for home missions alone, the Woman's Board had an annual budget of $1,068,091 and supervised the work of 451 missionaries at 78 stations, 24 boarding schools, 21 day schools, 8 medical centers, and

28 community stations.[11] Between 1873 and 1923, the sum total of women's gifts to mission work was approximately $45,000,000.[12]

The success of the women was phenomenal during this period, and they seemed well aware that their financial campaigns were a source of life-giving energy. One woman observed that local church societies that have no "direct financial responsibility tend to become lifeless agencies."[13] This period of financial independence and success among the women of the PCUSA was to be short-lived, however.

In 1923, all that the women of the church had worked for was taken away when the General Assembly of the PCUSA reorganized its ten boards into four new boards. As part of the reorganization, conceived and approved by men, the Woman's Board was dismantled and its property and assets divided between the Board of Foreign Missions and the Board of National Missions. As a consolation, the women were promised that one third of the membership of the new boards would be women. But that was little consolation to women who constituted 60 percent of the total membership of the church.

The women of the church would never recover their hard-earned property and assets or the power and prestige of those early glory days, and those losses would lead women to question, as never before, their status in the official leadership of the denomination.

With the women's organizations still intact at the presbytery and synod levels, the debate about a national organization for women went on for the next twenty years. Statements by women in the ensuing years were particularly caustic. In 1925, one woman assessed the situation this way: "This whole question seems to be about church dollars and politics. Until the women get in our whole church organization a much more representative organization, the men must willingly and by right give women their place." She concluded by observing, "I think the men are absolutely puzzled to death to know what to do with us, but I do believe that holding your own budget simply as a symbol of ability to carry a big task lovingly, prayerfully, and successfully has done more for the women of the Presbyterian Church than anything else has done."[14]

It is interesting to note that despite the bitterness of many women over the losses of 1923, their central concern for mission continued and their benevolence giving continued to increase until the 1930s. Women's share of the total benevolence giving of the church also continued to increase until the mid-1930s. This continued giving meant that women maintained a formidable profile in the church—formidable enough that, in 1933, five synods overtured the General Assembly to ask women who gave to women's societies to give to the church offering.[15] Either there was a lack of understanding that "women's giving" was by definition "second-mile giving," or women were actually ignoring the "second-mile" philosophy and giving the major portion of their money to the women's societies.

In 1943, amid assurances by the women that, if given a national organization, they would not remove their financial support from the existing denominational boards, the General Assembly approved a new national agency for women, the National Council of Women's Organizations of the Presbyterian Church in the United States of America, soon known as Presbyterian Women's Organization (PWO). Inez Moser, chair of the Council at the time of the 1943 General Assembly, remarked, "We were very clear that we wanted to be Church women—that our task was a Church task—that we would continue to give—and increase our giving—to the wide work of the Kingdom through the Church and its Boards and Agencies."[16]

By 1943, many local and regional women's groups had begun to move away from being strictly missionary societies to being more inclusive societies, with broader activities of study and service. This was partly in response to the church's broadening definition of mission, but many also felt that inclusive societies would attract younger women to local organizations. By the 1950s, the term and concept of "women's missionary societies" had been almost completely discarded, but the core financial commitment to church missions remained. An organization was usually termed "inclusive" when a portion of its benevolence money went to support the denomination's Board of Christian Education. Katherine Parker remarked that "the Board of Christian Education saw the amount of money that was coming through the women to the other Boards and really saw no reason . . . why some of the women's giving shouldn't go to the Board of Christian Education."[17]

The sense that if women did not support certain mission projects, no one would, still prevailed. Parker tells of Mrs. Russell Sage, who left some money in the control of women in the name of the Board of Foreign Missions. She recalls that the women representatives on the Board of Foreign Missions would hear of special needs and know that, as women, they were in a unique position to address those needs through the Sage funds. She also notes that the male treasurer of the board "absolutely hated that fund." In the face of such fears of female independence, Parker recalls that the women would "butter up" the men of the church with assurances that they wanted to be a part of the whole church.[18]

Most women did want to be included in the work of the whole church, but they also wanted some decision-making power, especially over their own considerable financial contributions. By 1951, the women had established the Opportunity Giving Program, in which the funds collected could be designated for special projects. When the PCUSA joined in 1958 with the United Presbyterian Church of North America (UPNA), and the new women's organization became United Presbyterian Women (UPW), the Thank Offering of the UPNA women was adopted. By 1965, another special offering, the Summer Medical Offering, had been organized. Slowly but surely the women of the church began to regain some control over their mission dollars through designated giving programs. But they never regained total control, and the major portion of their mission dollars continued to go, undesignated, to the regular mission programs of the church. The sense of ownership and the special personal relationships with mission workers, so prevalent in the missionary-society years and into the 1950s, was beginning to be lost.

The annual UPW report to General Assembly for 1966 noted that "United Presbyterian Women in 1966 found themselves more than ever integrated into the life and ministry of the entire church."[19] The following year, at the meeting of United Presbyterian Women at Purdue University, questions arose concerning the future of women's organizations. Interestingly, the questions were referred to the General Assembly Council for consideration. It is not surprising that the theme of the letter addressed to the Council was financial:

1. Shall women's giving continue to follow the present pattern?
2. Shall it be broadened to include other agencies of the church?
3. Shall it continue to be pledged by women's groups and paid to the agencies through the presbyterial treasurer?
4. Shall some form of unified budget be adopted and recommended for general use?
5. How can the church face the possible loss to our program agencies if the basic changes in women's giving are made?[20]

In response, the Council recommended that no changes be made in the procedures for women's giving, and the women continued, as before, to give the majority of their money, undesignated, to the regular mission of the church. Only a portion of the total giving would be designated through special offerings.

In 1972, de facto changes were made in women's giving as a result of another restructure of the denomination. Since 1923, women's undesignated mission contributions ("on-going giving") had been divided between the Board of National Missions, the Board of Foreign Missions (later the Commission on Ecumenical Mission and Relations [COEMAR]), and the Board of Christian Education. Through these boards, women had been able to continue supporting projects they had initiated and even owned before 1923. After 1972, women's impact on mission projects was removed one step farther when it was decided that their ongoing giving would be added into the churchwide income of the General Assembly general mission budget, which went to support programming and administrative costs, in addition to former mission institutions.[21]

Not only did the restructuring of 1972 have an impact on the tradition of women's giving, but UPW area field staff, formerly representatives of the denomination's three boards in five area offices, faced the possibility of having to submit to the authority of the new regional synod executives, whose offices were their bases of operation. Elizabeth Verdesi, a longtime activist in women's work, believes that some executives viewed the UPW staff as "potential competitors both for fund-raising and for providing resources for groups in the presbyteries within their synods."[22]

Between 1972 and 1974, the conflict over UPW area staff continued with meetings and political maneuvers. In 1974, the National Executive Committee (NEC) of UPW, citing UPW's "investment" in the new Program Agency, strongly recommended the employment of fifteen area staff responsible to UPW. According to Verdesi, the NEC also made the decision to make it known that if their recommendation failed, "they were prepared to set up their own administrative unit, finance their own staff, including area staff, and allocate their own mission funds." The threat was effective, and the General Assembly Mission Council finally agreed to fund the area staff. For many of the women involved, the success of the threat meant that their work was valued only "for its money," since it was only when they began to discuss withdrawing their funds that their requests were taken seriously.[23]

UPW's success in obtaining area staff was to be short-lived, however. Before the staff could be hired, a severe reduction in Program Agency receipts in 1973 necessitated the cutting of a variety of staff positions. UPW leaders reluctantly agreed that ten area staff would be adequate until funding levels increased. Receipts by the Program Agency did increase in 1976, however, and other staffing levels were increasing, but UPW never received its five area staff and chose not to fight the battle again. At the time of the reunion of the UPCUSA and PCUS churches in 1983, there were still only ten UPW area staff in place.

In 1982, just prior to reunion with the PCUS, United Presbyterian Women gave a total of $6,074,534 to mission. Sixty-nine percent ($4,197,906) was given, undesignated, to the denominational budget as "on-going giving"; 22 percent ($1,327,850) was designated for special projects through the UPW Opportunity Giving Program. The remaining 9 percent included a gift of $226,639 to the Presbyterian Hunger Fund and contributions of sewing and supplies valued at $322,139. While the giving by women in 1982 exceeded that of previous years, the total represented a diminishing percentage of the total denominational mission budget. Furthermore, by giving over two thirds of its mission dollars to other agencies, UPW continued, as in years before, to relinquish total control over women's mission giving (GA, UPCUSA, 1983, I, p. 483).

PCUS National Women's Organization

In the nineteenth century, PCUS women discovered their own skills of raising money for mission. One denominational publication noted that, in response to an 1868 denominational appeal, the women "raised in every case more than twice as much as was given by the whole congregation, to which they belonged, to the object; and in two cases at least, their contributions were truly magnificent."[24]

By the early twentieth century, some PCUS women were not averse to using money to gain some political leverage in the denomination. Arguing in a 1911 overture to the Synod of Missouri for the creation of a national women's organization, the Woman's Synodical Union of Missouri called attention to six facts, three of which are noteworthy. The first was that women constituted three fifths of the membership of the church. The second dealt with finances: "A large proportion of the mission money of our Church comes from Women's Societies." The final fact noted that the work of women was "greatly hampered by inefficient organization." It was also pointed out that simple organization had increased the offerings of the women of Virginia by three thousand dollars in one year.[25] The implication was clear—let women organize and there will be more dollars for mission.

The PCUS was one of the last major denominations in the United States to approve a national organization for women—a fact that was a source of shame for some women. Fears of granting authority and financial autonomy to women, however, remained widespread in the South. When the Synod of Missouri finally approved the overture to the General Assembly advocating the creation of a national women's organization, the women launched an educational campaign to allay those fears. Copies of the overture, as well as copies of "Reasons Why" and "The Nots" were circulated. In "The Nots," the women pleaded:

> We are NOT asking more AUTHORITY.
> We are NOT asking the HANDLING OF FUNDS.
> We are NOT asking the CREATION OF ANY NEW AGENCY.
> We ARE asking MORE EFFICIENCY through BETTER ORGANIZATION AND CLOSER UNION OF OUR FORCES [capitals in original].[26]

The campaign was successful, despite sometimes bitter opposition, and in 1912 the Woman's Auxiliary of the PCUS came into being, with the promise that it could generate mission funds for the whole church through better organization. The early leaders of the PCUS women acknowledged from the beginning that they were only an auxiliary to the denomination; nevertheless, a strong, independent spirit inspired their work.[27]

Until 1912, the women's missionary societies in the South had been concerned almost entirely with foreign missions. But when the Woman's Auxiliary was formed, pressure came from the male leadership to force women to divide their contributions "in harmony with the genius of the Assembly's plan" of assigned percentages (GA, PCUS,

1913, p. 39). To convince women to give to the other causes of the church—home missions, Christian education and ministerial relief, publications and Sunday school extension—was not an easy task. In her report of the Auxiliary, dated March 31, 1913, the first superintendent, Hallie Paxson Winsborough, wrote:

> The Woman's Society, to which all women shall belong, shall meet at least once a month to study, pray for and give to ALL THE MISSION CAUSES OF THE CHURCH. In proportioning their gifts to these causes we recommend the Assembly's proportion, as directed by the Supervisory Committee, EMPHAISSING [*sic*] HOWEVER, THAT ANY GIFTS WHICH THEY HAVE BEEN ACCUSTOMED TO GIVE TO ANY MISSION WORK OF THE CHURCH SHALL NOT BE LESSENED BUT IF POSSIBLE INCREASED; THAT THE OTHER CAUSES BE CONTRIBUTED TO FROM THE INCREASED GIFTS WHICH ALL ARE URGED TO GIVE. . . . NO PLEDGE CARRIED BY EITHER SOCIETY [Home or Foreign] BEFORE THE UNION IS TO BE DISTURBED OR SET ASIDE. Where but one society exists in a Church that society is asked to include all causes in its study, prayer and gifts, though no *former pledge is to be lessened* [capitals in original].[28]

The PCUS women, like their PCUSA sisters, were soon called upon to help pay the debts of one of the denominational boards (or committees, as they were called). As early as December 1912, Mrs. Winsborough noted that the women had been asked to help pay the debt of the Executive Committee of Foreign Missions. She wrote to her constituents, "Three months of consecrated and united effort along this line on the part of our societies throughout the church, will result in wiping out the debt and freeing the Foreign Mission office from its financial embarrassment."[29] The 1913 annual report of the Executive Committee of Foreign Missions noted,

> Through this new organization [the Woman's Auxiliary] great help has been r[e]ndered in the payment of the debt, the scope of the women's work has been enlarged, new

Synodicals and Presbyterials added, much excellent literature circulated, and greater unity and perfection of organization secured. Its capable leadership encourages us to look for yet larger things from the Woman's Auxiliary. Our pastors are urged to cooperate with it in every wise way (GA, PCUS, 1913, Executive Committee of Foreign Missions, p. 10).

Money, indeed, was buying support and recognition for the women of the PCUS.

By 1912, there were 2,606 PCUS woman's societies, with 66,684 members. Together, they contributed $401,519 to foreign, home, local, and other causes (PCUS GAM 1913, 70d-e). A footnote in the General Assembly *Minutes* notes that the total women's giving that year represented an "extraordinary effort" which had resulted in the women's paying 50 percent of the foreign-missions debt (GA, PCUS, 1914, p. 291).

Despite their considerable contributions, or perhaps because of them, PCUS women continued to experience strong opposition to their being organized. By 1916, a humiliating debate was raging in the General Assembly concerning "woman's position in the church." At the close of the debate, the 1916 Assembly voted to reaffirm its action of 1880 which barred women from speaking from church pulpits. But something new was added to the 1880 injunction: Even though women were still forbidden to preach, their other activities were to be left to the discretion of individual church sessions and the "enlightened consciences" of the women themselves (GA, PCUS, 1916, p. 48). The women's mission movement had not gone completely unnoticed; the status of PCUS women was beginning to change, if ever so slightly.

Even though the 1916 decree lessened restrictions on women's activities, particularly public speaking, the General Assembly leadership continued to show a need to control women's mission work through their finances. According to Winsborough, between 1914 and 1920 the question of how women were to give their mission money was frequently debated on the floor of the General Assembly.[30]

Apparently quite a few women were causing great consternation in their local churches by deducting the benevolence portion from their regular church pledge to give to the women's societies, because by 1920 the Assembly was loudly declaring that women must continue their regular contributions to local church collections. Only "self-denial and sacrificial" offerings beyond the regular contributions could be made to—and recorded by—the women's societies, said the General Assembly. The men also reiterated that women were not to be selective in their benevolences, but were to continue to give to all causes of the church, including the local budget, according to the recommended percentages (GA, PCUS, 1920, p. 70).

The 1921 General Assembly repeated that women were not to give any part of their regular church pledge to the auxiliary. Only gifts beyond the local pledge could be given to and reported by the auxiliary (GA, PCUS, 1921, p. 79). To encourage female cooperation, the Assembly declared that every church must set aside a portion of its annual budget to support the work of the auxiliary. In 1922, the General Assembly repeated that churches were to support their auxiliaries out of their regular budgets; in addition, it called special attention to local woman's auxiliary rules, which stated that no funds were to be given to any cause outside the denomination until the local church budget had been paid (GA, PCUS, 1922, p. 50).

Tensions over finances continued into 1925 when, in order to ease the strain between church sessions and women's auxiliaries, the General Assembly recommended that when local finance committees met to prepare the church budget for the upcoming year, a representative from each organization in the church be invited to attend the meeting. The intention was to include women in the budget preparation process, but the breadth of the recommendation, to include all church organizations, made its implementation too cumbersome. Twelve years later, Winsborough lamented the failure of the 1925 recommendation: "It would make a wonderful change in the work of the Church, however, if a few of the *well-informed missionary women* of the church could sit with the *Finance Com-*

mittee when it makes out the *budget for the coming year*" [italics in original].[31]

The financial plan for women's giving hammered out between 1912 and 1923 continued to be discussed and reaffirmed, in part and as a whole, in subsequent years, into the 1950s. The women's societies continued to be tied to regular church budgets through their required contributions as well as their receipt of programming funds from those budgets.

It had taken over a decade to secure the financial cooperation of women, who had argued in earlier years that they did not want to handle their own funds. Apparently many of them *did* want to manage their own mission dollars, for when presented with the option to give their money to the male leadership or to their own women's societies, many had chosen the women's societies—to the great frustration of men at all levels of the church. Yet, when the attempt by some women at securing independence by withdrawing part of their church pledges failed, they publicly, if not privately, resigned themselves to cooperating. In her closing comments on the Assembly's financial plan, Winsborough concluded that the plan had "borne the test of years successfully."[32]

In the ensuing years, the women of the South continued to study, pray for, and contribute to all the causes of the church. In 1961, Janie McGaughey, the executive secretary for women's work from 1929 to 1956, wrote that "basically the program of the women's work of the Church is the program of the Church. This was a foundation principle of the organization at its beginning, and has continued to be a guiding factor in all program planning."[33] Yet despite the commitment to remain auxiliary in nature, the Woman's Auxiliary, renamed in 1948 to be the Women of the Church (WOC), began to gain prominence and a larger measure of independence. By 1950, what had been the Department of Woman's Work (DWW) and later the Committee of Woman's Work (CWW) had become the Board of Women's Work (BWW), with full status as one of the denomination's five boards. Restructure of the PCUS into boards had actually benefited the Women of the Church.

By the 1950s, the Women's Board was managing receipts from the denominational budget, as well as donations by the women of the church, in excess of $250,000. In 1956, with seemingly no objection, the General Assembly granted permission for the Board of Women's Work to be incorporated. The board's annual report for 1956 simply noted that incorporation had taken place on November 2 (GA, PCUS, 1957, Board of Women's Work, p. 10). Status that had come only after a painful fight in the PCUSA in 1915 had quietly evolved in the PCUS, but forty-one years later.

Over the years, PCUS women also gained some control of the use of their mission dollars through the establishment of special funds, particularly the Honorary Life Membership Fund, begun by Hallie Winsborough and first spent in 1933, and the Birthday Offering, begun in 1922 to commemorate the tenth anniversary of the Woman's Auxiliary. Over the years the Women of the Church had given faithfully to all the approved causes of the church. Their annual reports give detailed statistics on their giving to the church's mission, including the local church, presbyteries, synods, and the General Assembly. But, as the years progressed, more and more of women's interest was focused on the Birthday Offering. Each year the women would raise money for the Birthday Offering, to be given to one to three mission projects. And although the money for the projects was given to one of the other denominational boards to administer, the offering gave women some measure of control, since they selected the causes to which their funds would go. By 1957 the Birthday Offering had attained such prominence among women that the Board of Women's Work no longer felt it necessary to require local groups to report their giving to any other cause of the church (GA, PCUS, 1958, Board of Women's Work, 2:37). The effect of this decision to eliminate paperwork was to consolidate women's giving into essentially one major offering, given to projects selected by women.

As in the PCUSA, the years of an incorporated Women's Board were numbered. The PCUSA board had lasted eight years (1915–1923) as an independent and incorporated entity; the PCUS board lasted seventeen years, until the 1973 restructuring of the General Assembly, when the Women's Board and its assets were taken over by the General Executive Board. In 1972, its last full year of operation, the Board of Women's Work had $225,656 in assets, including $158,371 in cash and $60,400 in property. In 1972, the board managed expenditures of $850,000 (GA, PCUS, 1973, 3:140–142) and had a full-time staff of twenty-three. The restructuring dealt a devastating blow to the PCUS women's organization. Staffing for women's work was reduced from twenty-three to one full-time person and a part-time secretary, with a program budget of $3,000.[34] Synodical presidents, so important in the Women of the Church network, were also eliminated by the new structure. Only local and presbytery programming continued relatively unscathed. The Birthday Offering continued and, interestingly, did not decrease in size.

At the time of restructure, the Board of Annuities and Relief had protested its inclusion in the new structure and was allowed to continue as a separate entity. Those on the Board of Women's Work, however, chose not to protest their part in the reorganization, despite the misgivings of many women in the church. One member of the Women's Board, Dorothy Barnard, commenting in 1985 on the effects of the restructure, noted that those on the board "affirmed the idea of coordination and unification for the good of the church. But we did not realize what a loss restructure would mean to the ongoing work of the former Board of Women's Work."[35]

UPCUSA and PCUS Reunion

In 1977, amid discussions of merging the UPCUSA and the PCUS, the women of both denominations cooperated in the production of the February issue of UPW's *Concern* magazine to address the topic of reunion in light of the histories of women in both denominations. It is not surprising that a key topic of discussion in the issue was that of finances. Differing financial practices were viewed as indicative of the basic difference in philosophies of the two organizations. The opening article by the editors summarized these financial differences: "In the PCUS, the women have limited their fund raising in recent years to one or two special offerings a year; otherwise, they are funded as any other local program might be. In the UPCUSA, women set giving goals for their organization and make decisions about the use of that money."[36]

The problem of reunion was seen by many as a problem of reconciling the auxiliary versus independent philosophies of the two women's organizations, perhaps an overly simplistic analysis, given the complex history of struggles for financial and administrative independence in both organizations. As it was, some women in the PCUS viewed reunion as an opportunity to recoup the losses of 1973,[37] whereas some UPCUSA women were fearful of losing what independence they had regained in the years since their losses of 1923. When the Plan for Reunion was finally published, the National Executive Committee of UPW firmly rejected it, primarily because it allowed exemptions for PCUS churches which refused to ordain women as elders, but also because it lacked a firm confessional base.[38] The PCUS women endorsed the Plan, which held the promise of greater status for them.

Over the objections of the UPW National Executive Committee, reunion became a reality in 1983. By 1985, the General Assembly of the newly united denomination approved a design for mission in which work would be divided into nine units, one of which would be the Women's Unit. The new Women's Unit has embraced not only the traditional women's organizations—Women of the Church and United Presbyterian Women—but also the other women's advocacy groups that had been organized in both denominations in the 1970s. Four areas of women's concerns are currently being addressed by the Women's Unit: Presbyterian Women (formerly WOC and UPW), Justice for Women Committee, Committee of Women of Color, and Women Employed by the Church.

The financial plan written by Presbyterian Women closely resembles that of the former UPW plan, in which support for mission and programming at the local, congregational, presbytery, and General Assembly levels comes primarily from women's giving. Women's groups from the former PCUS which prefer to receive some support from, and channel their mission dollars through, the regular church budget may do so; however, any benevolence giving beyond the regular church pledge and beyond women's special offerings, such as the Birthday Offering, is now channeled through the Women's Unit as "women's mission support for the worldwide mission of the PC(USA) through the General Assembly mission budget."[39]

Presbyterian Women are presently pledging and giving the major portion of their mission dollars, undesignated, to the regular General Assembly mission budget as "worldwide mission," formerly known in the UPW as "on-going giving." As in the past, women have retained some measure of control over their funds through designated giving programs, including the Thank Offering (embracing medical missions and creative mission), the Birthday Offering, and the ecumenical Least Coin Offering.

The Past and the Future of Presbyterian Women's Organizations

The history of Presbyterian women's organizations in the twentieth century is the story of a community of faith rich in relationships and gathered by a common commitment to the mission of the church. But it is also the story of money and power earned, and money and power taken away. It is the story of struggles by Presbyterian women for self-determination: struggles that were sometimes won, but more often lost.

Early in the century, women in both denominations seemed aware of the power and attention their fund-raising abilities gave them, particularly in the years when both denominations were trying to keep their national and foreign missions programs solvent. Some have said that women's giving saved the missionary movement, and that is probably true. But despite women's awareness of the power money gave them, they were often reluctant to use it.

In the early years, the PCUS women did use the promise of money to campaign for the establishment of a national women's organization, and women in local churches used their church pledges to indicate their desire for some autonomy. Yet, when their national organization was threatened with destruction in 1973, they chose not to use their money as a bargaining chip. Neither did the PCUSA women use their considerable financial power to save their organization in 1923. It was only in 1972 that women openly used their resources to bargain for their agenda; even then, having experienced success, they refused to continue to push to hold on to their achievement.

Over the years, women have been more likely to use their financial power in subtle hints and suggestions— what Lois Boyd and Douglas Brackenridge have called "influence."[40] Open confrontation, when it did occur, often happened outside the regular women's organization channels. In the '70s, confrontation was institutionalized in women's advocacy groups that were separate from, and sometimes in opposition to, traditional women's groups. One UPW leader said in 1974 that the confrontational tactics of one of those advocacy groups—the Council on Women and the Church (COWAC)—angered those active in UPW:

> As UPW we do feel some responsibility for the COWAC and at this time we regard some of their statements and advocacy as we do the actions of our children—who, when they can't obtain their elder's attention by good behavior, they deliberately misbehave because experience has already taught them that this usually gets fairly prompt reaction, although the resultant action may not be to their liking—as with children, we don't always like what they do, but they are ours and we must care for them.[41]

Despite these tensions, however, UPW found an ally in COWAC on the issue of UPW area staff, as well as the debate on requiring churches to elect women elders (Overture L) and the subsequent "women-elder" debates during UPCUSA and PCUS reunion negotiations. It is not clear, then, that the evolving relationship between traditional women's organizations and women's advocacy groups is necessarily an opposing one, though the latter do continue to be more confrontational.

Elizabeth Verdesi first identified the importance of money and power struggles in the history of Presbyterian women's organizations in her insightful book, *In but Still Out.* In that study, Verdesi identifies the process of cooptation in which, for the sake of administrative unity, a denomination absorbs women's groups into its main structure with the promise of participatory roles for women. It is clear that this process of cooptation occurred in the 1923 denominational restructure in the PCUSA and in the 1973 restructure in the PCUS. More subtle cooptation occurred at other times, as when the PCUS promised program funds to women in exchange for their submission to denominational control of their mission dollars. Subtle cooptation also occurred in the PCUSA in the '40s when the denomination allowed the formation of a national women's organization in exchange for promises that women would not withdraw their money from existing boards. The 1972 attempt by synod executives to coopt UPW area staff failed only because women were willing to use their financial leverage to promote their cause.

Women's struggle for independence in their work has always been confronted with the argument that women should participate in the unified programs of the church rather than work through their own separate organizations. The 1923 and 1973 restructures were occasions of the triumph of the philosophy of administrative unity. And yet structural purity has its dangers. One is the loss of human initiative and creativity, particularly for those groups that are disenfranchised, or, as in the case of women, groups that are reluctant to use the power they do have. The Feb-

ruary 1977 issue of *Concern* magazine credited Margaret
Shannon, a former national staff person for UPCUSA
women, with the opinion that, rather than disrupting denominational work, separate organizations strengthen that
work: "The church is most alive when it encourages movements or organizations to spring up on the periphery of the
institutional structures in response to some felt need—related enough to the total church to be responsible, free
enough to be creatively involved in mission in a way the
main institutional body cannot be."[42] Lillian McCulloch
Taylor, writing on the recent history of PCUS women, argues against structural unity on other grounds, saying that
only when women share equitably in the leadership of the
church will separate women's groups be unnecessary. "Until then," she says, "we do not do wisely to behave, either
in the church or in the world, as though the parousia has
already come."[43]

Since women still do not share equitably in the leadership of the church, separate women's organizations continue to have the potential to play a creative role in the
denomination. The question is whether the current organization of Presbyterian Women will survive to be one of
those groups.

Membership in Presbyterian women's organizations appears to be declining, as is membership in the denomination as a whole. If the average age of those attending the
July 1988 Gathering is indicative of local women's groups,
their constituencies are aging more rapidly than the denomination overall. But a declining and aging membership
does not necessarily mean the ultimate end of Presbyterian
women's organizations. Perhaps women's groups will develop, as many already have, smaller but committed constituencies of older women who are retired from the work
force. Perhaps younger women will begin to create groups
to address issues of particular concern to them.

Giving levels, another measure of the status of women's
organizations, are down when compared to years past. Accordingly, Presbyterian women seem to have less power on
the national level and less impact on the overall mission of

the church. The sense of unique purpose, so prominent in the early years when women's giving was essential to the survival of the mission movement, seems to have been lost in the intervening years. That loss of identity as an essential arm of the church has also meant a loss of status, and perhaps a loss of energy, for women's organizations in recent years.

But there is a tenacity about Presbyterian women's organizations and their desire to continue their work. Despair over the lack of interest of younger women, beginning as early as the turn of the century, has not resulted in the death of women's organizations. Institutional blows to women's work over the years have never seemed to be the cause of reduced giving or participation by women. Presbyterian women's organizations have survived, and it may be that, despite predictions of their ultimate demise, they will adjust to the changing conditions of church and society and persist in making solid and creative contributions to the life of the Presbyterian Church (U.S.A.).

9

Men and Mission: The Shifting Fortunes of Presbyterian Men's Organizations in the Twentieth Century

Dale E. Soden

In 1906, Presbyterian men from around the country gathered in Indianapolis, Indiana, to hear not only William Jennings Bryan but the Vice President, Charles Fairbanks, exhort them to fulfill their calling as leaders in their churches and to shape the communities in which they lived. In the 1950s, Presbyterian men confidently met by the thousands in national meetings at the Palmer House in Chicago to plan strategies and be renewed not only with regard to their role in the church, but also in their leadership in American society. Yet as strong as men's work has been at times, at other times it has struggled, particularly since the 1960s. Not even twenty years after the great meetings in the 1950s, the men's movement within the Presbyterian Church was nearly dead. The purpose here is to explore the history of this part of the Presbyterian experience in twentieth-century America.

There is no doubt that the leadership of the American Presbyterian Church has been largely dominated by white Anglo-Saxon males. Whether as pastors, deacons, trustees, or elders, men have historically wielded enormous influence over the direction of the church. Yet, as an identifiable group within the church, laymen have seemed much less visible than women. In Robert Wuthnow's recent study, *The Restructuring of American Religion,* women received prominent attention as an important subgroup, but men's groups did not appear. Aside from treating a few noteworthy individuals such as Robert Speer, religious historians have written very little regarding either laymen or organized men's activity in the church. Yet American Presbyterians have spent considerable time, effort, and resources attempting to organize groups of men in the church, motivate them into specific ministries, and invigorate a sense of purpose that would make the church a much more powerful institution in the twentieth century.[1]

Well intentioned, often well heeled with resources, and often able to gain the support of some of the most prominent political leaders in the United States, Presbyterian men's organizations have had many successes and a substantial impact on local congregations and communities. Conducting Bible studies, leadership training, youth work, social ministries, and education have been among the many ways in which men's groups have strengthened life in Presbyterian congregations across the country. Nevertheless, a certain element of frustration has accompanied the leaders of this movement since its beginning. In microcosm, the history of men's work reflects many of the problems facing mainstream Protestants in the twentieth century. Understanding why men's organizations have had difficulty sustaining themselves may reveal keys to the larger problems facing Presbyterians and other mainstream Protestants.

Presbyterian men's movements and organizations flourished in two separate periods in the twentieth century. The initial activity occurred from approximately the first decade of the twentieth century to the beginning of World War I. The second period was from the end of World War II to the mid-1960s. In no sense could men's activities be said to have ended completely during the years between the world wars or after the sixties. Yet clearly the level of activity diminished, particularly in congregations. The reasons for this ebb and flow are at times seemingly self-evident while at others they are more obscure and complex. The pattern in the Presbyterian Church in the U.S.A. (PCUSA) and, later, the UPCUSA, while similar to the pattern in the Presbyterian Church in the U.S. (PCUS) in many respects, differs in others. The activity and effectiveness of men's groups varied from congregation to congregation in the same city; efforts at the presbytery and synod level were far from uniform in a given period. The dynamic of lay leadership, clergy support (or lack thereof), and a host of other factors still contribute to the difficulty in making generalizations about the activity and work of such a broad group of people over an entire century.

Nevertheless, men's organizations and activity seemingly reached their greatest level when larger numbers of men perceived a direct connection between the mission of the church and broader social and political issues facing the nation as a whole. In the first period, during the height of the social gospel era, men's work, particularly in the PCUSA, attempted to reform social conditions in the larger metropolitan areas and in the missionary movement at home and abroad. In the second period, beginning in the mid-forties, men's organizations rallied around the notion that atheistic communism must be fought by a God-fearing America. Great numbers of men found purpose in meeting to discuss how that might be done more effectively and how they might make the church a vital force in American life. When the social gospel and missionary movements waned, so did men's organizations. When the consensus surrounding American civil religion faded in the 1960s, and considerable disagreement emerged concerning the role of politics in the church, men's work began to fragment. During the last two decades, it has had difficulty generating much force.

Early Men's Organizations

Several factors led to the development of organized men's work in the last part of the nineteenth and the early twentieth century. Certainly women's groups provided an important model for organization, as did the Young Men's

Christian Association. The intensification of missionary activity overseas proved also to be influential toward stimulating new men's activity. But perhaps most compelling were the voices of social gospel advocates in the context of the larger movement of progressivism in the early twentieth century. The belief that the church could reshape the urban and political environment, and the optimism associated with such reform, provided the motivation and energy for many men to participate.[2]

In the 1880s, largely due to the influence and success of the YMCA, increasing numbers of clergy and lay leaders called on churches to facilitate programs directed at saving America's youth from the perils of urbanization and industrialization. At the Congress of Religions, held in conjunction with the Chicago World's Fair in 1893, clergy and lay leaders pushed for more formal organization of men's activities. Yet, in most congregations throughout the country, men's organizations grew slowly. The vitality of congregational life centered largely in women's organizations. By 1895, the PCUSA General Assembly acknowledged that men were much less organized compared to women. In 1901, again the report lamented, "If the men in the churches were as the women, the Kingdom would come in by leaps and bounds."[3]

The one organization that did achieve some success in the last part of the nineteenth century was the Brotherhood of Andrew and Philip. Organized in the late 1880s by the Reverend Rufus Miller, the Brotherhood was not strictly a denominational organization. Its objective focused on spreading Christ's kingdom among men, especially young men. Asked to adhere to a rule of prayer and a rule of service, members were urged to pray daily for Christ's kingdom among men and for God's blessings on the Brotherhood. Secondarily, the Brotherhood required members to make an honest effort each week to bring at least one young man to hear the gospel of Jesus Christ. By the end of the 1890s, chapters were quite common in Presbyterian churches; several hundred chapters existed, mostly in the Northeast.[4]

At the turn of the century, pressure mounted at the General Assembly level in the PCUSA to develop more support for men's work, and in 1906 that body approved the formation of the Presbyterian Brotherhood, a group distinct from the Brotherhood of Andrew and Philip. Charles Holt, from Chicago, provided the initial leadership for the Brotherhood. National conventions were quickly organized to stimulate great enthusiasm for the Brotherhood. Held between 1906 and 1911, these remarkable gatherings reflected the close relationship between the PCUSA and major national political figures. The prospects for church participation in major reform movements at the city, state, and national levels were never stronger. Spokesmen for the social gospel addressed the challenge of making Christianity relevant to the needs of the working class and stressed how important it was that Christian values permeate public policy.[5]

For example, at the Indianapolis convention in 1906, speakers included not only Vice President Fairbanks and William Jennings Bryan but also many of the most prominent Presbyterians of the day, including Robert Speer, evangelist J. Wilbur Chapman, and the foremost Presbyterian advocate of the social gospel, Charles Stelzle. The convention speeches encouraged men's participation on a wide variety of fronts including Sunday evening services, ushers' associations, education, and leadership training. The organizers focused on the importance of the Brotherhood's catching a vision that would assist pastors in developing employment bureaus and sick and relief funds, on general issues of civic reform, and on temperance among boys. Speakers vehemently stressed the importance of evangelism, particularly to young boys. The charge was clear: More men should be brought to Christ and more energy must be expended on civic reform.[6]

By 1908, *Presbyterian Brotherhood* was published quarterly, with articles and news regarding affiliated chapters around the country. By that year over seven hundred chapters existed at the congregational level, claiming a membership of just over thirty-six thousand. The activity of the

Brotherhoods tended to focus on Bible study, assisting at services of worship, leadership training, and boys' work. The activity of many groups centered on civic affairs. For example, in 1909 at First Presbyterian Church in Elkhart, Indiana, the Brotherhood examined the question of "Where Your Taxes Go." The group mailed a copy of the tax pamphlet to every taxpayer in the city. Enthused about their ability to influence city planning, Brotherhood members authored a comprehensive plan for the entire city. Other men's groups from around the country held periodic programs on various issues associated with the progressive movement. By 1911, the Presbyterian Brotherhood, still under the direction of Charles Holt, supported an inter-denominational effort, the "Men and Religion Forward Movement." This effort exhorted men in metropolitan churches not only to evangelize but to become involved in social service. The movement lasted for one year, its leaders traveling throughout the country conducting rallies and organizing efforts to promote Christian service and civic reform.[7]

While the PCUSA took the lead in sponsoring men's activity, the United Presbyterian Church of North America also began formally to organize men's activity in 1906 on a model like the Brotherhood. In 1908, United Presbyterian Men sponsored a Nile mission boat and a home mission in Yakima, Washington, as well as one in Philadelphia. For the most part, however, men's work in the United Presbyterian Church centered on Bible study and leadership training.[8]

The Missionary Movement

While the social gospel and progressive movements strongly influenced men's activities, the missionary movement also had considerable impact. The Laymen's Missionary Movement was organized in 1907, with conferences in Washington, D.C., Los Angeles, and Chicago, with the sole purpose of generating support from the laymen for student missionaries overseas. The Laymen's Missionary Movement brought Theodore Roosevelt, William H. Taft, Woodrow Wilson, Alfred Thayer Mahan, governors, presidents of universities, and business leaders to speak before its gatherings. Attracting men from all over the country, the movement perhaps reached its peak when the Men's National Missionary Congress met in Chicago, May 3–6, 1910. The Congress was the culmination of seventy-five conventions from October 1909 to May 1910 that reached nearly a hundred thousand men.

The missionary movement had enormous influence in the PCUS as well. In fact, most men's activity in the PCUS centered on mission concerns rather than on the social gospel, although urban issues were not entirely absent. Charles Rowland helped orchestrate PCUS involvement in the Laymen's Missionary Movement. PCUS conventions were held in Birmingham, Memphis, Dallas, Chattanooga, and Charlotte over the next few years.[9]

Undergirding these conventions and the work at the congregational level was a spirit of what some have called "muscular Christianity." Both clergy and lay leaders attacked the notion that religion carried feminine associations. Men were encouraged to connect their faith with strength and virility. Pastors such as Mark Matthews, who built the largest Presbyterian church in the country in Seattle during this period, frequently exhorted congregations with sermons such as "Wanted: More Man in Men," and "The Manhood of Christianity in Civic Affairs."[10]

It is difficult to read the 620 pages of the proceedings of the Missionary Congress or the reports of the Presbyterian Brotherhood conventions and not feel that these were extraordinary moments in lay activity. There seemed little division between conservatives and liberals. Men from all walks of life felt called to articulate ways in which Christians might influence the debate over public policy as well as how to evangelize entire nations more effectively. The confidence in Western civilization, so evident in the United States and Western Europe prior to the First World War, was reflected in the zeal for missionary activity and men's work in particular. After the United States entered World War I and as energy was siphoned into other matters, the maintenance of men's activity in the church proved to be more difficult. The enthusiasm for social reform across the society waned; the impetus for social Christianity declined; and as missionary zeal ebbed, Presbyterian men's work entered a new phase, led largely by staff supported by the two General Assemblies.

Sustaining Men's Work in the Years Between the Wars

Although there are many exceptions, historically it has been more difficult to sustain men's organizations at the congregational level than women's. Certainly World War I was a major factor in diminished activity at the congregational level. But even prior to the war, in the midst of great enthusiasm generated at national conventions, men's activity at the local level began to show signs of waning. Several factors seemed to be at work. Presbyterians began to feel the divisive effects of the fundamentalist/modernist debate, and the social gospel and progressivism gradually lost vitality. The excitement surrounding civic reform, which gave great purpose to men's work, slowly dissipated. The case of Union Presbyterian Church Men's Club in Schenectady, New York, reveals the problem. Club minutes between 1911 and 1915 reflect the difficulty of maintaining enthusiasm at the local level. In February 1912, the men's groups sponsored a debate on the topic, "That the Trusts Are Responsible for the High Cost of Living." Later that month, the sixth annual Men's banquet featured the great Presbyterian layman Robert Speer as the speaker. But by April, there were not enough members present for a quorum. A ladies' night was held in May with a stereopticon lecture on Scotland. But by June there was no quorum again. Starting late in November, the meetings focused on suggestions for increasing attendance, more exciting programs, outings, refreshments. But by 1915 the group had apparently disbanded.[11]

The General Assemblies of the respective Presbyterian bodies increasingly recognized the difficulty during these years and made considerable effort to institutionalize the support for men's activity. The other emphasis in this period was on interdenominational activity. In 1912, the United Presbyterian Church of North America placed the support of the Brotherhood under the Division of Home Missions. By 1916, William Weir had been selected by the PCUSA to serve as general secretary of Men's Work, and he continued until 1931. Weir hoped to promote interdenominational cooperation and the development of printed materials, program helps, and general information that would assist the educational mission of men's organizations.[12]

Weir's belief that laymen, rather than clerics, could move denominations more rapidly to accept an ecumenical structure was shared widely after World War I. Even as the United States failed to join the newly formed League of Nations, men from around the country caught Woodrow Wilson's vision of a more internationally cooperative world. In religion this led to several ecumenical efforts. In 1923, largely through Weir's efforts, the Interdenominational Council on Men's Work was established, consisting of twenty-two Protestant denominations. In 1930, the Interdenominational Men's Congress met in Cincinnati with the hope that laymen might lead the Christian church into a more unified phase of its history. Although lacking much in the way of lasting success, the effort reflected the different direction that men's work took during the years between the wars.[13]

Weir also developed printed material for men's programs at the local level. This consisted primarily of suggested program ideas for men's groups. Everything from the program content itself to how to organize a group and lead a discussion was sent out to congregations on a monthly basis. In the twenties and thirties a newsletter entitled *Men's News* helped inform congregations of activity throughout the country. Local and regional conventions of men were held fairly regularly, but in general the years between the two world wars did not generate great enthusiasm for men's work. Pockets of activity continued to exist and in some cases thrived. Certainly Weir's efforts helped sustain men's work at a time when other cultural forces worked against the movement. The Depression further sapped energy and enthusiasm, and internal division over fundamentalism and the decline of the social gospel made Weir's task even more onerous.[14]

A similar situation faced Presbyterians in the PCUS following World War I. The General Assembly for the PCUS agreed to establish a Permanent Committee on Men's Work in 1922. The previous year they had conducted another survey; in the 431 churches returning questionnaires, 265 had some type of men's organization, of which 165 were Bible classes. The PCUS followed in the footsteps of the PCUSA, largely because its secretary of Men's Work, J. E. Purcell, had worked with Weir. Under Purcell, program suggestions were sent to the various men's organizations.[15]

Purcell deserves much of the credit for the development of an outstanding set of program helps for the men's programs. Prior to his efforts, aside from Bible study, men's work in the South had focused primarily on missionary efforts. Beginning in the late twenties and extending through the thirties, Purcell commissioned twelve separate programs each year. The programs centered on stewardship, church doctrine, occasionally church history, and oftentimes controversial issues such as the problems of lynching in the South or civil rights. How receptive local men's groups were to these program suggestions is difficult to say, yet one thing is clear—Purcell sought to raise the men's consciousness throughout the South regarding racial issues. In addition, Purcell focused on the need for better leadership training, more aggressive evangelism, and higher commitment to the broader life of the church.[16]

Besides formal programs provided by leaders such as Weir and Purcell, men's work in congregations continued to be sustained by Bible study and Sunday school courses. Exceptionally strong at the turn of the century, the Sunday school movement accounted for much of the leadership training in the Presbyterian Church. The continued success of Bible studies often depended on the organizational abilities of pastors and key laymen, but many groups developed a tradition of excellence that provided support for male involvement in the church as a whole.

Upon reflection, the years between the world wars marked a new direction for men's work within the Presbyterian Church. The General Assemblies provided support in the form of finances and personnel. Staff members worked diligently to provide program suggestions and encouragement in a variety of forms. Yet, for a variety of reasons, leaders of Presbyterian men's organizations found it more difficult to sustain enthusiasm at the congregational level. It would not be until the general resurgence of religious activity after World War II that men's organizations would gain new momentum. Increasingly, the element of American patriotism and civil religion would be a part of men's work in the postwar years.

Revitalization in the Forties and Fifties

In 1940, concerned about the lack of overall enthusiasm for men's organizations, a group of PCUS men met with the new director of Adult Education and Men's Work, Samuel Jasper Patterson, to devise a new strategy. Over the next few years, this group provided the impetus for reorganization and more concerted support from the General Assembly. In 1946, the General Assembly approved the formation of the Assembly Men's Council, which began to meet officially in Montreat, North Carolina, that same summer. Anxious to be seen as making a tangible difference, the Men's Council approved continued support for the Assembly's Radio Committee and urged that all synods plan and promote the holding of Negro Youth Conferences.[17]

By 1949, the Assembly Men's Council reported that there were 855 local men's groups, 69 presbytery rallies held, and 11 synod conferences. Momentum in the early fifties continued to build around several regional conventions in Greensboro, Jacksonville, Nashville, and Dallas.

The launching of the magazine *Presbyterian Men* stimulated interest, and new material for church officer training was published. In 1951 it was announced that a Division of Men's Work in the Board of Christian Education would be on a par with other divisions of the Board. Six conferences for Black youths were held in 1950 and more were urged. By 1952, PCUS statistics indicated that more than 200,000 men were members of 1,039 local men's organizations. One thousand copies of the bulletin, "Program Helps," were sent out each quarter. Assembly-wide conventions were held in Atlanta in 1949, New Orleans in 1954, Miami in 1957, and Dallas in 1963, reflecting the enthusiasm for men's work at that time. Aside from Patterson, men such as Andrew Bird, Jr., E. A. (Andy) Andrews, Jr., and Powell Fraser worked diligently to make men's work a vital part of the PCUS in the 1950s and early 1960s.[18]

The PCUSA men, perhaps taking their cue from their PCUS counterparts, established in 1944 a Special Lay Committee approved by the General Assembly. Led by Charles Turck, president of Macalester College, the committee made several recommendations to the General Assembly regarding lay activity, including the establishment of an Assembly-level men's organization. Accepted by the General Assembly, the recommendation bore fruit in 1948 when the National Council of Presbyterian Men convened a meeting in Chicago. In 1949, the United Presbyterian Church of North America also approved a men's organization.[19]

Several factors directly contributed to this revival of organization and enthusiasm in the late forties and early fifties throughout the country. One factor was the camaraderie created among men during World War II. Men returned from their military experience and rapidly integrated themselves into civilian life, but they also tried to preserve opportunities for fellowship that had been a part of the war. Another factor was the upsurge of enthusiasm for the work of the church after the war. Church attendance boomed, and the suburbanization of America produced an explosion of new churches.

In addition, the concern over the cold war helped provide a larger purpose, for men not only to belong to a church but to work for its growth and influence. During the last twenty years the phenomenon of civil religion has been widely studied in relation to the surge of religious activity following World War II. The identification of the United States with God's work, and specifically the role of the United States in battling atheistic communism, were important factors in stimulating men's activity from the mid-forties to the early sixties.[20]

Men seemed to find purpose in gathering to strengthen the work of the church in this worldwide struggle. The programs suggested by the national men's organizations clearly reflect this. Even during the war, men's organizations were encouraged by the boards of Christian Education to hold programs emphasizing patriotism. Program titles included "Defending the Bulwarks," "Building Up Home Morale," and "Planning for a Post-War World."[21]

In 1947, several suggested programs directly referred to the cold war. In the program "Christianity and Communism," the discussion leader was encouraged to stress the importance of supporting America's political leaders. "The Communistic influence, under its active mission of world-wide 'evangelism,' has spread its influence and sent its agents into all parts of the world. . . . Needless to say, the mission of the Christian Church in America and in the world at large is of tremendous importance. In fact, the successful accomplishment of this mission can be of controlling importance in the present struggle for world peace." The anxieties associated with the postwar world surfaced in discussions and generated enthusiasm for the work of the church.[22]

Men's programs in the PCUS periodically raised the issue of civil rights. For example, one program suggestion in 1947 was "The Golden Rule and Men of Every Color." The program directly attacked those who maintained the status quo in the South. Race relations in the South were compared to British rule of India; program leaders were asked to encourage their men's groups to seek actively "equal economic treatment" and "equal treatment in law courts and by police," and to "oppose all laws and customs that deny them the ballot solely because of their color."[23]

PCUSA men's activity was led in the late forties and throughout the fifties by Paul Moser. A distinguished lay leader in the 1940s, Moser served as executive secretary for the National Council of Presbyterian Men beginning in 1948. Over the next decade, the National Council met yearly at the Palmer House in Chicago. Its purpose was "to promote the Kingdom of God worldwide by encouraging Presbyterian Men to serve Jesus Christ in the work of the Church and to follow Him in the vocations of the common life."[24] Participants in these conventions heard national business leaders explain how they incorporated Christian principles into their everyday business practices. Inspired and stimulated to reflect a Christian ethos in the workplace, men returned to their communities believing that they were part of one of the great movements in the postwar world.

The sense of mission and desire for moral leadership during the late forties and through the fifties was exceptionally strong among men's groups throughout the PCUSA. Attendance at these conventions and gatherings grew significantly. In 1948, 370 men representing 245 presbyteries met at the Palmer House; John Foster Dulles spoke on the effectiveness of Soviet slogans in the Third World and the necessity to counter with a strengthened moral vision. The Reverend Louis Evans maligned the nation's universities for creating a moral vacuum and called on Presbyterian men to counter these influences. By the next year 600 men met at Palmer House; 900 in 1950; 1,400 in 1951; 1,900 in 1952; 2,100 in 1953; 2,652 in 1954; 7,400 met in regional conventions in Sacramento, New York, and Chicago in 1955. By 1957, 11,000 men were participating in area meetings of the National Council of Presbyterian Men.[25]

In 1958 the PCUSA and the United Presbyterian men's groups merged into the United Presbyterian Men in The United Presbyterian Church in the United States of

America (UPCUSA). But the late fifties represent the zenith of men's activities, the greatest activity since the early part of the century. Sustained by forces in American culture, men believed there was a larger purpose for their coming together and supporting the activity of the church (GA, UPCUSA, 1958, p. 220).

The Turbulent Sixties

At first glance, the best explanation for the decline of men's activity is related to the changing sociocultural climate in the 1960s. Social unrest did affect the problems afflicting men's organizations, but there are several indications that by the late fifties other difficulties began to contribute to declining interest and effectiveness. In 1957 the *Christian Century* editorialized that the Chicago meeting of the National Council of Presbyterian Men was not much more than a gathering of America's business elite hoping to cloak their activity in a religious mantle. Particularly dismaying to the editorial writer was the treatment of William Schnitzler, secretary-treasurer of the AFL-CIO, who asked for sensitivity to the plight of labor. "When Labor Leader Schnitzler lifted his lone (and admittedly, not too compelling) voice to plead the other side, he was received with unforgivable rudeness," reported the *Christian Century.* "There were insulting cries from the audience. . . . The moderator of the meeting at one point had to reprimand the delegates with a little lecture on courtesy."[26]

Criticisms of men's organizations began to surface more frequently. Charges that men carried on a kind of "fried chicken" theology referred to men's meetings as social gatherings. Pastors occasionally complained in national publications that they were apparently expected to lead meetings and provide the essential organization. "There is something both fascinating and discouraging in the man who holds a responsible job involving long range planning who, serving as Program Chairman of the Chapter, comes to the Pastor crying . . . 'Our Chapter meets next week.

We are planning our program. Do you know anyone we could get to speak? Or should we use that Rose Bowl film?' " reported one clergyman.[27] By 1961, an extensive report was delivered to the General Assembly detailing a number of the specific criticisms and urging structural changes as well as more coordination of national themes with congregations (GA, UPCUSA, 1961, p. 49).

In the PCUS, there was less overt criticism of men's programs. Perhaps this was due to the continued leadership of Andy Andrews, who succeeded Patterson in 1959 and remained in the position of executive secretary until 1964. But Andrews, by his own admission, struggled to find new avenues to invigorate men's work. After spending a year in Geneva, Switzerland, Andrews believed that the future of men's work rested with a European-style lay movement. He maintained that renewing the church through laymen's training centers, retreat houses, and "communities" would be the central purpose of men's organizations in the latter half of the twentieth century.[28]

But instead of revitalization and new vision, serious division emerged by the mid-sixties. In 1964, the Christian Education Committee of the Synod of Texas recommended eliminating organized men's work and absorbing its functions into adult work. Critics attacked the programming for being weak and irrelevant to the needs, particularly, of younger men. Often seen as just "knife and fork" clubs, men's organizations seemed ineffective in dealing with much other than the social needs of a few men. Some argued that it was anachronistic for men's programs to be responsible for church leadership training, when women were now officers as well. All agreed there was widespread ferment, from the congregation to the General Assembly, in both the UPCUSA and the PCUS regarding the purpose, organization, and effectiveness of men's organizations.[29]

As a result, the PCUS commissioned a thorough study of men's work. Forty interviewers were trained, and more than 750 men were questioned. These included laity, officers, and pastors from 119 churches in all synods across the denomination. The 1968 report found that the majority of men asserted "that the church and its role in today's world appear very unclear to them. And at the same time they expressed a great need for the church and feel that it should not be dismissed." The survey revealed a clear difference of opinion on a variety of topics between those over and those under the age of thirty-five. The younger men generally saw themselves and their role in the mission of the church much differently from those who were older. Younger men tended to be less satisfied with the church and expressed a need for renewal and for the church to be more relevant. Tension between clergymen and laymen surfaced repeatedly in the survey.[30]

Authors of the study concluded that the programs of study, worship, local men's programs, rallies, conferences, and conventions generally failed to convince men that they were adequately equipped for mission. The report urged that control and direction of lay programs be in the hands of the session; the General Assembly's newly formed Board of Lay Activities' role should be merely advisory. Flexibility, variety, creativity, experimentalism, relevancy, and responsiveness were encouraged in congregations. But the authors failed to offer much in the way of specific suggestions.[31]

The growing division over the role political issues should play in church life also tended to fragment men's organizations. As early as the late 1950s, differences in political outlook began to surface at national men's conventions. More conservative men increasingly resisted the call for social change desired by program leaders at the national level. By the late sixties, outside groups brought increasing pressure, particularly on the UPCUSA, to respond to the civil rights issues and the war in Vietnam and to open up church leadership to women. By 1969, in the wake of the King and Kennedy assassinations and the rioting at the Democratic National Convention in Chicago, the National Council of United Presbyterian Men urged much more involvement in politics. The publication *Call to Action* stressed that "Christ is in the midst of the fear, alienation, and bloodshed of our cities. . . . We presume to join him there . . . institutions perpetuate destructive forces such as poverty and injustice. . . . With joy and hope born of our faith in Christ, we commit ourselves and call upon you to join us in this commitment to action in this age of crisis so that we may witness together." The message was clear: Men in the church must have their consciousness raised and must seek ways to directly solve the social crises affecting the nation (GA, UPCUSA, 1969, pp. 376–377).

But the issue of how involved the church should be in political issues, and more specifically what stances should be taken, continued to fester in the late 1960s and exacerbated the already existing generation gap among men. Whereas in the postwar period a broad consensus unified the movement, that agreement ceased to exist by the late sixties. In a 1968 Gallup poll, one month after Martin Luther King, Jr.'s death, 53 percent of the Presbyterians polled argued that the church should stay out of politics altogether. This was an increase from the 44 percent who took this position in 1957. The number who argued that the church should express its political views dropped from 47 percent to 40 percent. Several editorials in *The Presbyterian Layman* spoke to the growing alienation among men because of the political positions of both the General Assembly and the National Council of United Presbyterian Men.[32]

The 1960s proved to be very difficult times not only for the church as a whole but for men's organizations in particular. The PCUS study revealed a broad generation gap, and the UPCUSA group struggled to find an appropriate stance in regard to the social unrest in major American cities. The growing women's movement tended to undermine the notion that men's groups should be responsible for leadership training and more subtly suggested that men's groups were bastions of continued sexism in the church. By the end of the decade, there were many who felt that men's organizations might have ceased serving a useful purpose.

Reorganization and Attempts at Revitalization in the Seventies and Eighties

By the mid-seventies the UPCUSA men acknowledged the serious problems facing their organization; hope dissipated that more flexibility and relevance could overcome the larger cultural forces and lack of focused mission. The United Presbyterian Men continued to meet, and a self-study resulted in the adoption of a fourfold program emphasis: Mission to Men, to Families, to Pastors, and to the World. More efforts were directed toward the redevelopment of organizations within the local congregation. By the late seventies and early eighties, moderate growth began again.

In 1972, staff support for men's work from the General Assembly of the PCUS was eliminated. Synods and presbyteries were charged with the responsibility of providing resources for congregations. In 1982, after two years of planning, PCUS men held a convention in Atlanta. The following year a new organization called the Men of the Church Council was established.[33]

The merger of the PCUS with UPCUSA provided the stimulus for the National Council of UPM to invite their PCUS counterparts in 1983 to form one organization. Created in 1984, the new organization, Presbyterian Men, held a major convention in New Orleans in 1987. One of the major efforts has been the development of fraternal relationships with men's movements in churches in other nations, particularly in Asia. Program emphases continued to vary: for example, the men of the Pittsburgh Presbytery assisted with Project Garden 5,000, which planted and harvested potatoes and corn for food banks. Concerns ranging from ministry to Mexican-Americans to the plight of the homeless were found in local men's programs around the country in the late eighties. Bible study remained a strong focus for many groups, and attempts to integrate Christianity into the workplace provided discussion topics for many men. Yet the seventies and eighties will surely be seen as a period of reorganization and reflection. The difficulty of sustaining activity at the congregational level continued. The efforts, largely sporadic, still depended heavily on the individual efforts of one or two persons in a given congregation (GA, UPCUSA, 1987, pp. 587–588).

Conclusions

Men's work and men's organizations have been an important but neglected part of the history of the Presbyterian Church. Their impact on the life of congregations and local communities has been significant. Yet the history of men's work is one of struggle and difficulty as well. When a broader consensus concerning larger social and political issues was achieved, such as existed prior to World War I and during the forties and fifties, men's organizations succeeded in attracting larger numbers of men into their ranks. When that consensus broke down, men's work experienced greater difficulty sustaining itself.

The comparison of Presbyterian men's work with that in other denominations, while it might prove fruitful in helping to determine the relative uniqueness of the Presbyterian experience, is beyond the scope of this article. It seems likely, however, that the historical Presbyterian effort to mold and shape American culture and public policy has had a significant impact on men's work. This engagement of American culture is not unique to Presbyterians, but it certainly has been greater than in many other Protestant groups.

In many ways, the intertwining of Presbyterianism with American culture has served men's work well; many Presbyterian business and political leaders have provided key leadership in their churches and communities. Yet in the period since the 1950s this may also help account for some of the difficulties faced by men's organizations. Without question, Presbyterian and mainstream Protestant influence in American culture as a whole has been waning. Men's work has been most successful when organizational leaders felt confident regarding the role of religion in society; that confidence has significantly eroded over the last two decades.

Two other factors will certainly influence future men's work. One is the feminist movement in American culture. Whether men's organizations can retain a separate identity without being perceived as sexist is difficult to say. Many clergy as well as Protestant lay leaders have attempted to eliminate all forms of sexism in the church. A second, more subtle factor is the influence of professionalization. As the middle class has increasingly developed professional organizations, some of the social needs that men's work in the church formerly met no longer exist. Again, the long-term influence is difficult to project. Nevertheless, the future health of the church does seem to depend heavily on finding ways in which the laity can serve in meaningful ministries. Men's organizations have historically provided such an avenue, and certainly that will remain their key challenge into the next century.

10

Special-Interest Groups and American Presbyterianism

Gary S. Eller

The session of First Presbyterian was enmeshed in a debate about the document, "Presbyterians and Peacemaking: Are We Now Called to Resistance?" The chair of the witness committee repeated emphatically, "It's just a study paper for prayerful consideration. Nobody said you have to agree with anything." "Is that right?" countered an elder across the table. "I understand from reading *The Presbyterian Layman* that 'they' are trying to put one over on the churches again with all this peacemaking business." "That's not what I saw," interjected a somewhat distressed clerk; "in *The Presbyterian Outlook* there is the whole story on that document, with pros and cons for everyone to see." "Well, now, who are you going to believe?" sighed a new elder. All eyes turned toward the perplexed pastor for guidance.[1]

Similar scenes are repeated in session meetings, officer retreats, private conversations, and fellowship dinners across the country. The voices competing for the support of Presbyterians have increased in number and intensity as special-interest groups related to the church have proliferated and promoted their views. Official publications of the Presbyterian Church (U.S.A.), such as *Presbyterian Survey* and *Monday Morning,* are often at variance with reports found in newsletters and publications of special-interest groups. What do the multiplicity of voices arising from these groups, commonly referred to as "Chapter Nine" organizations, signal for the PC(USA)? Who are the special-purpose groups? Where did they come from? What do they want? Are they here to stay? And what do they tell us about the Presbyterian capacity to incorporate often antagonistic groups with divided loyalties into a coherent and faithful Reformed witness?[2]

Historical Background

Special-interest groups are a contemporary expression of the historic interweaving of Reformed faith, politics, and spirituality. In *The Institutes of the Christian Religion,* John Calvin urged Christians to fulfill their particular responsibility to seek justice in a sinful world. Calvin's theology, based on his interpretation of scripture, was embodied in the government of Geneva. His views were stoutly resisted by advocates of a strict separation between ecclesiastical issues and affairs of state. Calvin's supporters agreed that there was nothing outside the potential concern of the church. To them, discipleship meant being constantly aware that "during one's whole life one has to do with God." Calvin's opponents urged the church to distinguish spiritual issues from politics.[3]

American Presbyterians have continued to wrestle with the proper relation of the church to politics. From pulpit and pew, Calvinists supported the American Revolution. When civil war threatened, southern Presbyterian theologians, such as James Henley Thornwell, defended slavery while other Reformed voices championed abolition. By 1861 the Presbyterian witness was divided North and South in a separation of the church that lasted for 122 years. Throughout those years a substantial number of southern Presbyterians remained convinced that the church should restrict its attention to spiritual nurture, apart from social and political issues.

Presbyterians still debated a host of public issues, such as entry into World War I, along with matters of personal morality, including the "Prohibition Amendment" of 1920. In each case, Presbyterians spoke as guardians of the basic convictions of American mainstream Protestant faith. Not everyone agreed with the Presbyterian positions—certainly not all Presbyterians—but Presbyterian convictions were heard and often heeded by political leaders. Presbyterians could not define American culture, but they could profoundly shape its contours.[4]

In the nineteenth century, benevolent societies developed outside the mainstream denominations. These independent organizations, such as the American Tract Society (1823) or the American Sunday School Union (1824), often coordinated their activities across denominational lines. Unlike contemporary special-interest groups, the benevolent societies were not restricted by denominational polity. They functioned independently or in concert with the denominations for particular ministries. When benevolent societies interacted with denominational boards and agencies, they were not focused on changing the direction or policies of the churches. In these significant ways the benevolent societies differed from today's denominational caucuses.

Advocacy groups formed gradually within the denominations. Specific provisions for "special organizations" reporting under the Form of Government to the Presbyterian Church date from the turn of the twentieth century. In 1902, at the 114th General Assembly of the Presbyterian Church in the United States of America (PCUSA), a new chapter was added to the Form of Government. Chapter XXIII (later changed to Chapter XXVIII) was entitled "Of the Organizations of the Church: Their Rights and Duties." The Assembly intended to establish some order among the growing number of special caucuses within the Presbyterian Church and to distinguish them from the proliferation of groups outside the denomination, such as the American Bible Society (1816) or the Gideons International (1899).[5] As Presbyterians defined their mission in contrast with these nondenominational societies, they soon discovered the high cost of building internal consensus. For example, when agreement could not be reached about the goal of foreign missions, J. Gresham Machen led a movement to found an independent board. By 1936, Machen was expelled from the PCUSA.

Modifications were made in the relationship between the Assembly and special-purpose groups during the 1960s and 1970s. The 179th General Assembly (1967) of The United Presbyterian Church in the U.S.A. (UPCUSA) tightened the "oversight and direction" process by requiring "organizations outside the judicatories of the church" to provide "at least an annual written report of activities and finances to the General Assembly through the Stated Clerk." In 1976, the Advisory Council on Discipleship and Worship was assigned by the General Assembly Mission Council of The United Presbyterian Church in the U.S.A. to serve as a liaison with Chapter XXVIII organizations to keep communications open between the Assembly and the caucuses. Three years later, the Special Committee to Study Chapter XXVIII of the Form of Government noted, "All subsequent General Assemblies have acted upon the reports of Chapter XXVIII organizations," either receiving them with or without exception, or rejecting them.[6] Also in 1979, a process for regular consultations between special-purpose groups and the Committee on Pluralism and Conflict was implemented by the same Advisory Council at the direction of the 191st General Assembly of the UPCUSA. While relations between the special groups and the Assembly were sometimes strained, a system for dialogue was established.

The pattern of relationships soon changed, with the 1983 reunion of the Presbyterian Church and the adoption of a new Constitution. The sections on special organizations acknowledged both their "Right to Organize" (G-9.0601) and the need for accountability by "Review and Control" (G-9.0602). The 196th General Assembly (1984) directed the Advisory Council on Discipleship and Worship to prepare standards for "G-9" organizations that would clarify the rights and duties of these groups. The council's response was adopted by the General Assembly of the PC(USA) in 1985. The guidelines called for an annual review of each special organization and a General Assembly vote whether each was "in compliance" or "not in compliance" for that year. The term "in compliance" would indicate "adherence to the Constitution of the Presbyterian Church (U.S.A.) and [the] guidelines, but does not imply the General Assembly's concurrence with, or endorsement of, the organization's position." To be found "not in compliance" carried disciplinary consequences. As the guidelines state:

> The "not in compliance" designation indicates a failure of the organization to adhere to the Constitution or these guidelines. The recommendation from the Committee on Pluralism and Conflict that a group receive the "not in compliance" designation must be accompanied by a statement to the General Assembly citing the irregularities and indicating the remedial action necessary for compliance. If the remedial action is not forthcoming before the next General Assembly, the special organization, while continuing to be accountable to the General Assembly, loses the privileges granted under compliance.[7]

Criteria for evaluating special organizations were developed along with a list of privileges for groups found "in compliance."

In the years before reunion, the Presbyterian Church in the U.S. (PCUS) witnessed similar organizations emerging to monitor the views of its councils, boards, and agencies. The caucuses formed even without constitutional provisions. As with the UPCUSA, PCUS special-interest groups generally preferred reform of the denomination to any division. Controversies were nevertheless keen. With the approach of reunion, the activity of many of these special-interest groups increased significantly. Thus in 1983, when the new *Book of Order* of the Presbyterian Church (U.S.A.) was adopted, Presbyterians from both denominations were concerned with the status of special-purpose groups and how they would influence the reunited church.

The key portions of the *Book of Order* provided for "members of a particular church or churches" to associate together "to conduct special tasks of witness, service, nurture, or other appropriate endeavors" (G-9.0600–.0602). These special organizations, called "Chapter Nine" organizations, were subject to the direction, control, and oversight of the session, the presbytery or synod, or the General Assembly, according to their geographical territory. Special-purpose groups were permitted to select their own names, adopt their particular bylaws, elect officers, and solicit funds, all subject to the power of review of the governing bodies under whose jurisdiction they resided. They were required to submit annual financial reports to the appropriate judicatory. This model assumed that the governing body's right of review and oversight would be the proper course for monitoring special organizations. The caucuses found "in compliance" each year would be granted their rights as "loving critics" to make governing bodies aware of the "special tasks of witness, service, [and] nurture" facing the denomination. While the locus of authority would remain with the appropriate judicatory, special-interest groups were granted recognition and a role in the reunited church from its inception in 1983.

This was a crucial decision. The Form of Government constitutionally legitimized organized advocacy groups within the PC(USA) during the same eight-year period, 1983–1991, in which there would be major transitions for the new church. Those transitions would include a new Brief Statement of Faith, a new hymnbook, controversies about the mission of the church, decisions on the ownership of church property, and intense social debates. As the constituency and identity of the reunited PC(USA) emerged, internal interest groups were given a dramatic opportunity, far greater than the weight of their numbers, to steer the church toward different agendas.

By 1988 all officers of special organizations were required by the Assembly to read and endorse the *Book of Order,* G-9.0600–.0602, to affirm the recommended "Guidelines for Special Organizations," including detailed annual financial reports, and to observe the "Statement of Ethics and Standards for Professional Practice of the Associated Press." The 200th General Assembly (1988) adopted revisions in the language of G-9.0601, shifting the emphasis from direction and control to recognition and dialogue. Presbyterians for Biblical Concerns commended these changes, calling them a "new emphasis on communication" which "represents a giant leap forward in recognizing the valuable contributions and insights of the Chapter IX groups."[8] Not everyone was content. Resistance to "guidelines" remained so intense from the Presbyterian Lay Committee that the 1989 General Assembly voted to strike section G-9.0602 from the Form of Government. The presbyteries approved the Assembly's action. All that remained of chapter 9 in the *1989–90 Book of Order* was a single paragraph, G-9.0601, emphasizing the rights and responsibilities of special-purpose groups.

The exact wording of these provisions was still debated. At a minimum, the *Book of Order* stressed that special organizations "are not official agencies of the Presbyterian Church (U.S.A.)" and that "they bear alone responsibility for their views and actions." In particular, special-purpose groups were subject to the discipline of the church if their activities compromised the "decency, order, peace and unity of the church." Advocacy groups, however, could hardly avoid disturbing the church. Thus the *Book of Order* allowed considerable latitude in interpreting exactly what level of discord was permitted and what required disciplinary action.

When the PC(USA) General Assembly met in 1990, the role of special-interest groups was a major agenda item. By an overwhelming count of 422–104, the Assembly voted to eliminate Chapter Nine provisions, amid both criticism and support of the action. The Committee on Worship and Diversity recognized that Chapter Nine status implied official status for the caucuses in the minds of many Presbyterians. While the *Book of Order* specifically stated that this was not the case, the only resolution appeared to be the elimination of the provision. A minority report cited the church's need for self-critical dissent. The denomination had no effective way of monitoring the caucuses. Some groups, such as the Presbyterian Lay Committee, defied attempts at control. Extremely diverse groups, even without official status, proved more powerful than the PC(USA) could handle without fragmenting or polarizing. Even if the presbyteries vote to support the Assembly's action during 1990–1991 the potential for schism remains.

At present, twenty-two Chapter Nine groups are recognized by the General Assembly. The range and growth of these organizations since the 1960s have been remarkable. Membership figures may reflect contributors or simply the active participants on a governing board. Totals vary from six families in the New Earth Covenant Community or the thirteen-member Board of Trustees of Presbyterians for Biblical Sexuality to the 37,600 listed as contributors to the Presbyterian Lay Committee, Inc., during 1987 (GA, PC(USA), 1988, I, pp. 1119-1143).

A few special organizations have very modest budgets, while others have substantial financial resources. Presbyterians for Democracy and Religious Freedom (PDRF), based in Nashville, had an operating budget of nearly $100,000 for 1988. More than $1 million annually is channeled into mission projects by the Outreach Foundation, based in Charlotte, North Carolina. Accurate, annual financial reports for all groups are not readily accessible. Detailed membership demographics indicating the age grouping, financial circumstances, and geographical location of supporters are unavailable. Most of the special-interest groups are self-defined as evangelical coalitions of lay and ordained Presbyterians advocating biblical Christianity, lay renewal, spiritual renewal, and evangelism. Some of the most influential evangelical groups, such as the Presbyterian Lay Committee, are extremely critical of the national leadership of the PC(USA). Their newsletters and journals implore readers to help end the alleged "liberal bias" of the denominational policymakers. Ordinarily, even the most critical special-purpose groups are not openly schismatic. *The Presbyterian Layman* declared in a 1989 editorial, "Loving, Not Leaving It":

> We've said it before, but it bears saying again: We choose to remain members of the Presbyterian Church (USA). We have no intention of leaving, and we fervently hope that our words will not encourage any of our readers to leave.

> It is incumbent upon a critic, it seems to us, to be clear about his loyalty, lest the point of his proclamation be misunderstood. The Presbyterian Lay Committee was formed to counter a disastrous trend in our national church. Believing that the social activist hegemony which captured control of this denomination would, if allowed to continue unabated, eviscerate the church, the Presbyterian Lay Committee gave birth to a critical voice.[9]

That "critical voice" from within the PC(USA) is shared with other groups. Consistently, their stated goals are the spiritual renewal of the PC(USA) and a reinvigorated Reformed witness for Jesus Christ. Unfortunately, the process of renewal demands a spirit of compassion and cooperation which is often lacking in the exchanges between the Assembly and its harshest critics.

A few special organizations are not composed of evangelical Presbyterians. The Witherspoon Society, founded in 1973 within the UPCUSA, addresses concerns for "inclusiveness in church and society, social and economic justice, lifestyle concerns, and just international relations" from a Reformed, confessional, but considerably more liberal point of view. In its profile statement, the Witherspoon Society expresses its prophetic role and social justice commitments so that

> Presbyterians and their Church continue to hear and heed God's call to empower the powerless; to speak of God's justice and mercy to a world in need of repentance; to raise to the consciousness of the Church the concerns of the poor and the disenfranchised; to call the Church to reformation when it falls short of God's demand for right relation in its own life.[10]

These commitments are expressed in support of causes strongly opposed by evangelicals like the Presbyterian Lay Committee. Witherspooners support the sanctuary movement, urge freedom of access and choice in birth control, endorse the National Council of Churches and the World Council of Churches, and invite the church to end discrimination against lesbians and gay men who suffer the injustices of homophobia. These are just a few examples of the volatile issues that widely separate Witherspooners from evangelicals.

Still other special organizations center their efforts on more narrowly defined single-issue concerns that are neither exclusively evangelical nor liberal agendas. The Presbyterian Network on Alcohol and Other Drug Abuse (PNAODA), which serves as a resource to the greater church, is one such group. Its activities include a broad ministry of compassion and education that both evangelicals and liberals within the PC(USA) ordinarily support. By its own choice, this group is no longer a Chapter Nine caucus, but continues its ministries in relation to the PC(USA).[11]

The emergence of new special organizations and the reformation of ongoing groups continue to affect their structure and mission. The Presbyterian Evangelical Coalition (PEC), founded in 1985 but later denied Chapter Nine status, was formed to coordinate the "fellowship, nurture, and collaboration of organizations that normally refer to themselves as evangelicals" (GA, PC(USA), 1986, Part I, pp. 949–970). No other umbrella group for evangelicals or liberals has since emerged. Some major groups have combined their resources. In April 1989, Presbyterians for Renewal (PFR) was born in St. Louis from the combination of Presbyterians for Biblical Concerns (formerly recognized by the UPCUSA) and the Covenant Fellowship of Presbyterians (originally related to the PCUS). PFR's membership includes many moderate Presbyterians who seek a centrist orientation for the church.

The variety and dynamics of special organizations make simple generalizations tenuous. Although an overwhelming majority can be broadly classified as "evangelical" associations, the following categories more adequately describe Presbyterian special-purpose groups:

Prophetic/social action—may be either evangelical or liberal, single issue or multiple concern:
>   Presbyterians for Biblical Sexuality
>   Presbyterians for Lesbian/Gay Concerns
>   Presbyterian Peace Fellowship
>   Presbyterians Pro-Life Research, Education
>   and Care, Inc.
>   The New Earth Covenant Community
>   The Witherspoon Society

Evangelical/centrist—emerging single-issue or multiple-concern organizations with growing numbers of theological moderates joining their ranks:
>   Covenant Fellowship of
>   Presbyterians   united as
>   Presbyterians for Biblical   Presbyterians
>   Concerns   for Renewal
>   Presbyterians for Democracy and
>   Religious Freedom

Evangelical/conservative—single-issue or multiple-concern caucuses, not currently moving toward a more centrist position:
>   The Presbyterian Lay Committee, Inc.

Evangelical/mission—caucuses whose particular thrust is spreading the gospel at home or abroad through traditional approaches such as mission evangelists, literacy programs, or medical mission:
>   Association of Presbyterians in Cross-Cultural
>   Mission
>   Literacy and Evangelism International
>   Presbyterian Center for Mission Studies
>   Presbyterian Frontier Fellowship
>   Presbyterian Order for World Evangelization
>   The Outreach Foundation of the Presbyterian
>   Church, Inc.

Evangelical/renewal—organizations whose primary pur-
pose is spiritual reawakening by prayer, Bible study,
and acts of personal piety:
Presbyterian Elders in Prayer
Presbyterian Renewal Ministries
Reformed Order of Discipleship

This ordering of special-interest groups, if even roughly
accurate, suggests that the development of these organizations shows:

1. A preponderance of evangelical caucuses focusing on
evangelism and mission as first priorities for the reunited
church

2. The movement of formerly evangelical/conservative
groups—Presbyterians for Biblical Concerns and the Covenant Fellowship of Presbyterians—to an evangelical/
centrist position that is attracting many moderates to PFR
who were not members of either previous organization

3. A greater number of prophetic/social action groups
arising from theologically and politically conservative
groups such as Presbyterians for Biblical Sexuality

4. An increase in spiritual renewal groups from evangelical circles at the same time that spirituality has become a
major interest of many moderate and liberal Presbyterians. Perhaps one of the next new Chapter Nine groups
will be a renewal group with a predominately moderate
constituency.

The birth and realignment of special-purpose groups reflects massive changes in American society and denominational life. Presbyterians are part of a widely documented
cultural and religious shift that calls forth and sustains advocacy groups. In the next section we will survey the
American religious landscape that contributes so much to
the emergence of special organizations.

The Landscape

Robert Wuthnow's study *The Restructuring of American
Religion: Society and Faith Since World War II* astutely

examines religious trends and activities that have contributed to the rise of advocacy groups inside and outside
mainstream denominations. Wuthnow's thesis is that
American mainstream religion is undergoing a momentous
identity crisis. This crisis is the result of traditional religious institutions confronting the politics and technologies
of the late twentieth century. In the wake of that engagement, a major "cleavage" has appeared between liberals
and conservatives within Protestant, Catholic, and Jewish
groups. Divisions within the Protestant house are deep
and intensely defended. On both sides are earnest, faithful
people committed to the well-being of their church. Their
disagreements with sisters and brothers within their own
denomination are family feuds, carried out primarily
within the confines of the denominational house rather
than through nondenominational or para-church organizations. The impact of these family quarrels upon the broad
realignment of the churches after the 1960s, Wuthnow argues, will profoundly affect the vitality and witness of the
church for decades to come.[12]

The dynamics of the present realignment differ from the
debates of the 1920s. Today conservatives and liberals are
separated not only by theology, but also by social agendas
and leadership styles. Most conservatives maintain that
values lead to behavior, while liberals insist that values are
of secondary importance to the structured forces that control behavior. Conservatives concentrate on building
mechanisms for evangelism, while liberals are more focused on peace and justice issues. Neither group tends to
promote schism. Both conservatives and liberals usually
remain inside the denominational fold as they struggle
fiercely for control. While growing in unprecedented numbers inside and outside denominations, these partisan organizations have cultivated broad-based support from
denominational memberships. They compete with one another to define the issues and approaches their denominations will take to myriad problems. These special-interest
groups often command the primary loyalty of their mem-

bers; indeed, denominational ties are frequently weaker than members' bonds to special groups.

Since World War II denominational loyalty has eroded, partly because of the blurring of denominational distinctiveness. Many Protestants believe that there are no significant differences between denominations.[13] Religious commitments are not faring very well in competition with optional leisure activities. This observation is particularly true of the "baby-boom" generation, who were keenly influenced by the upheaval of the sixties and the materialism of the eighties. However, religious commitment does not run as deep among middle or older adults either as it did in the 1950s. What characterizes the contemporary scene is a general perplexity among laypersons as to what it means to be a Presbyterian, for example. American Presbyterian congregations are typically diverse combinations of members from many different denominational traditions.

In such a complex cultural and religious environment, special-interest groups can provide a haven for those who feel threatened by too much rapid change and a voice for those who want drastic changes. Mainstream Protestants are living, says sociologist Wade Clark Roof, in a "postestablishment era." American society is no longer a "melting pot," but a "centrifuge." In a centrifuge the center of a substance "collapses and elements regroup in a different more fragmented constellation." Churches, which historically have provided a "bridging institution," nurturing society toward some "meaningful whole," now find their own identity diffused. The churches do not yet have the language or the metaphors to construct a coherent theological vision to interpret a postestablishment world.[14] In the absence of a consensus about basic issues, tension between liberals and conservatives has escalated and produced more special-interest caucuses.

Jack B. Rogers, formerly Associate Director of the PC(USA)'s Theology and Worship Ministry Unit, has argued that historically a bell curve describes the distribution of liberals and conservatives in the church. According

to Rogers, there are never more than 10 percent of Presbyterians who, at any one time, could be properly classified
as "liberals." Conservatives, he added, are never more
than 15 percent. Across the decades most Presbyterians
fall between those two extremes. The middle 75 percent of
Presbyterians, past and present, struggle to keep complex
issues in balance. In such a system, the groups to the left or
to the right are only as powerful as the number of persons
from the middle they enlist to their causes.[15] The contest
between liberals and conservatives is, first, a battle for the
support of moderates to strengthen targeted causes. Neither liberals nor conservatives are likely to be swayed by
the arguments of the other. They offer a point of view
which they hope will draw moderates to their side. Moderates seldom have an articulate voice, so the great majority
of Presbyterians either take no clear position on issues or
adopt the views of a far smaller but vocal group to the left
or right of them.

Special-interest groups can cultivate disquiet, give their
causes a name, and provide a means for addressing perceived problems. That is part of the appeal of special-
interest groups. They also offer support and guidance
during a transitional period in American religious life.

The effect of the special-interest groups on the PC(USA)
is ambiguous. On the one hand, they are agents of change
and renewal. On the other hand, they also have the potential of further fragmenting and blurring the identity of the
denomination and increasing the level of divisiveness on
controversial issues. A case study of one of the newest
groups, Presbyterians for Renewal, illuminates both the
promise and the peril of the special-interest groups.

Presbyterians for Renewal

This group, founded in April 1989, is essentially a combination of Presbyterians for Biblical Concerns (PBC) of
the former UPCUSA and the Covenant Fellowship of
Presbyterians (CFP) from the PCUS. Presbyterians for
Biblical Concerns began in 1965, when evangelical clergy

and laity met in Chicago to debate the proposed Confession of 1967's view on the authority of scripture. According to Dwight A. White, the last president of PBC, the caucus originally adopted the name "Presbyterians United for Biblical Confession" (PUBC). The group was conceived as an ad hoc association, for the sole purpose of ensuring that the new confession would affirm an evangelical point of view.[16] The founders planned to dissolve the caucus after the adoption of the confession by the UPCUSA.

PUBC's leaders soon discovered, however, that they could effectively influence major decisions by the Presbyterian Church. This realization led to the ongoing life of PUBC for nearly a quarter of century. Several other renewal groups were generated by PUBC as the founding caucus engaged a variety of issues after a modified Confession of 1967 was adopted. PUBC's commitment to "biblical renewal" identified the organization with "evangelical renewalists." They described themselves as rooted in the "Protestant Reformation and the spiritual movements of purification subsequent to the Reformation: Pietism, Puritanism and the evangelical awakenings of the 18th and 19th centuries." Specifically, they affirmed "Scripture as the only infallible rule of faith and practice, the source of wisdom and authority above all worldly ones." Their "balanced theology" emphasized:

- the full deity and humanity of Jesus Christ
- the gravity of our sinful condition as human beings
- our lostness and need for salvation
- redemption provided by Christ's atoning death and bodily resurrection
- salvation by faith alone through the agency of the Holy Spirit
- the equipping and enabling of the body of Christ through the power of the Holy Spirit
- and a comprehensive and holistic mission of personal evangelism and social justice worldwide

This theological agenda was pursued as a "catalytic agent

of reconciliation, reformation, and renewal within" the UPCUSA.[17] PUBC began to publish *The Presbyterian Communique* as a quarterly magazine distributed across the nation and to expand its programs. By 1988 approximately sixteen hundred individuals were members of PBC, representing some 250 congregations and three contributing foundations.

A movement toward reorganization began in 1983, when the board of PBC indicated an openness to "merge with others of a like mind, or if God so led, to disband thus enabling some new movement of the Spirit." According to *The Presbyterian Communique,* the board of directors of PBC (the "United" was dropped after reunion) met in April 1988 and "authorized its representatives to explore" these options with others.[18] The result was the decision to join with the Covenant Fellowship of Presbyterians in a new renewal group.

This second partner in the alliance, the Covenant Fellowship of Presbyterians, began in 1967, when thirty PCUS leaders met with William M. Elliot, Jr., pastor of Highland Park Church in Dallas, Texas. The group signed "An Open Letter to the Church," which cited the potential for division between a "liberal coalition" (associated with the views expressed by Aubrey Brown of *The Presbyterian Outlook*) and a "conservative coalition" (which included Concerned Presbyterians, Presbyterian Churchmen United, Presbyterian Evangelistic Fellowship, and *Southern Presbyterian Journal*). The newsletter *The Open Letter* would declare: "We recognize and value the contributions of both groups. . . . We believe, however, that neither of these emphases, standing by itself, truly represents 'the whole counsel of God' as set forth in the Scriptures. Both are important aspects of the truth and neither is complete without the other."[19] The group covenanted to work together through the courts of the church and to resolve differences "through communication marked by respect, understanding, and trust among persons who are all alike committed to the service of our Lord and Savior."[20] Further, they asked others to join them in this covenant, yet they made no plans to formally organize.

During 1969 and 1970 evangelical PCUS church leaders met out of a dual concern for the restoration of the Presbyterian Church and for reconciliation within the denomination. From their meetings CFP was born. *The Open Letter* became the regular forum for CFP in 1971. Commenting on the early concerns of CFP, Harry S. Hassall, once editor of the newsletter, writes:

> In 1970 the issues which attracted our attention included the following: synod restructuring (which we opposed), increasing of lay representation (which we supported), and broadening of union talks to include five other major Presbyterian bodies in this nation. Others included rejection of a Brazos Presbytery overture limiting local autonomy over local church property (Assembly rejected this overture), support of the adequacy of the Westminster theological standards, support of the Black Presbyterian Leadership Caucus's inclusion in the church structure, opposition to COCU, willingness to consider any reformed church union based on the merits of that plan of union, opposition to any pre-union merging of boards/agencies design until after union vote, opposition to any new statement of faith but support for a rewrite and modernization of Westminster, rejection of union presbyteries, support for sharing of power with the disenfranchised, and eventually a strong opposition to the inclusion in the 1973 Plan of Union of an escape clause which would have allowed conservatives to vote for union and then to stay out—a plan we saw as really a blueprint for the deliberate carving up of the PCUS by the Left and Right in cahoots. This last issue proved to be our most difficult issue.[21]

While CFP opposed schism and acted as a moderately conservative critical voice within the PCUS, many staunch conservatives did split from the PCUS in 1973 to form the Presbyterian Church in America (PCA). The conservatives who did remain part of the PCUS continued to exercise their influence, often through CFP, whose political power base was centered in the presbyteries. CFP led conservative opposition to a proposed *Book of Confessions* and a

"Declaration of Faith" for the PCUS in the mid-1970s. They also battled against the ordination of practicing homosexuals and objected to "weighted voting" by presbyteries. Even so, CFP maintained its special-organization status in the PCUS. As reunion approached it helped reshape the Plan for Reunion (1981) to make the Plan more acceptable to conservatives when further divisions threatened reunion.

The theological themes most often cited by CFP commentators in describing CFP's relation to the PCUS and in the negotiations for reunion were "restoration" and "reconciliation." In their judgment, CFP served as a "loving critic," keeping a "theological balance" in the PCUS during an eventful twenty years. When liberals contested with conservatives, CFP provided a moderately conservative, denominationally loyal, evangelical voice on the presenting issues.

After reunion the need for a new evangelical caucus emerged. On May 16–18, 1988, seventy-three clergy and laity met in Dallas, Texas, to share their concerns and hopes for the Presbyterian Church (U.S.A.). The conference was publicized as "A Call to Renewal." The three conveners were evangelical pastors: J. Murray Marshall of First Presbyterian Church, Seattle, Washington; John Huffman of St. Andrew's Presbyterian Church, Newport Beach, California; and B. Clayton Bell, of Highland Park Presbyterian Church, Dallas. A two-page release states:

> We gathered in Dallas because we love our church and because we believe that we are in a unique moment of crisis and opportunity. The crisis we sense is theological, ethical, and in its deepest dimension, spiritual. Among its symptoms are a well-publicized continuing decline in membership and mounting financial difficulties. These pressures have brought our structures to the point where positive change is necessary and, we believe, possible. The opportunity for renewal in our church is of equal magnitude to the crisis that confronts it.[22]

Added to this statement were a series of confessions and affirmations, including:

> We confess that we have contributed to the problems within
> our denomination by our isolationism, our prideful indepen-
> dence, and our greater concern with our congregations and
> local spheres of influence than with the connectional witness
> of the church.[23]

The paper continued with a four-part statement on the
uniqueness of Christ, the authority of scripture, the holy
life, and the church. The paper ended with an appeal that
the issues named in the document might be a "rallying
point for those who share" their hopes and vision for
reformation and renewal in the Presbyterian Church
(U.S.A.).[24]

When almost a thousand guests arrived in St. Louis in
April 1989 for the founding meeting of Presbyterians for
Renewal, the concerns of the Call for Renewal group were
sufficiently strong to support a new special-interest group.
Attending the conference were former members of PBC
and CFP, along with a host of visitors, reporters, speakers,
and denominational leaders. At the opening assembly the
crowd was welcomed and introduced to a threefold
agenda: "To acknowledge that our church is ill, to accept
the prescription for that illness, and to act together to reform the Presbyterian Church so that it is biblically based,
theologically sound and socially relevant."[25] Just how a
new coalition would pursue that agenda was still being
decided late into the evening after the general meetings
adjourned.

During the general meetings, keynote addresses were
made to the delegates. Jack B. Rogers, an evangelical
leader and a General Assembly staff member, asserted,
"The leadership and membership of the Presbyterian
Church have generally differing views of what the church
should be about." In essence, the General Assembly staff,
he said, have opted for structure and public pronouncement while the membership longs for personal spiritual
growth. Rogers therefore urged all Presbyterians to work
diligently for "the synthesis of the personal piety and social justice agendas into a pluralistic doctrine of the
church."[26]

The hope for a new coalition of moderates yielded "A Covenant of Renewal." It was presented at the first meeting of PFR and signed by approximately one thousand attendees. The covenant is a nine-part declaration of the church's need for spiritual reawakening through celebration, confession, and commitment. The covenant affirms salvation through Jesus Christ alone, the necessity of personal piety for a "holy life," the authority of scripture, the importance of the Great Commission, and a willingness to "pursue social justice and righteousness to combat racism and sexism."[27] The document contains no specific program agendas. Instead, it offers a foundational covenant around which an evangelical/centrist coalition might be formed that would provide a voice for the largely silent 75 percent of the Presbyterian Church.

The impact of PFR on the whole church may be considerable. PFR was conceived as an "attempt to coalesce Presbyterians of a middle way." Born during a season of decline for the PC(USA), PFR has not yet proposed an alternative social agenda to what many evangelicals consider "the liberal Presbyterian establishment." Instead, it called for the spiritual renewal of individuals and local congregations. J. Murray Marshall, speaking for PFR, commented, "Renewal is not right positions on a series of particular issues. Our primary agenda is God's renewal of individuals and the church."[28] The founders of PFR envisioned more hope for a unified Presbyterian witness in the future as a renewed church. The future will tell the whole church whether they were right.

Theological Reflections

In a major report to the 200th General Assembly entitled "Is Christ Divided?" the theological diversity of the Presbyterian Church was celebrated as "one of the glories" of the church and lamented as leading "to the decline of the denomination."[29] The Task Force on Theological Pluralism Within the Presbyterian Community of Faith, which prepared the document between 1985 and 1987, examined the unity and diversity within the church and found that they "are not polar opposites. Diversity does not destroy unity; unity does not destroy diversity. Rather, unity and diversity are complementary realities in the community of faith."[30]

Certain theological themes appear frequently in the report, such as the following affirmation: "The Christian community of faith is formed in ongoing encounter with Jesus Christ, the crucified and risen Lord. This encounter is God's gift, which leads to new life in the Spirit."[31] Such unity is not accomplished by revising the polity of the church; it demands, instead, that theology be taken seriously.

The report adds that the Presbyterian Church—still a predominantly white, middle-class denomination—is not as diverse as it thinks. Indeed, the church is arguably no more pluralistic now than when Presbyterians debated with Independents about the "visible church" at the Westminster Assembly. What is most needed, said the Task Force, is the recognition that too often the Presbyterian Church has avoided the challenges of its diversity by urging "unity in mission" before "unity in theology." The result has been "unity in neither."[32]

In particular, many of the present controversies within the church grow out of a misunderstanding of the principle that "God alone is Lord of the conscience." The abuse of that conviction is manifested when "the grace of conscience (is) perverted into the arrogance of dogmatism." When the broad community of faith is forsaken in favor of "compact communities of those whose experience and expression of faith are particularly compatible," there is a strengthening of group conscience by mutual affirmation, and the very great danger of cultivating an "exclusive certainty" within the compact community that eventually leads to isolation and schism.[33]

The erosion of a theological center in the church, such as a basic agreement about the elusive "essential tenets" of Reformed faith, "leads to self-righteous dismissal of those with whom we disagree."[34] This is precisely what has occurred in the Presbyterian Church. Since we have often been unable to sustain constructive theological discourse, we have tended to imitate the political culture of our society and formed compact communities "on the basis of power" to address our internal conflicts. The Task Force added:

> In the Presbyterian Church, the centralization of denominational structures and the proliferation of Ch. 9 and other special-interest groups are but two sides of the same institutional coin. Hope is placed in the operation of structures to preserve the truth. Many of the current Ch. 9 Special Organizations were formed out of the perceived inability of certain theological positions to gain an adequate hearing within the structures of the denomination, both at governing body and agency levels. There is little doubt that the perception was correct, that open theological discourse was lacking in an institutional structure that displayed theological and ethical certitude. Yet the response led not to new theological openness but to a calcifying of theological positions in institutional form. The emerging Special Organizations were as certain of their truth as denominational structures were of theirs. Thus the Presbyterian Church experiences a kind of theological Balkanization in which various groups are convinced that the faithfulness of the Presbyterian Church depends upon their action to preserve the gospel. Strangely, the witness of many groups within the church is a negative one, more concerned to identify the errors of other groups than to proclaim the good news of God's grace and a vision of Christian life. Perhaps this is inevitable when theological discourse is reduced to competing claims made by competing structures.[35]

There is a widespread concern within the Presbyterian Church that many special organizations are great dangers to the peace and harmony of the church. Would the PC(USA) be strengthened by the abolition of Chapter Nine organizations? Not in every case. Some special-interest groups are primarily extended fellowships who provide support for an enhanced spiritual life through acts of traditional piety such as prayer. Those groups which are most like "struggle groups" or "pressure groups," however, may divide the church far more often than they heal the body. Wuthnow cites an editorial in *The Presbyterian Layman* which predicts, "The church will be changed by a proliferation of sharply focused, single-issue groups, each of which is willing to get down in the trenches and fight."[36] The result of such protracted conflict, in the face of diminishing human, financial, and spiritual resources, would virtually guarantee the decline of the Presbyterian Church. Wuthnow comments, "The cleavage between liberal and conservative Presbyterians is . . . both serious and unfortunate. Although it may, at its best, ensure that different points of view are heard in denominational bureaucracies, it has become a means to an end that often overshadows the end itself. Certainly, the biblical image of love, or more modern ideals of community and reconciliation, are difficult to see amidst the turmoil that divides liberals and conservatives."[37]

What might the more issue-focused special organizations offer the Presbyterian Church that could contribute to its faithful witness into the next century? First, special-interest groups can provide an arena for voicing dissent from within the denomination in such a way that genuine dialogue is encouraged and schism avoided. Special-purpose groups provide an alternative structure where dissent can be registered constructively so that the essential "peace and harmony" of the church is preserved. Second, they can organize the huge majority of Presbyterians, who are neither liberal nor conservative, so that the numerical mainstream of the church can take a more active and informed leadership role in the future. Presbyterians for Renewal, for example, has the potential for articulating an evangelical/centrist position that could galvanize the typically silent mainstream majority of Presbyterian congregations. Third, special organizations, such as the Outreach Foundation, may well be able to mobilize resources beyond the ordinary contributions made to denominational missions. They have cultivated a high level of trust within their constituencies at precisely the time when denominational identity has been diffused by reunion. Such groups will extend the traditional ministries of the church, particularly in evangelism, new church development, and medical missions. They will be advocates for these ministries while remaining clearly loyal to the denomination.

Can special-purpose groups be agents of reconciliation within the Presbyterian Church? Only if strident debates between contending factions are replaced by a respectful dialogue and concern for the welfare of the whole Presbyterian family while working together to pursue the mission of the church. If this is done in the power of the Spirit, the "theological Balkanization" of the Presbyterian Church can end, the identity of the new church can be firmly established, and authentic ministries of faithfulness can begin.

11

The Emerging Importance
of Presbyterian Polity

David B. McCarthy

The Presbyterian Church in the twentieth century has witnessed an increasing theological pluralism and diversity among its members. A recent survey of the Presbyterian Church (U.S.A.) found that fewer than half (43 percent) of its members and only 61 percent of the pastors had been Presbyterians all their lives; many of today's Presbyterians were once members of Methodist, Baptist, Lutheran, United Church of Christ, Roman Catholic, or other churches.[1] Another recent study found that 45 percent of those Americans who had been brought up as Presbyterians have since "dropped out" or joined another denomination. The theological identity of the Presbyterian Church has become blurred, as the "boundaries" between Presbyterianism and other major denominations have become less distinct during the past decades.[2]

In 1729, the Westminster Confession and Catechisms were officially adopted by the Presbyterian Church as confessional standards, but the church has moved away from those standards in the intervening years. Even when the Westminster standards were first adopted, provisions were made to allow ministers to disagree, as long as their disagreement was "only about articles not Essential and necessary."[3] As it became apparent that not every Presbyterian—or even every Presbyterian minister—could subscribe to those standards, the Presbyterian Church attempted first to amend the Confession, and then to define its "essential" articles. As early as 1788,[4] both the Westminster Confession and Catechisms were amended by the Presbyterian Church, and the Presbyterian Church U.S. amended the Westminster Confession as late as 1963. More recently, the church has realized the futility either of amending a historical document or of attempting a definitive interpretation of its essential articles.

In the past few decades, this decline of confessionalism led to a legitimation of theological pluralism in both of the major branches of American Presbyterianism—the United Presbyterian Church in the U.S.A. (UPCUSA) and the Presbyterian Church in the United States (PCUS). In recent years, each denomination considered or adopted a contemporary confession of faith. Each denomination considered or adopted a multi-confessional *Book of Confessions*. Each denomination changed its ordination vows to relax the question about confessional subscription.[5]

American Presbyterianism has seen many changes since its beginnings in the seventeenth and eighteenth centuries. Amidst an increasing theological pluralism and diversity, the polity of the Presbyterian Church has become more important to its self-identity than its theology. No longer can it be assumed that a Presbyterian believes every article of the Westminster Confession or Catechisms, or even its five "essential and necessary" articles—if, indeed, it ever could have been. No longer can it be said that most Presbyterians have a particular doctrine, be it "Calvinism" or "predestination," that unites them. No longer can a "Presbyterian theology" be identified that distinguishes the Presbyterian denomination from other American Protestant denominations. Rather, the distinctiveness of the Presbyterian Church today lies in its polity.

As the theological diversity of the Presbyterian Church has become more apparent, the role of polity in mediating those differences has become increasingly important. Sev-

eral debates within the denomination, including some decisions of the General Assembly Permanent Judicial
Commission (the PJC), have served to clarify the respective roles of theology and polity.

This essay examines first the ascendance of polity in several instances where polity, rather than theology, proved
the deciding factor in resolving questions widely seen as
theological in nature: these cases include the debate surrounding a grant to help defray the legal expenses of Angela Davis, the judicial decision denying ministerial
ordination to Walter Wynn Kenyon because of his refusal
to ordain women as church officers, and Boston Presbytery's appeal to matters of order rather than doctrine in
investigating its ministers' involvement in Cape Cod's
Community of Jesus. Next, two judicial cases that saw polity attenuated and theology reaffirmed will be discussed:
the Ellis case in the PCUS, which affirmed a minister's
right to disagree with the denomination's polity, and the
twice-tried Kaseman case, which recognized the theoretical limits of orthodoxy but reaffirmed the presbytery's
right to be the judge of those limits. Finally, a look at polity in the reunited church will suggest that theological issues of order, equality, and accountability are reflected in
Presbyterian polity.

The Ascendance of Polity

Theological consensus may once have been important to
denominational unity, but it has given way to other criteria in the face of increasing pluralism within the Presbyterian Church. During the past two decades, several
questions facing the United Presbyterian Church were decided on polity concerns rather than on their theological
merits, despite the apparent theological nature of those
questions. Throughout that time, many people found
themselves "subtly shifting the mode of religious authority
from doctrinal validation to procedural validation."[6] Increasingly, the Presbyterian Church appealed to polity and
procedures to resolve issues that previous generations

would have debated on their theological merits. Presbyterian polity was clearly emerging in its importance to the life of the church.

The Angela Davis Debate

One of the controversies that first signaled the growing importance of polity was the debate surrounding a $10,000 grant to help defray the legal expenses of Angela Davis. The grant divided the church along theological lines, but it was defended by an appeal to polity. In March 1971, the Emergency Fund for Legal Aid of the Council on Church and Race (COCAR) contributed $10,000 to the Marin County Black Defense Fund for the defense of Angela Davis, a professed Communist, a member of the Black Panther party, and an atheist.[7] On Wednesday, May 19, news of the grant leaked out to the General Assembly; the official report, presented on May 24, was hotly debated. The Reverend William Al Walmsey moved "that the 183rd General Assembly (1971) communicate to the Council on Church and Race its serious question concerning the propriety of allocating $10,000 to the Marin County Black Defense Fund," and the General Assembly concurred by a vote of 347 to 303.[8]

Much of the subsequent debate in the church at large focused on theological and ideological issues, including the nature and mission of the church and the church's involvement in the political arena. Four months after the news broke at the General Assembly, COCAR had amassed more than ten thousand letters from members of sessions of United Presbyterian churches, 85 percent of which opposed the grant. Many of those letters mentioned Angela Davis's atheism, more than half mentioned her communism, and one fourth indicated that other priorities should be more important to the church. None of the reasons listed in COCAR's report even mentioned the procedures of the Emergency Fund for Legal Aid in their arguments.[9]

While the church at large debated the Davis grant on its ideological and theological merits, COCAR was being attacked within the church hierarchy for the impropriety of its administrative procedures. The Fund's stated purpose was "for legal aid purposes in relation to racial and cultural justice . . . in cases where there is some judicatory participation, including endorsement and shared funding where possible" (GA, UPCUSA, 1971, 571). It soon appeared, however, that no lower judicatory had endorsed any such request: "The St. Andrew's Church in Marin County issued a statement in December, 1970. It was a position paper . . . [which] made no request." The synod executive sent a copy of the statement to COCAR, although the church had made no such request:

> *Technically* he was transmitting a request for legal aid from a local church session, although there was no explicit request for funds in the St. Andrew's statement. *Technically* the fact that he made the transmission signifies a concurrence with the request, although he made no request either. *Technically* a grant to the Marin County Defense Fund was approvable because it met the guidelines of the emergency fund requiring it to come from lower judicatories through higher judicatories to COCAR.
>
> For every technically, however, there were alternating technicallys.[10]

Despite the general outcry about the theological issues at stake, "mostly the controversy was not carried on theologically. It was an ecclesiastical-organizational matter and discussed in those terms."[11] Thus, conformity to polity became a forum for discussing an issue that had sharply divided the church along theological lines.

The Council on Church and Race weathered the storm, although it emerged restructured. General Assembly Moderator Lois Stair distanced herself from the Angela Davis grant, but she expressed her satisfaction "that those who did have authority to make this grant acted in accordance with the procedure set forth by the 1970 Assembly establishing the Emergency Legal Aid Defense Fund [*sic*]."[12] COCAR responded at length to the General Assembly's directive to study the propriety of the grant, defending both the merit of its action and its adherence to procedures (GA, UPCUSA, 1972, pp. 747–749, 992–998).

Although the issues surrounding Angela Davis and COCAR's grant on her behalf were never considered by a judicial commission, polity was clearly playing a more important role in deciding matters that many people saw as theological issues. Only a few years later, a case was to come to the attention of the General Assembly PJC that brought the conflict between theology and polity to a head.

The Kenyon Case

On February 14, 1974, Pittsburgh Presbytery's Committee on Candidates and Credentials recommended that Walter Wynn Kenyon, a graduate of Pittsburgh Theological Seminary, not be ordained. The committee reported that "the primary issue concerned the candidate's vows of ordination, particularly his endorsing the Church's government and honoring its discipline." Kenyon had told the committee that if women were elected to the session of his congregation, he would not ordain them. "He would have been willing to work with women in the church, and he would have been willing to have someone else come into his church to ordain any duly elected women elders, but he himself would not have been willing to ordain women" (GA, UPCUSA, 1975, 255).[13]

Overruling the committee's recommendation, Pittsburgh Presbytery examined Kenyon and voted (147 to 133) to sustain his examination and ordain him. Fifty-five members of the presbytery dissented, and on February 25 the Reverend Jack M. Maxwell filed an official complaint against Pittsburgh Presbytery. A "stay of execution" was filed on March 6, forestalling Kenyon's ordination pending the final outcome of the case.

On April 19, 1974, the synod PJC reversed the action of Pittsburgh Presbytery, ruling that it had been irregular and that the presbytery had, in effect, granted an exception to the constitutional provision of the Form of Government, namely, the ordination vow which asked in part: "Do you endorse our Church's government, and will you honor its discipline?" Kenyon had indeed answered the question in the affirmative before the presbytery, but the synod ruled that his answers to the presbytery's previous questions had, in effect, compromised his responses. Pittsburgh appealed the case to the PJC of the General Assembly, which rendered its decision on November 18, 1974, siding with the synod and voting not to sustain the appeal. On Wednesday, May 21, 1975, the General Assembly adopted the PJC's report, thereby ratifying its decision (GA, UPCUSA, 1975, pp. 254–259, 178).

Throughout the debate, many of Kenyon's supporters saw the issue as one of conscience: the Assembly PJC's report notes that "Mr. Kenyon . . . seeks to refrain from violating his own conscience by performing an act contrary to that interpretation" (GA, UPCUSA, 1975, p. 259). The March 1975 issue of *Christianity Today* reported the PJC's decision under the headline "United Presbyterians: An Issue of Conscience."[14] Later that year, the president of the Presbyterian Lay Committee, Paul J. Cupp, told the national convention of the Presbyterian Lay Committee that "the issue now is freedom of conscience, and it affects not only the seminarian, Walter Wynn Kenyon, a talented Christian who must go elsewhere if he stays in the ministry."[15] Even *A.D.,* the official Presbyterian magazine, first reported that Kenyon had been denied ordination "because he believes that the Bible forbids him to ordain women as elders."[16]

Writing after the synod decision of April 1974 but before the General Assembly decision, a General Assembly subcommittee advised that a minister having Kenyon's views, regardless of how quiet or cooperative, could disagree in doctrine, but could not refuse to participate in the ordination of women. Such a refusal, no matter how conscientiously formulated, "might be construed as a refusal to perform an action usually expected of the pastor of a congregation."[17] The PJC concurred: "In considering the gravity of the question, we are mindful that conscience can be in conflict with polity. But it is important to recall that the decision to present oneself as a candidate for ordination is voluntary. A candidate who chooses not to subscribe to the polity of this church may be a more useful servant of our Lord in some other fellowship whose polity is in harmony with the candidate's conscience" (GA, UPCUSA, 1975, p. 257). In other words, Kenyon could disagree in conscience with the UPCUSA, but he could not ignore the duties its government imposed on him, even for the sake of his conscience.

Kenyon's opponents raised the issue of women's rights. Soon after a sympathetic announcement of the PJC's decision appeared in *A.D.* ("A splendid young minister" and "a son of the manse . . . denied the place in which he has dreamed of serving"), several letters to the editor appeared in subsequent issues, denouncing the flavor of the article and raising the issue of women's equality in the church.[18] It eventually became clear from the decision that the "ordination of women is no longer an issue within the United Presbyterian Church," according to Mayo Smith, an *A.D.* columnist. "Its propriety is taken for granted by most of our ministers and members."[19] Even Kenyon himself "recognized the ecclesiastical right of women to be elders in his congregation."[20] The PJC was particularly explicit on this very point, stating that "there is no question that refusal to ordain women on the basis of their sex is contrary to the Constitution" (GA, UPCUSA, 1977, p. 258).

The PJC affirmed the presbytery's right to ordain, a right which the General Assembly had recently reaffirmed.[21] Presbyterian and Reformed churches have traditionally upheld the right of the people to elect their own officers,[22] but the presbytery must exercise its authority "in conformity to constitutional requirements," as the PJC had ruled in 1935 (quoted in GA, UPCUSA, 1975, p. 258).

Finally, the freedom of conscience, the right to ordain women, and the right of presbytery to ordain were not factors in the PJC's final decision; rather, they were emotionally charged issues used to rally support for one side or the other. *Christianity Today* rightly identified the primary issue in its announcement of the decision headlined

"United Presbyterians: A Clash of Polity and Doctrine."[23]
Stated Clerk William P. Thompson also advised that the
PJC's decision "is based upon the premise that the issue
before it was one of church government rather than of
doctrine."[24]

Polity has long been an important and integral part of
the Presbyterian Church and ministers have always been
subordinate to the polity of the church,[25] but polity had
also traditionally been subordinated to the gospel.[26] With
the decline of theological consensus in the United Presbyterian Church, the importance of polity was on the rise.
One commentator on the Kenyon case observed:

> There is a growing awareness of the necessary distinction
> between statements in the *Book of Confessions* and the man-
> datory directives of the *Book of Order*. They are not and
> cannot be of equal weight.
>
> The United Presbyterian Church is no longer a confes-
> sional church in the strict sense; we do not have a single
> document with which every ordained person must agree in
> every detail. We have a *Book of Confessions* originating in
> different times and places. In the constitutional questions
> that every candidate for ordination or installation must an-
> swer, he or she promises to be "instructed" and "guided" by
> the confessions. That is quite different from having to agree
> with every word or sentence.
>
> The situation is necessarily different with governmental
> provisions. A sentence defining what constitutes a quorum of
> a judicatory or affirming that women are eligible for ordina-
> tion is not ambiguous; it must be either accepted or rejected.
> Again, the constitutional question reflects this distinction:
> "Do you endorse our church's government, and will you
> honor its discipline?" The candidate who cannot in good
> faith and without exception answer that question is not de-
> prived of liberty. He or she need not seek office in a volun-
> tary organization, the United Presbyterian Church.[27]

But not everyone welcomed this emphasis on polity.

One critic saw this emphasis on polity as "unnecessarily
legalistic,"[28] and another called the decision a "triumph of
legalism over doctrine and freedom of conscience";[29] yet
another said that "the issue forces people into a fundamen-

talist constitutionalism."[30] At its February 1975 annual
meeting, Presbyterians United for Biblical Concerns approved an open letter expressing their concern that the
Kenyon decision would "precipitate a series of heresy trials."[31] At least one Kenyon sympathizer expressed a concern that his "brethren" would react to the Kenyon case
with a backlash of their own "heresy trials."[32] Boston Presbytery responded to the Kenyon decision with an open
letter to its members, acknowledging that "there are ways
in which the Kenyon decision could be legalistically interpreted and enforced at the presbytery level" and urging the
presbytery "to act with grace and follow the intent rather
than the letter of the law."[33]

The irony in the fear of "heresy trials" can hardly be
ignored. Whereas heresy trials had previously been conducted for theological unorthodoxy, they were now threatened for departures from points of polity. Richard Lovelace
feared that "the church might find itself in the position of
'asking the ordinand to bring his [or her] conscience captive
to . . . a conviction "into which the Holy Spirit has led the
whole church." ' Now this is a very unPresbyterian thing to
do."[34] Some feared a potential legalism in the ordination
vow which asked the ordinand to "endorse" the church's
government. Responding to an inquiry about the Kenyon
case, Stated Clerk William P. Thompson advised that "the
word 'endorse' as used in the question means 'to express
approval of, publicly and definitely; to give support to; to
sanction; to affirm.' "[35] The Presbytery of Seattle subsequently overtured the General Assembly to amend the
wording of that ordination vow, claiming that it "requires
subscription to every provision under the *Form of Government* and that the word 'endorse' . . . can be interpreted to
imply intellectual assent" (GA, UPCUSA, 1977, p. 746
[Overture 43]). The Presbytery of Pittsburgh also overtured
the General Assembly that year, claiming that the word
"endorse" was "open to a narrow and restrictive interpretation" (GA, UPCUSA, 1977, p. 752 [Overture 53]). Both
overtures proposed the substitution of the word "submit"
instead of "endorse." The General Assembly did not pass

either overture, thus defeating two attempts to broaden the
ordination vow's required subscription to discipline (GA,
UPCUSA, 1977, p. 92). The subscription that had once
been required of the Westminster Confession was now
clearly required of Presbyterian polity.

The Community of Jesus Controversy

The same concern for polity as a means of settling a
theological disagreement appeared several years later. In
September 1981, the Presbytery of Boston established a
Task Force to Study the Community of Jesus, a community based in Cape Cod and said to have disrupted some
congregations and individuals within the Boston Presbytery. The Task Force's final report characterized the Community of Jesus as a charismatic fellowship begun in 1958
which had since developed into "an incorporated (1970)
non-profit residential religious community, functioning as
a retreat center in Orleans [Massachusetts] and connected
to a facility in Bermuda as well as to a school in Ontario,
Canada."[36] According to another report, about 250 res-
idents lived there in "25 or so houses . . . clustered on 35
acres in the Rock Harbor section of Orleans," and "an
additional 60 people, most of them from New England and
Canada, [were] nonresident or associate members." The
Community's influence extended far beyond the geographical boundaries of Cape Cod, however. It was associated
with the 3D diet program (Diet, Discipline, and Discipleship), which had involved "more than 100,000 people in
5,000 churches." More than 150,000 copies of the book
3D were in circulation. Peter Marshall, son of the well-
known chaplain to the U.S. Senate and of the author Cath-
erine Marshall, had been intermittently involved with the
Community of Jesus since 1965.[37]

At the conclusion of its study, the Task Force found "evidence that involvement with and within the Community
of Jesus [was] frequently incompatible with Presbyterian
commitments of doctrine and order."[38] During the debate
on the floor of the Boston Presbytery meeting of October

24, 1982, one commissioner questioned the propriety of the inclusion of the word "doctrine" in their report, arguing that only issues of order had been addressed by the Task Force. Perhaps doctrinal issues were indeed encountered by the Task Force, but the difficulties encountered with the Community of Jesus were eventually resolved chiefly through appeal to issues of discipline and order.

The chief objection to lay participation in the Community of Jesus concerned the potentially abrasive nature of the live-in encounter groups in the Community, an objection that also applied to clergy who became personally involved in the Community.[39] The literature of the Community stressed "the counseling authority of the entire community." At the heart of its counseling was the "light group"—"a style of encounter therapy used extensively by the Community of Jesus which spills over into the small groups basic to the 3D experience. Viewed by the community as a form of Christian honesty and 'tough love,' 'light groups' are said to be based on I John 1:7, 'If we walk in the light, as he is in the light, we have fellowship with one another and the blood of Jesus his Son cleanses us from all sin.' "[40]

A former member of the Community of Jesus said that members of light groups would confront each other "with any sort of supposed deviance [the group] can think of"; he had seen physical violence in light groups ("a person knocked off his chair") and isolation punishment ("One community member sat daily in the basement of one of the houses for six months"). The power of these "light groups" extended even to family life:

> Husbands and wives have been separated for periods of up to six months, and children are often removed from their parents. Most children over the age of 12 live separately from their families. Peter Hamilton was once denied the right to watch a television appearance by a daughter outside the Community of Jesus by one of the ministers who said, "You see, you are making an idol of your child."
>
> Families have been permanently separated by community involvement when one adult decided to enter and the other

did not, or when one departed and the other did not. Once
one has left the Community of Jesus, very little contact is
allowed with the remaining family members.[41]

The Boston Task Force expressed its concerns about the
practices of the Community of Jesus in terms of "caveats"
to the individuals involved.

Despite the many potential dangers the Community of
Jesus might pose to individual church members who might
become involved with it, the Task Force was mainly concerned with involvement by clergy,[42] a concern that the
Synod of the Northeast would reiterate in its report five
years later.[43] The Task Force's report focused its discussion
of clergy participation in the Community around the fifth
ordination vow—the same one at issue in the Kenyon
case—which asks the ordinand to "endorse our church's
government" and "honor its discipline." The Task Force
understood that vow to mean that "an individual minister
owes primary ecclesiastical loyalty to the presbytery, and
has expressed free agreement to 'honor its discipline' in the
vows of ordination." The repeated refusal of the involved
clergy to disclose the vows they had made to the Community of Jesus led the Task Force to conclude that "lacking a
full and reasonable understanding of the minister's ecclesiastical standing vis-à-vis the Community, the Presbytery
cannot carry out the ministerial oversight mandated by our
Constitution." On the basis of that finding, the Task Force
reported, and the presbytery concurred, that the "Presbytery of Boston may be seriously remiss in its responsibilities
if further actions are taken to transfer ministers with specific calls to the Community of Jesus to the Presbytery of
Southern New England." Despite the very serious theological and doctrinal issues raised about the Community of Jesus, the final method of dealing with the Community was an
insistence on strict adherence to the church's discipline.[44]

Polity Attenuated and Theology Reaffirmed

Although the Angela Davis debate, the Kenyon case, and
the Community of Jesus controversy witnessed the ascen-

dance of polity, two more recent judicial cases saw polity attenuated and theology reaffirmed. The Ellis case in the PCUS affirmed a minister's right to disagree with the church's polity that women be ordained to church office, and the twice-tried Kaseman case in the UPCUSA recognized theoretical limits of orthodoxy but reaffirmed the presbytery's right to be the judge of those limits. The Ellis case represented a retreat from the strict endorsement of polity implied by the decision in the Kenyon case, and the Kaseman cases reasserted the theology of a candidate as a proper concern of the ordaining or installing presbytery.

The Ellis Case

In 1977, a case very similar to the UPCUSA Kenyon case was decided differently by the PCUS Permanent Judicial Commission when it ruled that the Reverend Thomas T. Ellis could be installed as a pastor despite his views on the ordination of women. Ellis had been an ordained minister of the PCUS since 1966, but his acceptance of a new call meant that he would have to reaffirm his ordination vows upon his installation. Would the reaffirmation of his "approval of the government and discipline of the Presbyterian Church, U.S." imply (as it had for Kenyon and all who followed him in the UPCUSA) that Ellis could not disagree with the church's decision to ordain women as ministers, elders, or deacons?

In 1975, Atlanta's Capitol View Presbyterian Church called Ellis to be its pastor. Ellis consulted a member of the Atlanta Presbytery about his reservations concerning women's ordination, and was told that his views would not obstruct his reception by the presbytery.[45] Unaware of Ellis's beliefs about the ordination of women, the Commission on the Minister recommended at the June 10, 1975, adjourned meeting of the Presbytery of Atlanta that the call be found in order, but his examination was referred back to the Commission on a substitute motion by the Reverend J. Randolph Taylor.[46] At a called meeting on July 8, 1975, after Ellis "presented a written discourse on his views in Church Government," the Presbytery of Atlanta examined Ellis and voted 109 to 44 to sustain his examination.[47]

Eight members of the presbytery filed a complaint on July 16, bringing the issue before the Synod of the Southeast and eventually the General Assembly. The synod PJC saw the "degree of flexibility concerning doctrine and government" as an underlying issue; their decision maintained that subscription to the doctrinal "system" "does not imply subscription to every detail of doctrine. It also maintains that to 'approve' the government and discipline of the Presbyterian Church, U.S. does not imply approval of every detail of government and discipline."[48] Both the synod and the General Assembly PJC sustained the reception of Mr. Ellis.

Responding to questions from the floor of the General Assembly, the PJC chairperson indicated the situation would have been different if Ellis had "acted to block the ordination of women."[49] However reluctantly, Ellis had agreed that he would ordain women if requested. As one observer interpreted the decision, "If a man in his wisdom still finds himself conscientiously unable to participate in ordaining women, that belief should be no bar to his own ordination. He should simply make himself scarce when women are to be ordained."[50] In its opinion, the General Assembly PJC agreed with the synod that the question "was not primarily what the candidate *thinks,* but what he *does.* The issue is one of *freedom of conscience* versus invidious *action.* Belief or *conviction* versus *conduct*" (GA, PCUS, 1977, p. 115). In making this distinction between beliefs and actions, the Commission concluded that "dissenting *views,* as opposed to destructive *action,* may be tolerated if the Presbytery or the Synod find that those views may be held by a minister without destroying his [or her] effectiveness in carrying out Church policy." (GA, PCUS, 1977, p. 116).

In both the Ellis case and the Kenyon case, the respective PJC's had ruled that the theological beliefs of the individual were not the deciding issue. The UPCUSA had ruled that the ordinand must ordain women to the offices of the church, and Kenyon had not been willing to do that. Although Ellis agreed with Kenyon that women should not be ordained, he was willing to participate in the ordination if requested. Thus, polity was a factor in both decisions, and both cases hinged on whether the individual was willing to set aside personal theological beliefs in order to participate in the established polity of ordaining women to the offices of the Presbyterian Church.[51]

The Ellis decision seemed to attenuate the understanding of the ordinand's assent to Presbyterian polity. Whereas the critics of the Kenyon decision feared that the ordination vow's "endorsement" implied total agreement with UPCUSA polity, the PCUS decision in the Ellis case made it clear that their ordination vows left room for individual disagreement with church polity. The "approval" of the church's government required by the PCUS was apparently less binding on the individual than the "endorsement" mandated by the UPCUSA. As the PJC noted: "It is the freedom of conscience and the *right to work for change* of any established principle which brought about in fact the right of women to be church officers—the very provision of the *Book of Church Order* now under debate. If action to challenge and change the *Book of Church Order* had been stifled by the authorities, the very right of women to be church officers could never have come into being!" (GA, PCUS, 1977, p. 116). In other words, if subscription to polity were enforced as strictly as some feared might happen in the UPCUSA, "women would never have gained the right to ordination, since it would have been impossible to question the church's original stance."[52]

Lest its decision appear to weaken the church's commitment to the ordination of women, the Commission was anxious to reaffirm the constitutional stand on the ordination of women, and reiterated its previous "Advisory Opinion" of 1976:

> "Women are children of God.
> "To Jesus they were not less worthy than men.
> "In God's Church they equal men.

"Under the Constitution of our Church ... women are entitled, equally with men, to hold church office and to serve Christ thereby.

"No minister—and no Presbytery—is entitled to deny or frustrate this equal right and duty of women in our Church" (GA, PCUS, 1977, p. 115, quoting GA, PCUS, 1976, pp. 159–160).

When later asked to clarify what might "deny or frustrate this equal right," the Commission reported that it was inadvisable "to delineate what particular words would constitute a violation of [the constitutional provisions] without having full knowledge of all of the facts and circumstances surrounding a particular case" (GA, PCUS, 1979, p. 282). The PJC concluded that the acceptability of a candidate's polity beliefs should be "determined initially by the Presbytery, and subject to review by higher courts" (GA, PCUS, 1977, p. 115). By distinguishing between belief and action and by granting more discretion to the presbytery in individual instances, the nuances of the decision in the Ellis case established a balance between polity and theology.

The Kaseman Case

If the decision in the Ellis case seemed to attenuate the primacy of polity, the decision in the Kaseman case a few years later seemed to reaffirm the role of theology as a proper concern of the Presbyterian Church. Even this decision, however, was decided on the basis of polity.

The Reverend Mansfield M. Kaseman had been ordained to the ministry in the United Church of Christ and was subsequently called to serve a union church (UCC and UPCUSA) in Rockville, Maryland. The National Capital Union Presbytery (which had dual standing as a presbytery in both the UPCUSA and the PCUS churches) examined and enrolled Kaseman on March 20, 1979. During his examination, however, Kaseman did not affirm the deity of Christ to the satisfaction of some of those present.[53]

A complaint was filed with the Synod of the Piedmont,

which sustained the presbytery on June 16, 1979. The General Assembly PJC gave its decision on January 21, 1980, reversing the synod and instructing the presbytery to reexamine Kaseman. Its decision reaffirmed the importance of the Presbyterian confessional heritage:

> The adoption of the Book of Confessions as a part of our Constitution brought together expressions of a long history regarding doctrines of the Trinity and of the Person of Christ that have long been sources of controversy within the Christian Church. The centrality of these doctrines, variously set forth in the Book of Confessions, is not an issue. All who seek ordination or enrollment in a presbytery must receive these Confessions and be guided by them (GA, UPCUSA, 1980, p. 94).

This judgment did not imply that Kaseman's theology was insufficient or in error, however; they merely found that the presbytery's examination of Kaseman "was not sufficiently thorough and concise as to comply with the constitutional responsibilities" (GA, UPCUSA, 1980, p. 94). As one report noted, the Commission had ruled "not on the merits of the allegations but on the grounds of 'irregularities' in the examination."[54] The decision did establish, however, that it was still possible to conceive of theological boundaries to the Presbyterian Church, outside of which an individual might not be ordained. Whether or not Kaseman had crossed those boundaries had yet to be determined, and was now the issue before the National Capital Union Presbytery once again.

Nearly a year after his first appearance before the presbytery, Kaseman was reexamined on March 18, 1980. The original half hour allotted for the examination grew to almost four hours as Kaseman defended his statement of faith and fielded questions from the floor. Near the conclusion of his statement, he said: "For me, the God worth knowing is found more in the integrity of love than in the purity of doctrine, more in the question of liberation than the pursuit of orthodoxy, and more in the process of becoming than in the satisfaction of having arrived. I value theological plurality and the necessity to use theological concepts; however, these concepts require continual re-forming."[55] During the subsequent debate, one minister asked Kaseman a series of questions:

> "Can we expect a fuller revelation of God's love than we have in Christ?" Reply: "I don't want to set any parameters on God's love and God's revelation." Question: "Can you affirm the bodily resurrection of Christ?" Answer: "I believe in the resurrection without necessarily in the bodily resurrection. We all have our own ways of understanding that." Question: "Do you believe he ascended into heaven?" Answer: "He is one with God. One in eternity."[56]

The presbytery subsequently voted 165 to 58 to receive Kaseman.[57] Still not satisfied with Kaseman's orthodoxy, members of the presbytery again filed a complaint.

On June 9, 1980, the synod PJC found that "most extraordinary reasons do not exist for review of Presbytery's actions," and concluded that the presbytery had "reasonably and properly exercised its Constitutional rights, power and obligations." In its decision, it reaffirmed the theological diversity of the United Presbyterian Church:

> Theological pluralism is a reality which is both desirable and present in our midst. Whether one begins his/her quest for truth with faith and experience as the path that leads to knowledge (creedal or otherwise), or whether one begins the quest with knowledge (creeds) that lead to faith, is not an important issue. There is room in the Church for both approaches to reality, and for the honest difference of opinion that will result. Tolerance is called for—tolerance, sympathy, understanding and mutual respect and love in Christ.[58]

The General Assembly PJC reviewed the case on January 26, 1981, and sustained the synod. The complainants saw the issue as theological, challenging "the authority of the presbytery to confirm Mr. Kaseman as a continuing member of Presbytery because of the alleged failure of his theology to fall within the confessional standards." Noting the shift from the Westminster standards to the multi-confessional *Book of Confessions,* the PJC acknowledged:

"The centrality of these Confessions to the issues presented in this appeal is without question. The United Presbyterian Church is a Confessional Church that takes its doctrines seriously" (GA, UPCUSA, 1981, pp. 114, 115).

The PJC also reviewed the changes in the ordination vows and reaffirmed their legitimation of theological pluralism:

> In this tradition the adoption of the new ordination and installation questions expresses an expanded understanding of the Church's views regarding the function and purpose of our Confessions in the work and witness of our Church. . . .
>
> Formerly the Constitution prescribed empirical standards, as set out in the vows, the Westminster Confession, and the Larger and Shorter Catechisms, by which the candidate's theology was judged. Now the constitution places the primary focus of the candidate's examination not on his or her conformity with theological prescriptions but rather on the candidate's willingness and commitment to be instructed by the confessions of our church and continually guided by them in leading the people of God (GA, UPCUSA, 1981, p. 115).

With respect to theology, this decision had two effects. First, it legitimated the theological pluralism that had evolved during the 1960s. The adoption of multi-confessional standards and the loosening of the ordination subscription vows clearly allowed for more latitude within the confessional stance of the UPCUSA. Secondly, this decision reaffirmed the recognition implicit in the previous Kaseman decision, namely, that theoretical boundaries for the denomination's confessional stance could still be imagined. What those boundaries were, however, was no more clearly established by this decision.

With respect to polity, this decision reaffirmed the powers of the presbytery and strengthened the role of polity in decisions before the church. As the PJC indicated:

> The Presbytery, after examinations of unprecedented length, determined by a vote of almost 3 to 1 that Mr. Kaseman affirms the doctrines about which questions are raised in this case and that differences apparent in his personal wording of

> his answers were not denials of the doctrines. This is a judg-
> ment the Presbytery was best qualified to make. While an-
> swers to some questions may appear to be weak, or less than
> wholly adequate, we reaffirm the principle that we are not to
> substitute our own judgment for that of the lower judicatory,
> which is best able to judge. The Commission is satisfied that
> . . . Presbytery acted reasonably, responsibly, and deliber-
> ately within the constitution of the Church (GA, UPCUSA,
> 1981, p. 116).

The PJC's decisions in the Kaseman cases of 1980 and
again in 1981 were contingent on polity issues: In the first
case, they found that the presbytery had not properly exercised its duty, whereas in the second case, they determined
that the presbytery had indeed properly examined
Kaseman.

Polity in the Reunited Church

On June 10, 1983, the PCUS and the UPCUSA officially
set aside their differences of 122 years and merged to form
the Presbyterian Church (U.S.A.). Would this new church
interpret the role of polity more strictly, as the Kenyon
case might indicate, or would the new church, as in the
Ellis case, be more lenient in its interpretation of polity?

One factor that affects any consideration of polity versus
theology in the reunited church arises from the ordination
vows of the new *Book of Order.* The reunion has done what
no overture to the UPCUSA General Assembly could do:
the word "endorse," implying intellectual subscription to
the discipline and polity of the church, is gone from the
ordination vow. Gone, too, is the word "approve," which
figured in the PCUS ordination vow. The fifth ordination
vow now reads: "Will you be governed by our Church's
polity, and will you abide by its discipline? Will you be a
friend among your colleagues in ministry, working with
them, subject to the ordering of God's Word and Spirit?"[59]
The PC(USA), like the UPCUSA before it, has a multi-
confessional *Book of Confessions,* with the Westminster
Larger Catechism and a Brief Statement of Faith joining

those confessions already known to United Presbyterians. The new church affirms the Confession of 1967 with its explicit affirmations of the relative nature of confessions and creeds. It continues to ask that its ordinands be "guided" by the confessions of the church, no longer seeking the total subscription once required of all ordained officers of the church.

The Ellis Case Retried

The issue of polity and its relation to theology soon came before the reunited church. The Reverend Thomas T. Ellis, whose reception and installation by the Presbytery of Atlanta had been favorably ruled upon by the PCUS in 1977, again came before a presbytery as he accepted a call to the Northshore Presbyterian Church of Jacksonville, Florida. Several members of presbytery subsequently filed a complaint alleging that Ellis had told the presbytery that the Confession of 1967 "is not a statement of the Reformed Faith by which he would be instructed, led or guided in the fulfillment of his office," that "in his view, women should not be ordained as ministers, elders or deacons," and that "he did not agree . . . that unconfirmed baptized children who are being nurtured and instructed should be invited to partake of the Lord's Supper."[60] (PC(USA) 1985, 115). The synod subsequently upheld Suwanee Presbytery in receiving Mr. Ellis, and in its decision of October 1984 the General Assembly PJC concurred.

On the first point, the General Assembly PJC found that, given Ellis's acceptance of the Westminster standards, "his apparent rejection of the Confession of 1967 is insufficient grounds to override the decision of the Presbytery to receive him." Regarding the second point, the PJC cited the previous decision of the 1977 PCUS Judicial Commission in the Ellis case (establishing Ellis's willingness to ordain women despite his beliefs), and found that "the complainants have not established that Mr. Ellis has repudiated this position." As to the third point, it had not been proven that Ellis's views about not admitting baptized but unconfirmed children to the Lord's Table was irreconcilable with the *Book of Order* (GA, PC(USA), 1985, p. 116).

Two members of the PJC abstained from the decision, and three were absent. Five others submitted a lengthy dissenting opinion, acknowledging that "Mr. Ellis holds to the essential tenets of the Reformed faith as traditionally expressed," but pointing out that he "specifically refused to be 'guided and led' " by the Confession of 1967:

> Confessions of faith differ. They do not all address the same issues or theological questions. Rather, they reflect the issues and areas of Christian concern that are pertinent to the time in which they are written. It is this living characteristic that makes confessions useful.
>
> The Christian faith is alive because it follows a Living Lord. It therefore repeatedly finds new expressions in its Confessions. A relevant ministry thus requires the minister be "led" by even that with which he or she may not agree (GA, PC(USA), 1985, p. 117).

Whereas in the Kenyon case conservative elements in the church were upset that polity considerations had proved weightier than any confessional stance, now it was to the dismay of many liberals that the confessional issue had again been subsumed to polity, this time in the Ellis case. If subscription to conservative confessions was irrelevant to the outcome of the Kenyon case, subscription to the more liberal Confession of 1967 was likewise irrelevant to the outcome of the Ellis case.

The acceptance of the previous decision in the Ellis case is significant: it has now become a precedent for the re-united PC(USA). Of the two possible resolutions of this issue, the newly constituted PJC appears to have chosen the more lenient interpretation of the ordination vows which was established by the Ellis case in the PCUS, rather than the stricter interpretation indicated by the precedent of the Kenyon case in the UPCUSA.

In the PC(USA), the continued legitimation of theological pluralism is assured, and the ascendance of polity has been accepted, albeit attenuated. While both liberals and conservatives feared "heresy trials" resulting from the strict interpretation of the fifth ordination vow, the new formulation would not seem to allow for such legalism. The balance between creed and polity is a fine one, and undoubtedly several years will pass before their respective roles in the new church become clear.

Polity Versus Theology, or Polity as Theology?

As the Presbyterian churches in America—first the UPCUSA and the PCUS and now the PC(USA)—have moved away from a confessional stance toward an affirmation of theological pluralism, polity has come to the forefront. While it may appear that polity and theology have sometimes been juxtaposed in apparent opposition, theological and ethical issues are, in fact, at stake in Presbyterian polity. Presbyterians have traditionally affirmed the Westminster Confession's dictum that "God alone is Lord of the conscience."[61] That affirmation becomes an issue, however, when people within the church disagree in good conscience on theological matters. How those disagreements between individuals are mediated is an ethical issue, and inasmuch as ethics are informed by theology, the mediation of conflicts within the church becomes a theological issue as well. Hence, "polity is a matter of theological, as well as practical importance for the life of the Church."[62] As a 1983 PC(USA) General Assembly report argued: "The basis of Presbyterian polity is theological. Our polity is not just a convenient way of getting things done; it is rather, the ordering of our corporate life which expresses what we believe. The connection between faith and order is inseparable. At its heart, the polity of the church expresses our Reformed theology. What we do and the way we do it is an expression of how we understand our faith."[63]

If polity constitutes the means whereby Presbyterians adjudicate their theological differences, it is appropriate that polity should become more important in the face of increasing religious pluralism. Any "endorsement" or "approval" of Presbyterian polity, however, should not be absolute. John Calvin, to whom Presbyterianism owes much of its polity, acknowledged the flexible nature of church polity, recognizing that church organization must change "according to the varying condition of the times."[64] Amid these changes, however, some "general rules"[65] and theological principles of polity can be discerned, and among those are order, equality, and accountability.

One of the theological principles of Presbyterian polity, from Calvin onward, has been order. Calvin was a lawyer by training, and had a high regard for church government;[66] he believed the life of the church should be "well ordered and maintained."[67] Attention to matters of order is a recognition that the means to an end are often as important as the end itself. In other words, an individual choosing "a course of advocacy" must "try to be as careful for truth and civility in the ways and means of argument as about judging the merits of the cause."[68] No individual, agency, or governing body of the Presbyterian Church can set aside the requirements of church polity. The principle of order is threatened in the Presbyterian Church when political means are subverted to a private end, no matter how praiseworthy the end.

A second theological principle of Presbyterian polity lies in the equality of all people before God. As Calvin wrote, "All are brought under the same regulation" in the church.[69] In the Presbyterian Church, ministers, elders, and deacons differ from other members only in function; this "parity of the clergy and laity" has long been a cornerstone of Presbyterian polity.[70] Just as everyone in the Presbyterian Church is equal in that no one person has any power over another, so also everyone is equal in the sense that no one is exempt from the polity provisions of the church. The appeal to individual conscience clearly does not exonerate anyone from fulfilling the requirements of church government.

As far back as 1758, the Presbyterian Church faced the problem of "conscientious objectors" when the "Old Side" and the "New Side" factions ended their schism; their Plan of Union provided that every member should either "actively concur" or "passively submit" to the majority, or "peaceably withdraw."[71] Freedom of conscience must be exercised "within certain bounds," which are the "responsibility of the governing body" to determine.[72] As the 195th General Assembly recognized,

> Freedom of conscience does not require that the conscientious opinion of every member of the church will prevail. Where there are differences of opinion, our church recognizes that the ways of resolving conflict between the freedom of individual conscience and the requirements of our polity are compromise, acquiescence by one group or another, or withdrawal without causing schism. Therefore freedom of conscience is not abridged by the requirements of our constitution.[73]

The equality of all people in the Presbyterian Church is thus assured. All who seek office in the Presbyterian Church must agree to "be governed by our church's polity" and "abide by its discipline."[74]

A third theological principle of Presbyterian polity is accountability. In Calvin's church, every member was accountable to the consistory or session;[75] Calvin also instituted an annual visit to the pastors of Geneva's outlying churches; these pastors were accountable to the seigneury, much as our pastors are accountable to the presbytery.[76] In practice, members of a local Presbyterian church are not often held accountable to their session today, but the Presbyterian Church still affirms that a minister "is always accountable and therefore subject to the jurisdiction of the presbytery of which he or she is a member" (GA, UPCUSA, 1980, p. 291). More recently, the General Assembly affirmed that "Church officers are accountable to governing bodies and the questions asked in ordination and installation are the formal acknowledgment of that accountability" (GA, PC(USA), 1983, p. 150).

Accountability reflects a long-standing Reformed concern with discipline. Calvin listed discipline as one of the "three things on which the safety of the Church is founded and supported."[77] One of Calvin's contemporaries at Strasbourg, Martin Bucer, listed the administration of discipline as one of the three duties of the ministry.[78] Another of Calvin's contemporaries, John Knox, listed "ecclesiastical discipline uprightly administered" as one of the three marks of the church.[79]

With the legitimation of theological pluralism in the 1960s and 1970s, it is more difficult today to hold ministers accountable for their theology, although the Kaseman cases reaffirmed the continuing existence of theoretical boundaries to orthodoxy. Ministers do remain accountable, however, for their actions. A refusal to carry out the constitutionally mandated policies of the Presbyterian Church constitutes sufficient ground to bar an individual from holding church office. This shift in accountability from orthodoxy to orthopraxis was recognized by the 1983 General Assembly, which concluded that "ultimately officers must conform their actions—not necessarily their beliefs or opinions—to the church's practice in those areas where the church has determined that uniformity is necessary or desirable."[80]

The increasing theological pluralism and diversity of twentieth-century Presbyterianism led to the ascendance of polity, as polity became increasingly important in resolving theological differences. Several issues in the church were decided on the basis of polity rather than theology, despite the apparent theological nature of many of the discussions. Among these events which established the ascendance of polity were the debate surrounding a grant for Angela Davis, the PJC's decision to withhold ordination from Walter Kenyon, and Boston Presbytery's appeal to matters of order in dealing with its ministers who were involved in the Community of Jesus.

If the ascendance of polity evoked fears of "heresy trials" for unacceptable polity, two subsequent cases retreated from this strict interpretation and saw polity attenuated and theology reaffirmed. By distinguishing between belief and action, the nuances of the Ellis decision indicated that it was indeed possible to disagree with church polity, provided one acted in accordance with church law. By recognizing the continued potential for distinguishing orthodoxy from unorthodoxy, the Kaseman decision indicated that a candidate's theology was still a valid issue in the PC(USA).

The newly reunited PC(USA) has continued the legitimation of theological pluralism by its adoption of the contemporary Confession of 1967, of the inclusive *Book of Confessions,* and of an ordination vow that is more lenient regarding the church's confessions. The PC(USA) appears, however, to have taken the more attenuated approach to church polity. By ratifying the 1977 Ellis decision in its reconsideration of the issue, the PJC indicated that its interpretation of polity would tend more toward the relatively lenient approach taken by the PCUS in the earlier Ellis case, rather than the stricter course previously taken in the Kenyon case.

As the Presbyterian Church moves away from a unified confessional stance, polity becomes increasingly important as a source of denominational identity. Theology is not less important than polity; it is simply no longer possible to identify a single, coherent Presbyterian theology. As one General Assembly report declares, "The fact that the church permits diversity of theological beliefs but in many areas requires uniformity of practice does not exalt polity over theology. It is simply a recognition that in at least some areas practice must be uniform in order to define the church's identity."[81] Indeed, theological issues of order, equality, and accountability are at stake in Presbyterian polity. In an era of increasing theological pluralism and growing ecumenical relationships with other churches, the enduring contribution of the Presbyterian Church may well lie in its polity.

12

The National Organizational Structures of Protestant Denominations: An Invitation to a Conversation

Craig Dykstra and
James Hudnut-Beumler

Introduction

This essay is an invitation to a conversation. We want to suggest a series of metaphors that describe changing patterns of denominational life over the past 150 years in order to see if these metaphors have any power to illuminate the nature of some of the frustrations that we sense are widely experienced in mainstream Protestant denominational life. In doing so, we hope to ask about the whole range of denominational institutional life, but to focus especially on how denominations are organized and governed at a national level.

This is an invitation to a conversation because we really want to ask whether these metaphors are useful. We are raising a question to which we hope others will respond. It is a question to history. We are asking whether this way of describing the developing shape of denominational ecologies is true to the events of the past and illuminates patterns in that past in a way that provides fresh insight.

The series of metaphors we want to suggest is the following. First, we suggest that for the period from the late eighteenth century to the late nineteenth century, denominational governance can be understood best by the metaphor of *constitutional confederacy*. Second, we believe that during the late nineteenth century and, with increasing momentum, the early twentieth, denominations became organized into bureaucracies that are best described by the metaphor of the *corporation*. Then, third, beginning probably in the mid- to late 1960s, the nature of these bureaucracies shifted in an important way, so that they have become less like corporations and more like *regulatory agencies*.

In this study we will try to say what we mean by each of these metaphors and provide some historical evidence to justify these descriptions. It is clear that mainstream Protestant denominations are facing serious difficulties today, and we acknowledge that we think the current, dominant form of national denominational governance is in important ways dysfunctional. Ways to move beyond that form into an alternative dominant image and structure must be found. But we also want to stress that this is not one of those pessimistic histories like the Puritan declension sermons that narrate past events in a litany of regress toward "our present troubles." The simple truth about the history of American denominations is that national-level bodies have taken on different forms over time according to the religious and social needs and pressures of the times. It is neither good nor bad that they took particular forms except to the extent that those forms did or did not meet the legitimate needs of the people and the gospel. In every case, including the present, the forms that have prevailed have both strengths and weaknesses.

The Constitutional Confederacy

As hard as it might be to conceive for those of us who are accustomed to thinking about religion denominationally, denominations as such were a peculiarly American innovation when they came into being in the 1780s and 1790s. From the founding of Jamestown in 1607, and for another 180 years, the intention of those who brought Old World faith to the English colonies in America was to perpetuate "in the new land" religious patterns to which the mother country had grown accustomed.[1] The practical problem with this intention was, of course, that the American colonies were host not only to transplanted churches from different "mother" countries but also to different theological and ecclesiastical arrangements of single European traditions. Thus Congregationalists in New England and Anglicans in Virginia could both see themselves as legitimate expressions of the Church of England.

Just over a century ago, Philip Schaff argued that religious liberty arose because the Congress really had no choice. If there was to be a nation, then there necessarily must be no national church. That much seems true; but it also was true conversely that the fact of nationhood forced the emergence of a new understanding as to the acceptable forms of the church in the new United States. Prior to 1776 the religious groups of the colonies were largely dependent on the metropolitan centers of Europe. Dutch Reformed ministers in New York were members of a classis in the Netherlands. German Reformed pastors in Pennsylvania belonged to a German classis. Most Presbyterian clergy in the middle colonies had been ordained in Scotland or northern Ireland. All Anglican and Catholic priests were ordained by bishops on the other side of the Atlantic. Gathered churches such as the Baptists and the Congregationalists had an organizational advantage because their congregations called and ordained their own ministers and teachers. Even so, these groups did not form national-level bodies until after the Declaration of Independence forced the issue of national identity. The Declaration of Independence had religious as well as political implications. If the nation was to be free, then American Methodists could no longer maintain the fiction kept alive in Britain that Methodism was just an outreach ministry of the Church of England.

John Wesley opposed the separation of Methodism from Anglicanism but ended up bowing late in life to the logic of a separate identity, which was forcefully articulated in the 1780s by American Methodists Thomas Coke and Francis Asbury. The so-called Christmas conference of 1784 in Baltimore, where Asbury was elected as the first Methodist bishop, is regarded as the date on which the organized Methodist Church was founded as an ecclesiastical organization. Not coincidentally, this occurred the year after it became clear that the British could no longer reverse the process of nation-forming and withdrew in defeat from their former colonies. The revolution also forced the hands of other churches into forming national organizations. Many Anglican priests fled back to England, but many Episcopalian lay people stayed, along with enough priests to rebuild the church. In that context they developed a strong argument for the ordination of at least three Anglican bishops for the United States so that the church might ordain its ministers without a transatlantic sojourn and indeed might perpetuate the episcopacy itself.

The initiative to solve the ecclesiastical problem of the Anglican communion came from the clergy of Connecticut. In 1783, ten Episcopal priests met and chose one of their own number, Samuel Seabury, who, after much difficulty, was consecrated a bishop by three Anglican bishops in Aberdeen, Scotland, in 1784. Over the next few years, William White was consecrated as Bishop of Pennsylvania and Samuel Provoost was made Bishop of New York, and a new denomination, the Protestant Episcopal Church in the United States of America, was formed in 1789.

The Presbyterians likewise formed themselves into a self-consciously American national body in 1789 when the Synod of New York and Philadelphia met to adopt the Westminster Confession as its standard of faith—with appropriate modifications in the sections about civil government—and a Form of Government as the standard by which to conduct its affairs throughout the new nation. This was the beginning of the Presbyterian Church in the U.S.A. and of its General Assembly.

Other churches continued to be missionary extensions of

their European counterparts well into the nineteenth century. While Congregationalism in New England continued to exist as an established church into the 1830s, it too had reasons to think denominationally outside the context of its home states. The national crisis for the Congregationalists was the same one that had been brewing since the Great Awakening in the 1730s: how to deal with not being an American state church, or at least how to deal with the existence of dissenters in their midst. The acceptance of religious toleration by the Standing Order was, therefore, Congregationalism's first act of capitulation to the rise of the denominational system.

With all these developments it is crucial to recognize, nonetheless, that the formation of national-level church bodies in the earliest years of the republic did *not* involve the formation of large-scale bureaucratic denominations as we know them today. They responded to the ecclesiastical problems of ministerial succession, guidance, and governance brought on by the fact of America's emergence as a separate nation, but the forms they used were not bureaucratic; they were constitutional. Churches became national bodies by constituting themselves as confederations.

At the same time as American politicians were writing state and federal constitutions, the lay and clergy church leaders were composing the Presbyterian Form of Government, the Methodist Book of Discipline, and the Constitution and Canons of the Protestant Episcopal Church. Constitutions were written, but things did not go much further than this. There was no perceived need for national action on social issues or even for collective coordination of charitable work. These denominations had no professional staff, nor were they charged with the production of any national goods or services, not even Sunday school materials.

All politics, it is often said, is local. At least in the churches of the colonial and early national periods, church politics was certainly largely local. Churches looked to a national-level body mainly for consistency in supply of ministers and common agreement on a framework in which to conduct local (namely, congregational and regional) church political affairs.

We have observed that church constitutions and national political constitutions were being created at the same time in the late eighteenth century. It is also instructive to note the parallels between the institutions that emerged from those creative acts. As the nation created frames of government—state and federal constitutions—without creating strong governmental agencies, so too did the churches create frameworks for interaction without actually creating a national program. Though the federal constitution allowed for the possibility of a federal department of health, education, and welfare, none was created. Likewise, the churches did not create boards of foreign or home missions or boards of Christian education.

The Corporation

The early national churches had developed into denominations as a response to the needs of the time. The next step in our story comes out of the growth of Jacksonian democracy in the life of the new nation. During what Henry Steele Commager designated "the era of reform," 1830–1860, Americans began to take on a wide variety of social issues and activities growing out of a faith in democracy (the belief that every person could and should take an active role in determining his or her destiny) and acceptance of the evangelical premises of the Second Great Awakening (the Arminian principle that all individuals could respond to God by free exercise of the will and thus effect their salvation). These two great notions, democracy and religious voluntarism, were the forces that created the America that Alexis de Tocqueville found so striking in his travels to America in the 1820s.

In *Democracy in America* (1835), Tocqueville voiced his belief that it was participation in voluntary associations, especially religious ones, that provided the key to the vitality of American democracy. These institutions allowed

Americans of like mind to come together to discuss and act on the issues that affected them most deeply, including those that affected their religious and moral sensibilities. Postrevolutionary France, Tocqueville's home, had already moved in the direction of a bureaucratic corporatist state. When there was a problem with roads or sewers or the growing number of hungry orphans, the response of the French individual was to ask what the government was doing about it. No wonder, then, that Tocqueville found it amazing that the typical American response was to form a group and take up a collection.

The voluntary societies formed by American Christians in the early nineteenth century were the next great step toward the corporate denomination so familiar to us today. But the most interesting aspects of their character are the ways in which they differed from modern denominations. They were, first of all, independent of local, regional, and national church bodies. Organized by groups of Christians to address needs unmet by church or society, the antislavery societies, the tract societies, the Bible societies, the prohibitionist societies, and even the home and foreign mission societies might or might not be associated with the members of a particular faith tradition.[2] Thus the ecclesiastical form of choice in the antebellum period was a weak central church government with a modest set of responsibilities coupled with a wide range of loosely related societies for Christian endeavors. This situation reflects a number of key social facts of our collective history.

On the positive side, as Tocqueville was quick to notice, the prevalence of voluntary religious societies reflected a belief in the power of individuals to organize for collective action. Their dominance also reflected a reluctance to solve large-scale problems through national bureaucracies. Remember, if you will, that it was during these same years that the country's banking system was in a perpetual state of chaos while all rational proposals for a central bank were routinely defeated.

More disturbing, though, the limited-function denomination and the spectrum of voluntary associations indicated deep tensions in American society and its churches. Many of the most important issues of nineteenth-century American religious life could not be safely discussed in national church meetings. The attempt to address the question of whether a Christian could hold slaves and still be served Communion, let alone remain in a state of grace, caused such pain to the 1818 Presbyterian General Assembly that it was decided that General Assemblies should not discuss such "political" issues. When, after eighteen years, northern evangelicals from New York and the Western Reserve could hold their tongues no longer, their insistence on going on record against slavery caused the church to split into the Old and New Schools. Methodists were similarly divided in 1844, and the weak alliance of Baptists to raise funds for missions was split in 1845 when Baptists from nine states withdrew and formed the Southern Baptist Convention.

After the Civil War, work for Reconstruction engaged a new set of voluntary organizations, the "freedmen's bureaus." These largely northern groups were responsible for hundreds of schools for the newly freed slaves. The amount of money that was collected, the urgency of the task, and the scale of activity undertaken helped nudge denominations further down the path of bureaucratic organization. Sidney Mead argues that these voluntary organizations—from the American Board of Commissioners for Foreign Missions to the relatively newer Student Volunteer Movement—all constituted a challenge to the role of churches in public life. Their success in enlisting the hearts and minds and dollars of religious individuals virtually guaranteed that from the late nineteenth century onward, religious bodies would seek more effective ways to represent themselves in public affairs.[3]

Transformations taking place in the larger culture also helped to effect the change. The theory of institutional isomorphism associated with sociologist Paul DiMaggio suggests that institutions developed in different fields within a culture in the same period will assume remarkably similar shapes. This, along with what we know about changes in

American government and business at the turn of the century, suggests that "religious bureaucratization stemmed, at least in part, from the bureaucratization and rationalization of other parts of society."[4] This was the age of trusts, collectives, and, above all, vertically integrated corporations. Is it surprising that religious denominations, led by clergy and business elites accustomed to thinking in the organizational categories of their time, should reorganize themselves on lines parallel to the worlds of business and government?

We do not mean to suggest that Protestant denominations chose to reorganize themselves to resemble business corporations merely because they wanted to be like business corporations. Timothy L. Smith has made the argument that the modern denomination evolved out of necessity as "a structural super-organization designed to give guidance, support, and discipline to local congregations" and not out of a design to meet some "high doctrine of denominationalism." He further argues that "the fulfillment of its functions required, however, a specific rationale, a permanent structure, and a leadership dedicated not only to serving the congregations but to perpetuating both the larger institution and their own place in it."[5] Smith's points about the leadership's interest in perpetuating the bureaucracy will occupy our attention shortly, but here we want to take slight issue with Smith over his statement that there was no "high doctrine of denominationalism" at work promoting the rise of the corporate church.

Social gospel leaders during this critical bureaucracy-formation period often made arguments for a reform politics that involved the application of "sound business principles" to governmental activities. They employed the same rhetoric when discussing their churches. A typical turn-of-the-century argument for denominationalism was made by no less a theologian than the modernist Baptist Shailer Mathews, who in a 1910 article entitled "Why I Am a Denominationalist" gave these among other reasons:

Why am I a denominationalist? I am a denominationalist, in the first place, because a man cannot engage effectively in church work without belonging to a denomination. As Christianity is organized today, a man who wishes to share in any really large Christian movement can work best in connection with the great societies which have been organized along denominational lines. In the second place, because each great body of Protestant Christians perpetuates the momentum of its past. There persists a denominational esprit de corps, which is a great reinforcement for the more fundamental Christian esprit de corps. In the third place, because I believe denominations are a desirable and practical method of organizing the church universal. Such a division insures the maintenance of certain aspects of Christian truth which might pass into desuetude if they did not mark out the task for definite groups of men and women.[6]

As we can see, Mathews was arguing for the modern, complex, mission- and service-oriented denomination as *the* correct expression of the church in the twentieth century, and he was doing so on much more than purely pragmatic grounds.

Thus, by 1900, for both practical and ideological reasons, the die had been cast for a corporate bureaucratic form of organization that would characterize American Protestantism at the national level for most of this century. Corporations are in the business of providing goods and services, and the modern denomination was no exception to this rule.

The first thing denominations typically did in the process of bureaucratic rationalization was to bring all mission boards, publications groups, even temperance associations related to the church under central control. Part of the issue here was efficiency and coordination of effort, but that was probably not the crux of the matter. Though there may have been some competition and duplication of effort on the mission field; for example, missionaries generally tended to be accommodating toward each other. The larger issue was denominational control of the foreign mission institutions' budgets—especially the income, which was considerable and much easier to raise than monies for domestic mission activities. The move to-

ward central control also resulted in a more denominationally oriented sense of programmatic accountability. So the
first product, if you will, of the corporate denomination
was a centralized mission effort, which, compared to its
predecessor efforts, was more broadly coordinated and
more clearly identified with the denomination. Where
there had been an Armenian mission appealing to every
congregation within the denomination, there was now a
unified giving campaign that highlighted the Armenian
mission activities as but one part of the total overseas mission of the church.

Other principal goods and services that the new religious
conglomerates provided included: Sunday school curriculum materials and boards of Christian education, providing guidance and resources; denominational magazines
and newspapers (alongside the many independent, denominationally related periodicals that continued to exist); departments of church architecture, which provided building
plans and advice; pension funds to provide for the clergy
in retirement (a relatively new concept in the twentieth
century in all but a few denominations); a pooled-risk in-
surance fund for the property of local churches; and even
agencies to help local churches raise funds and to provide
them with the offering envelopes to bring in those pledges
week after week.

The general conventions and assemblies of the denominations became, in effect, stockholders' meetings. Participants voted on actions prepared between meetings by
denominational executives. Unlike the typical large corporation, there was still some room for controversy and initiative, but given the complexity of these new national
organizations, the most that the voting groups representing
the local churches usually could do was to ratify or reject
agenda items controlled by someone else. Managers of
business corporations had church analogues in the field
and home secretaries, the presiding bishops, and the presidents and stated clerks of the denominations. Corporate
trustees were paralleled by the ministers and lay people,
almost always men, who came to headquarters several

times a year from the largest and wealthiest congregations
to serve on the boards and councils of the denominations.

This model managed to deliver an incredible array of
goods and services that "sold" in the sense that they were
well received by the market. At its peak in the 1950s, *Presbyterian Life* had a larger paid subscription list than *News-
week:* more than a million copies per issue. Members of all
the mainline churches between 1900 and 1960 could point
with pride to ever-increasing numbers of missionaries in
the field. The average church member was happy with his
or her association with the national church, since that association had multiple dimensions and most of them were
experienced positively. News of missionaries, denominational magazine stories of brave Christians standing up to
the forces of evil in China, and colorful Christian education materials with lots of pictures of happy children could
easily offset the occasionally disagreeable social pronouncement. Even the Fundamentalist-Modernist controversy of the 1920s did little damage to national-level
church prestige, since lay people tended toward a much
greater pragmatism in their theological stances than clergy
did.[7]

The Regulatory Agency

Beginning about 1960, the corporate model began to
break down. This happened for a variety of reasons. Some
of it had to do with decisions made concerning the goods
and services the corporation provided. For decades, a general consensus had prevailed between the corporate managers and trustees on the one hand and the people in the
pew on the other. In the 1960s and early '70s, this consensus began to crumble—and around issues that polarized
the larger society. For example, thoughtful American
Christians in mainline denominations began to be sensi-
tive both to American political and economic imperialism
and to the first-world Christian chauvinism present in so
much of the churches' own historical mission activities
abroad. At the same time, and perhaps for similar reasons,

these denominations began to experience a decline in personnel who chose traditional missionary roles. Thus, for some very good reasons, the mainline denominations began to call the missionaries home, dismantle their more evangelical enterprises, spin off overseas synods, conferences, and dioceses as independent churches, and invite the new sister churches to send their own missionaries to the United States as partners in mission.

While done for valid reasons relating to self-determination, cutting these traditional foreign missions activities was unpopular with the rank and file. Similar decisions were made—with similar effect—in the late 1960s to turn national missions activity over to local groups working with Indians, orphans, alcoholics, pregnant teenagers, and African-American schoolchildren. Especially important were decisions to abandon large-scale national youth ministry programs. To speak in marketing terms, the national churches were divesting themselves of some of their most popular products. Given this process alone, one could expect that the national appeal to the pocketbooks of church members would begin to diminish. But that was not all that diminished resources available to the national church bodies.

Membership in the mainline denominations peaked in the years 1965–1966, just after the tail end of the baby boom. Denominational bureaucracies had swelled in size during the 1950s as the popularity of religion fueled increases in religious giving that far exceeded the rate of growth in a very robust postwar economy. In the later 1960s and throughout the 1970s, however, the economy would slow its rate of growth, and religious giving would drop in relative, though not absolute, terms. Financing a sizeable church bureaucracy during these inflationary years on gifts diminishing in real value proved impossible. In most cases, the result was a vicious cycle of cuts of popular services and greater membership dissatisfaction.

As the corporation began to cut back the scope of the goods and services it was able to offer and as "consumer satisfaction" began to fall, a whole new constellation of cottage industries was formed to provide those services which once were provided by the corporate-model denomination. The Alban Institute is one example. It provides an array of consultancy services that denominational staff were once expected to offer—but now "on the market" and for a fee. Pony Express, a stewardship campaign that local churches can buy to raise funds the old-fashioned way, is another. In the 1970s, more and more local churches began to opt out of their own denomination's Sunday school curriculum materials. Sometimes it was a case of choosing to use another denomination's products; more often it was a decision to use a commercial curriculum from an independent house such as David C. Cook on the conservative side or Winston Press on the liberal.

The denominational corporations gave ground as initiators and sponsors not just in the production of goods and services but also in the initiation of issue-oriented and personal growth groups and activities as well. Locally based movements rather than nationally organized and maintained programs carried the day. The 1970s and 1980s saw a tremendous rise in the number and kinds of affinity and special-interest groups in American society in general. Among members of the denominations, such groups also caught on. These groups crossed the political spectrum and included everything from anti-war to pro-life groups. Affinity groups for gay and lesbian Christians as well as "twelve-step" self-help associations for those struggling with dependency patterns in their lives emerged. Educational and spiritual formation groupings cropped up across the landscape, often completely outside denominational sponsorship or even, at times, awareness.

Some of these groups emerged to fill perceived gaps in the denominations' programs and services. Some of them developed in protest against what the denominations were doing and providing. The denominational leadership took stands on public issues and provided resources for their discussion and debate that were not welcome in every quarter. In a time of considerable social transformation and profound political debate in the nation at large, the churches, too, found themselves in a period of conflict over what their denominations ought to believe and do. In many cases, then, particular goods and services provided from the denominational headquarters were being subjected to a kind and intensity of critical scrutiny that was new to all concerned. Thus, at the same time that financial resources for the corporation were declining in relative terms, consensus was breaking down about what the corporation would and should do and produce. In the process, the corporate model of denominational organization began to give way to a new form: the regulatory agency model.

The fact that the corporate model "gave way" to the regulatory agency is important to emphasize. This was a different kind of transition than the nineteenth-century transition to the development of the corporation. In that case, the corporate model had strong, positive advocates who believed the denomination should be intentionally structured along corporate lines. The shift to the regulatory model has had more the character of an inadvertent acceptance than an enthusiastic embrace. While many in the denominations have fought for *particular* strong regulations of aspects of denominational life, no one has argued that the denomination should become more like regulatory agencies in their fundamental structures. Rather, the shift has taken place through a slow accumulation of regulatory activity in a context of both the retrenchment of the corporation and the absence of a compelling constructive alternative. Because this transformation has been largely passive in nature, it is only recently that observers have become aware that a fundamental structural shift has, in fact, occurred.

The regulatory nature of the current denominational structure has two dimensions. First, in the face of competition over a steadily shrinking financial pie, regulation consists of the development of procedures and policies for adjudicating the distribution of dwindling resources. Second, regulation consists of the development of patterns of governance and control over the budgets and activities of

denominationally related institutions that the former corporation no longer can support and influence through the
provision of funds and services.

The rise of the regulatory agency pattern in denominational life is the (perhaps predictable) outcome of the decline in funding and personnel resources that the corporate
bureaucracies have suffered. Indeed, an economic understanding of the emergence of regulatory agencies in general
is illuminating in this case. One way that societies—and
institutions within them—can get the results they want
from organized activity is to allow price mechanisms to
function. Thus corporations and entrepreneurs compete in
a market. But markets will not always produce desired results. Virtually everyone in our society recognizes the need
for public defenders, for example, but individuals will not
pay for them personally. Therefore, agencies are created
and given the power to tax in order to provide the policing
forces and judiciaries we all need to regulate our common
life. The regulatory function of these agencies includes
making some things illegal, enacting a rule that says, for
example, "No smoking in public places." It also includes
making some things mandatory; for example, "All public
schools shall have teachers certified by the state."

Thus far the development of regulatory agencies seems a
straightforward means to address a broad social need. The
story gets more complicated, however. Because regulatory
mechanisms work so well to produce so many desirable
social outcomes, they are readily embraced by the regulatory agency itself as ways of "beating the market" on other
outcomes that the bureaucracy wishes to achieve. Indeed,
even when market solutions are available, regulation is often cheaper and more expedient than the alternatives. The
temptation to use them is thus often extremely difficult to
resist.

The same dynamic operates in denominational bureaucracies. Denominations "tax" themselves in order to provide a denominational infrastructure. It, too, has powers
of regulation. It may make some things illegal: "Non-
ordained persons shall not preside over Communion." It

can also make some things mandatory: "All ordained pastors shall have an accredited seminary degree." Denominations have exercised these powers from their beginnings. But like public bureaucracies that have regulatory powers, denominational agencies also find the temptation to "beat the market" hard to resist. Thus, when denominational leaders find they no longer have adequate educational resources or persuasive powers to influence social and ecclesiastical change, they attempt to mandate it through regulation.

Saying that the bureaucracies have found regulatory approaches difficult to resist may make it appear that we are arguing that denominational officials choose these mechanisms because they like them. Our argument ascribes no such intent to denominational leaders. Instead, it is our view that the denominational propensity toward regulation is the result primarily of structurally circumscribed options. In the current denominational ethos, if church leaders are to fulfill their assigned functions, they will almost necessarily find themselves resorting to regulation. Understanding the economic and social uses and limitations of regulation, therefore, is crucial for comprehending the contemporary denomination.

When regulatory powers are exercised in an economic market, especially by institutions that lack the financial power to enforce those regulations, anomalies may arise. In the Presbyterian Church, for example, one recent General Assembly mandated that the church's seminaries be made handicapped-accessible. The denomination, however, is no longer financially able to support much of what the seminaries normally do, and it contributed no additional funds to make this particular worthy goal financially feasible. Here regulation and the real authorization of action are split. Or, to take another example, a Presbyterian General Assembly also issued a social policy statement calling on all employers in society to provide workers with full health-care benefits. Unfortunately, this pronouncement came from a church that two years later concluded it was having a hard enough time administering a clergy health plan without taking on the burden of providing benefits for the thousands of low-paid secretaries and janitors working in its churches.

Other sorts of new dilemmas are faced by whole denominational systems when the turn to regulation becomes an institutional habit on the part of the bureaucracy. Take, for example, the issue of gender and racial inclusiveness. In many denominations, congregations are now required to give full consideration to women and minority candidates whenever they conduct a search for a pastor. In being forced by regulation to interview women and minority candidates, congregations have often discovered that a woman or minority candidate is indeed the best person for the job. And the regulations have provided important support for the transition to a more heterogeneous pastoral leadership in these denominations.

The effectiveness of this procedure should not, however, obscure the fact that force is being applied. Regulation is being used to compel a procedure, and there seems to be a cost. The cost often takes the form of a deepening resistance not only to the procedure required but, in some cases, also to the larger justice aim for the sake of which the procedure was designed in the first place. It may also breed resentment and even rebellion against the regulating body. Congregations may, for example, agree that everyone should be fairly considered for ordained office but at the same time resent being compelled to that consideration if they sense that their right to a certain degree of autonomy is being violated. In this context, a sense of alienation toward the denomination can grow.

This is a true dilemma for all concerned. Ethical and procedural justice often conflict in some ways, and it is difficult to determine in any particular case where regulation is necessary and where it will have diminishing returns or even overall unhappy consequences. The dilemma is sharp enough in the example we have given. Most mainstream Protestants generally agree with this particular ethical justice objective that regulation has been employed to achieve, yet even here, the strains that regulatory compulsion generates are great. The matter becomes even more difficult when regulation is used to pursue less broadly accepted or clear ethical aims.

The place of special-interest groups in the regulation-oriented denomination can be understood in part in this context. Special-interest groups are small-scale voluntary associations within which people may work together and exercise initiative in a manner almost impossible within a centralized bureaucracy. There have always been such groups in denominations, and they are usually set up to pursue some cause in the society or to provide some service in which their members (sometimes passionately) believe. In the regulatory situation, however, the energies of these groups are often bent in on the denominational regulatory function itself, to press or block action that the denomination is taking. That is, in addition to providing an outlet for volunteerism, such groups often act, in the context of regulation, like political action committees fighting guerilla wars within the denomination so that their views might prevail.[8] In reaction, the regulatory agency regulates further. This in turn creates a cycle of suspicion and conflict concerning the legitimacy of the interest groups themselves.

We can see this in the history of what the Presbyterian Church calls Chapter Nine organizations. These voluntary organizations receive some status and legitimacy by being officially recognized by the denomination. In turn, however, they place themselves, as chapter 9 of the denomination's *Book of Order* states, "subject always to the power of review and control vested by the Constitution in the several governing bodies of the church" (G-9.0602). Attempts at actual regulation by the denominational bureaucracy often generate resentment, and the groups plead for relief. Thus the action at the 1990 General Assembly, which seeks to eliminate chapter 9 from the *Book of Order* altogether, can be seen as an admission that the current regulatory patterns are not working.

The question, then, is not whether denominations should exercise powers of regulation. The question concerns how the necessary and appropriate function of regulation can be exercised most judiciously and in company with other powers of mutual influence and encouragement. The issue also revolves around the question of how denominational leadership can lead without the organization becoming defined primarily by mandatory regulation. Bureaucracies, especially in the context of voluntary association, are much more likely to thrive, we would suggest, when they are very cautious about *commanding* loyalties that can and should be earned by admittedly much slower and more expensive efforts of education, local communal deliberation, and persuasive appeal to the best instincts of the faithful.

Judicious restraint in regulation is difficult in the situation we have been describing, however, since regulation, as we have seen, is more an institutional habit under certain social and economic conditions than it is a personal inclination. All bureaucracies—public and private, corporate and regulatory—develop patterns of internal inertia. The sociologist Theda Skocpol was one of the first to note that the usual Marxian analysis (which saw politics as consisting of the contention between the masses and capitalists) had left out an important group—one that has interests and objectives of its own.[9] She argued that one would never understand Soviet Communism, or the United States government for that matter, until one noticed that bureaucracies were pursuing agendas of their own. And as one of the most powerful groups in the political system, they would often win.

Skocpol's basic point is instructive for denominational life, for there has arisen during the period of corporate and regulatory bureaucratization a virtual profession of "denominational executive." Often without meaning to or even wanting to, these executives find themselves pursuing an agenda relatively independent of local churches and even of the aggregate interests of the church on a national level. Members of this more or less permanent group of denominational officials often move from position to position within the national agency. Their primary colleagues are their peers in the bureaucracy and in other like organizations. And their interests tend to be focused on issues internal to the survival of the bureaucratic organization itself.

Under these conditions, it is not difficult to imagine that patterns of isolation from the larger church might emerge. This is reinforced in the *regulatory* bureaucracy in several ways. First, of course, the very interplay of regulation places officials in situations that are much more conflictual than does the interplay of providing goods and services. Our human distaste for such conflict naturally encourages us to avoid our opponents. Second, many denominational officials are now entering into national church work at a younger age and with less pastoral and local church experience than their counterparts earlier in the century. Denominational officials in the 1940s and 1950s typically came to national church work after having proven themselves in parish life or in the missionary field. Officials often still come by that traditional route, but many now enter into this specialized ministry directly from seminary or from secular employment. Third, denominational officials, like those who lead most bureaucracies in our society, are characteristically members of what some scholars have described as "the new middle class": people who receive their income not from the production of goods and services ("the old middle class"), but through the production and manipulation of information. Studies indicate that this broad group is typically possessed of a worldview that is quite distinct from those of both blue-collar workers and the business sector of society.[10] And while liberal social and political attitudes characterize this group, the cultural and economic chasm dividing the middle class as a whole from the poor still pertains in this case as well.

All these factors conspire to reinforce the development of the relatively separate regulatory agency institutions that have emerged within denominations largely due to broad economic and social conditions in mainstream Protestantism. Work under these conditions is often difficult. The patterns that have emerged often have a dispiriting effect on the very people who are officials within the bureaucracy itself. Those who have taken up positions in the denominational headquarters have done so precisely in order to minister with integrity in and for the sake of the larger church and world. They go there not to regulate but to provide essential resources and services and to exercise leadership. What they find, however, is an organization whose very structure and momentum virtually prohibit them from doing what they themselves often most want to do. Rather than producing valued and valuable goods and services, they find their time and energies consumed by participation in meetings and consultations internal to the bureaucracy itself, by engagement in conflicts among various parties in the larger system, and by the production of policy papers, regulations, sanctions, and inducements designed to keep the organization in a state of controlled equilibrium. When these activities dominate the lives of persons who go into this work with different intentions in mind, the effect on morale and perhaps even health is predictable. When the regulatory dynamics we have been describing become dominant in a bureaucratic organization, especially one situated in the context of a larger voluntary association whose fundamental purposes and powers are not essentially regulatory, even those responsible to lead it feel trapped.

Conclusion

In this essay, we have put forward three metaphors for describing changing patterns of national denominational organization in the United States over the past century and a half. Each of these metaphors points to an interplay between organizational structure and function. We suggest that in different historical periods, certain functions and structures tend to dominate.

In the earliest period of denominational development, the ascendant function was to create a polity and identity on grounds other than that of a state church model. The constitutional confederacy, borrowed in a sense from the larger nation-building that was simultaneously taking place, provided the structure to accomplish this function. Later, as churches mobilized for the efficient and effective production of broad-scale goods and services in a rapidly expanding nation, denominations again borrowed from the larger culture. This time the corporate structure seemed to meet its needs. In our current period, the regulatory function seems dominant, and the larger society's own expanding infrastructure of regulatory agencies, designed to adjudicate the distribution of limited centralized funds and to shape patterns of social, economic, and cultural interaction, seems again to have influenced Protestant denominational life.

The three functions we have outlined are functions that every large-scale organization will always have. Protestant denominations have always had regulatory responsibilities. They have in every era produced goods and services. And a constitutional polity marks them in every period. Our hypothesis is not that one such function is ever carried out to the exclusion of the others. Rather, it is that in various periods one or another seems to dominate. It molds the structure—and sets the prevailing tone—for the national denominational organization as a whole. But never does a complex organization such as a denomination carry out just one function. Nor does a denomination ever *become* a constitutional confederacy, a corporation, or a regulatory agency. Denominations are denominations, religious bodies. They are intrinsically different from all other large-scale organizations, no matter how much *like* other institutions they may be in certain important respects.

Our strategy in this chapter has been to lift up certain metaphors. We are asking whether we might get some purchase on the dilemmas that mainstream Protestant denominations now face by thinking metaphorically about institutional structures. Many denominational leaders with whom we have shared these ideas in private conversation—a fair number of "bureaucrats" among them—have said that this history of denominational organization rings true to them. They say it describes what they have been living through. To the extent that it does so, this exposition may be helpful to practitioners of church leadership, of whom much will be required in the years ahead.

We hope it may also prove a hypothesis worthy of a more careful exploration by historians and sociologists. Is this story a reasonable telling, and does it help make sense of events that seem anomalous outside its frame? Does it bring to our attention or lift into new significance data that have heretofore been left unattended? If so, then it will have served the heuristic purposes for which it is intended.

This essay is an invitation to conversation, both to church leaders and to researchers. But it is an invitation we issue with some sense of urgency. As we look at contemporary mainstream Protestant churches, it appears to us that the regulatory agency model is not working well enough to provide for the kind of national institutional governance our times require. Some way is needed out of the cycle of dissatisfaction that our current situation seems to breed. We suspect that the way will be found only as some new and compelling vision emerges of what a national denominational organization might fruitfully be.

Perhaps an alternative metaphor is just beyond our horizon. If the past is any indication, the churches may well borrow again from institutional patterns alive in the larger society. We seem to be living in a time of social structural change that runs fairly deep. What this means for us, we will have to wait and see. We can be sure, however, that the fashioning of new patterns of organizational life from whatever materials are at hand will require a good deal of imagination, care, and even courage.

A time of transition such as our own need not be a time of despair or of fear. We believe that the decade of the 1990s presents mainstream Protestant denominations with an enormous opportunity. Among other things, a large generation of young people is now coming into adulthood. Many of these are asking religious questions anew and seeking afresh to participate in communities whose sense of meaning and history runs deep. The mainstream Protestant denominations are blessed with theological, communal, and organizational resources of immense power, which in a new day and probably in a new way will be shaped for the good of many.

Notes

Series Foreword

1. Arthur M. Schlesinger, Sr., "A Critical Period in American Religion, 1875–1900," first appeared in the *Massachusetts Historical Society Proceedings* 64 (1930–32) and is reprinted in John M. Mulder and John F. Wilson, eds., *Religion in American History: Interpretive Essays* (Englewood Cliffs, N.J.: Prentice-Hall, 1978), pp. 302–317.

2. Robert T. Handy, "The American Religious Depression, 1925–1935," *Church History* 29 (1960), 3–16, reprinted in Mulder and Wilson, *Religion in American History,* pp. 431–444; Handy, *A Christian America: Protestant Hopes and Historical Realities,* 2nd ed. (New York: Oxford University Press, 1984), pp. 159–184.

3. Sydney E. Ahlstrom, "The Radical Turn in Theology and Ethics: Why It Occurred in the 1960s," *Annals of the American Academy of Political and Social Science* 387 (1970), 1–13, reprinted in Mulder and Wilson, *Religion in American History,* pp. 445–456; Ahlstrom, "The Traumatic Years: American Religion and Culture in the 1960s and 1970s," *Theology Today* 26 (1980), 504–522; Ahlstrom, *A Religious History of the American People* (New Haven, Conn.: Yale University Press, 1972), pp. 1079–1096.

4. Wade Clark Roof and William McKinney, *American Mainline Religion: Its Changing Shape and Future* (New Brunswick,

N.J.: Rutgers University Press, 1987); Robert Wuthnow, *The Restructuring of American Religion: Society and Faith Since World War II* (Princeton, N.J.: Princeton University Press, 1988).

5. John V. Taylor, *The Primal Vision: Christian Presence Amid African Religion* (Philadelphia: Fortress Press, 1964), chapter 13, "The Practice of Presence" pp. 196–205.

Introduction

1. Robert T. Handy, *A Christian America: Protestant Hopes and Historical Realities,* rev. ed. (New York: Oxford University Press, 1984), pp. 3–23; Perry Miller, *Nature's Nation* (Cambridge, Mass.: Harvard University Press, 1967), pp. 150–162.

2. H. Richard Niebuhr, *The Social Sources of Denominationalism* (New York, Henry Holt & Co., 1929).

3. Russell E. Richey, ed., *Denominationalism* (Nashville: Abingdon Press, 1977); Sidney E. Mead, *The Lively Experiment: The Shaping of Christianity in America* (New York: Harper & Row, 1963), pp. 16–37, 103–188; Andrew M. Greeley, *The Denominational Society* (Glenview, Ill.: Scott, Foresman & Co., 1972).

4. A noteworthy exception is Paul M. Harrison, *Authority and Power in the Free Church Tradition* (Princeton, N.J.: Princeton University Press, 1959).

5. *Chronicle of Higher Education,* July 11, 1990.

6. Peter Drucker, *The New Realities: In Government and Politics, in Economics and Society, in Business, Technology, and World View* (New York: Harper & Row, 1989).

7. Robert H. Wiebe, *The Search for Order, 1877–1920* (New York: Hill & Wang, 1967).

8. Robert H. Bremner, *American Philanthropy* (Chicago: University of Chicago Press, 1960).

9. Nesbitt, James D. "1963–1983: United Presbyterian Giving . . . " (table), revised June 26, 1984, in

10. Robert Wuthnow, *The Restructuring of American Religion: Society and Faith Since World War II* (Princeton, N.J.: Princeton University Press, 1988), pp. 71–99; Wade Clark Roof and William McKinney, *American Mainline Religion: Its Changing Shape and Future* (New Brunswick, N.J.: Rutgers University Press, 1987); as well as the essays by Donald Luidens, C. Kirk Hadaway, and Jon Robert Stone in *The Mainstream Protestant "Decline": The Presbyterian Pattern,* Milton J Coalter, John M.

Mulder, Louis B. Weeks, eds. (Louisville, Ky.: Westminster/John Knox Press, 1990).

11. Wuthnow, *The Restructuring of American Religion.*

12. See the essays edited by Milton J Coalter, John M. Mulder, and Louis B. Weeks, eds., in *The Confessional Mosaic: Presbyterians and Twentieth-Century Theology* (Louisville, Ky.: Westminster/John Knox Press, 1990) and in *The Pluralistic Vision: Presbyterians and Mainstream Protestant Education and Leadership* (Louisville, Ky.: Westminster/John Knox Press, 1991).

1: The Incorporation of the Presbyterians

1. I am deeply indebted to the works of a number of scholars, including Alan Trachtenberg, *The Incorporation of America: Culture and Society in the Gilded Age* (New York: Hill & Wang, 1982); Richard Reifsnyder, "The Reorganizational Impulse in American Protestantism: The Presbyterian Church (U.S.A.) as a Case Study (1783–1983)," Ph.D. dissertation, Princeton Theological Seminary, 1984; Ben Primer, *Protestants and American Business Methods* (U.M.I. Press, 1979); Alfred Chandler, *The Visible Hand: The Managerial Revolution in American Business* (Cambridge, Mass.: Harvard University Press, 1977); Robert Wiebe, *The Search for Order, 1877–1920* (New York: Hill & Wang, 1967); and Martin E. Marty, *Modern American Religion,* vol. 1: *The Irony of It All, 1893–1919* (Chicago: University of Chicago Press, 1986). Many others contributed to my thinking and to the text itself, especially John M. Mulder, Milton J Coalter, and Joel Alvis.

2. Leonard Trinterud, *The Forming of an American Tradition: A Re-examination of Colonial Presbyterianism* (Philadelphia: Westminster Press, 1949); John T. McNeill, *The History and Character of Calvinism* (New York: Oxford University Press, 1954).

3. Presbyterian Church U.S.A., *Book of Order* (Philadelphia: Thomas Bradford, 1789), pp. 138, 139.

4. Clifford S. Griffin, *Their Brothers' Keepers: Moral Stewardship in the United States, 1800–1865* (New Brunswick, N.J.: Rutgers University Press, 1960), especially "Organized for Control," pp. 23–43; Donald Mathews, "The Second Great Awakening as an Organizing Process, 1780–1830," *Religion in American History: Interpretive Essays,* John M. Mulder and John F. Wilson, eds. (Englewood Cliffs, N.J.: Prentice-Hall, 1978), pp. 199–217.

5. Fred J. Hood, "Presbyterianism and the New American Nation, 1783–1826" (Ph.D. dissertation, Princeton University, 1968), reoffered as *Reformed America: The Middle and Southern States, 1783–1837* (Tuscaloosa, Ala.: University of Alabama Press, 1980).

6. See my articles "The Presbyterian Church, Inc." and "Social Witness, Social Service, and Social Policy: Charles Stelzle and the Presbyterians," available in the Ernest White Library, Louisville Presbyterian Seminary.

7. Max Weber, *Theory of Social and Economic Organization,* Talcott Parsons, trans. (New York: Oxford University Press, 1947). See especially II. 2: "Legal Authority with a Bureaucratic Administrative Staff."

8. Chandler, *The Visible Hand;* see also his "Entrepreneurial Opportunity in Nineteenth Century America," in *Explorations in Entrepreneurial History* (Cambridge, Mass.: M.I.T. Press, 1962).

9. Wiebe, *The Search for Order,* pp. 44–75.

10. Ibid., chap. 6, "The Revolution in Values," pp. 133–163. Wiebe focuses on the change in Christian reliance on the doctrine of "providence" as one indication, pp. 133–134.

11. Chandler, *The Visible Hand,* pp. 484–500.

12. Trachtenberg, *The Incorporation of America.*

13. Ibid., pp. 236–238, 412–416.

14. Trachtenberg, *The Incorporation of America,* pp. 6–7. See also David Nachmias and David H. Rosenbloom, *Bureaucratic Government, USA* (New York: St. Martin's Press, 1980), chapter 9, "The Evolving Bureaucratic Citizen."

15. Interestingly, the sports events took place mainly on Sundays, and Presbyterian General Assemblies decried Sabbath violations until well into the 1920s.

16. Trachtenberg, *The Incorporation of America,* pp. 70–100.

17. Ibid.; see also George de Mare, with Joanne Summerfield, *Corporate Lives* (New York: Van Nostrand, Reinhold, 1982).

18. Kathy Ferguson, *The Feminist Case Against Bureaucracy* (Philadelphia: Temple University Press, 1984).

19. In this period, particularly, the term "bluestocking" was used to describe Presbyterians in popular literature. See my "Presbyterian Culture: Views from the Edge," in Jackson Carroll and Wade Clark Roof, eds., *Denominational Culture* (forthcoming) for an update on the "elitism."

20. Charles Stelzle, *The Church and Labor* (Boston: Houghton, Mifflin, 1907), pp. 20–21.

21. Chandler, *The Visible Hand,* passim.

22. Bruce David Forbes, "William Henry Roberts: Resistance to Change and Bureaucratic Adaptation," *Journal of Presbyterian History* 54 (1976), pp. 405–421. The penchant for Stated Clerks' sharing legal expertise certainly continued with more recent, annually re-edited publications of *Presbyterian Law for Local Sessions* and *Presbyterian Law for Presbyteries and Synods,* by both Eugene Carson Blake and William P. Thompson.

23. In the Presbyterian Church U.S.A., for example, *Minutes* of the 1880 Assembly consisted of a total of 496 pages. Those of the General Assembly of 1915 ran to more than 1,052. Reports of the permanent committees multiplied three times and more in size—from 508 pages in 1880 to 1,790 in 1915. Beyond the mere bulk, the prose became more convoluted, more laced with references to administrators, and more detailed regarding finances.

See also Ben Primer, *Protestants and American Business Methods.* Primer concerned himself with the Christian Church (Disciples of Christ), the Episcopalians, the Methodists, and the Southern Baptist Convention during the first decades of the twentieth century.

24. Again, the already perceptible trends increased in intensity.

25. James S. Coleman, *Power and the Structure of Society* (New York: W. W. Norton & Co., 1974).

26. *Minutes of the General Assembly of the Presbyterian Church in the United States of America* [cited hereafter in text as GA, PCUSA], 1879, pp. 621–623.

27. Reifsnyder, *The Reorganizational Impulse,* p. 294.

28. See Albert McGarrah, "Lecturer on Church Efficiency in McCormick Theological Seminary," *A Modern Church Program: A Study in Efficiency* (New York: Fleming H. Revell Co., 1915); *Modern Church Management* (New York: Fleming H. Revell Co., 1917); also Henry F. Cope, *Efficiency in the Sunday School* (New York: E. P. Dutton, n.d.).

29. Annual Report, bound as Part II, GA, PCUSA, 1871, p. 6.

30. Both also began the era with decidedly less involvement in the mainstream of American Christianity than did the PCUSA.

31. In fact, the study of congregations generally has trailed the study of most other aspects and "levels" of Presbyterianism. Even such incisive works as James F. Hopewell, *Congregation: Stories and Structures,* Barbara Wheeler, ed. (Philadelphia: Fortress Press, 1987) pay little attention to the prevalent bureaucratization and its effects on communal life.

32. Robert Bellah et al., *Habits of the Heart: Individualism and Commitment in American Life* (University of California Press, 1985), pp. 176–179, makes the point more broadly. According to that study, a second language of moral responsibility has also been lost, as well as the loss of communal expectations toward the "town fathers."

33. Robert W. Lynn and Elliott Wright, *The Big Little School* (Nashville: Abingdon Press, 1971, 1980), p. 107, cites the perspective of John Wanamaker as an example of efficiency in Sunday school and retail sales alike. See also *The Development of the Sunday Schools, 1780–1905* (Boston: Executive Committee of the International Sunday School Association, 1905) for a study of the classification of programs. Wallace M. Alston, "A History of Young People's Work in the Presbyterian Church (1861–1938)," Th.D. dissertation, Union Theological Seminary (Richmond, 1943). By 1910, the pressure for using the same scripture lessons in all age groups had become significant.

34. Such institutions as the YMCA and the YWCA later spun off from their earlier, evangelical Christian orientation. See Wade Clark Roof and William McKinney, *American Mainline Religion: Its Changing Shape and Future* (New Brunswick, N.J.: Rutgers University Press, 1987), pp. 40–71, for discussion of the more recent breakdown of ascriptive loyalties and the process of extravasation.

35. How such committees functioned would make a fascinating research topic, but the data would be difficult to obtain.

36. Moody was the one who made of revivalism "big business," according to William G. McLoughlin, *Modern Revivalism: Charles G. Finney to Billy Graham* (New York: Ronald Press, 1959), pp. 166–216. Moody established organizational criteria to determine selection of locations for his revival campaigns, among them sound financial support, the completion of the tabernacle, the suspension of "competing activities," and a promise that all mainline Protestant denominations in the area would be cooperative. See James F. Findlay, *Dwight L. Moody, American Evangelist, 1837–1899* (Chicago: University of Chicago Press, 1969), pp. 195–197.

37. I followed the *Christian Observer* after a Louisville revival and read of continuing revivals and "special meetings" lasting into a second year.

38. Archibald Davison, *Protestant Church Music in America* (Boston: E. C. Schirmer, 1933) for a study of attitudes and con-

ditions in the early part of the century. Leonard Ellinwood, *The History of American Church Music* (New York: Morehouse-Gorham, 1950) asserts that in some churches quartets had become popular much earlier in the century.

39. The minutes of various congregations I have studied show great attention to choir directors, musicians' requests, budget considerations regarding the organ, and other such matters.

40. That seems the time when congregations that could afford 50 percent for benevolence offerings became the paradigms for generosity.

41. Robert E. Thompson, *A History of the Presbyterian Church in the United States* (*sic*) (New York: Charles Scribner's Sons, 1895), pp. 230–231. He calls the section, "Polypragmatic Pastors."

42. Gary Smith, "The Spirit of Capitalism Revisited: Calvinists in the Industrial Revolution," *Journal of Presbyterian History* 59 (1981), pp. 481–497.

43. Herman C. Weber, *Statistics, Presbyterian Church, USA, 1826–1926* (n.p.: Board of Christian Education, 1927). The PCUSA grew from 578,671 in 1880 to 1,513,240 in 1915. The PCUS grew from 120,028 to 332,339 during the same period.

44. Indeed, the preparation of the design chart for General Assembly organization required the services of a consulting firm and the work of at least fifteen committees, together with numerous discussions and modifications in the General Assembly Council.

45. Weber, *Statistics,* p. 142; also, GA, PCUSA, 1870, 1871.

46. Ibid., pp. 51, 56. He related major growth to revival efforts, and he designated declines as resulting from wars and times of controversy. He also named the influenza epidemic of 1918–1919 as a major cause of membership decline.

47. Charles Stelzle, *A Son of the Bowery* (New York: George H. Doran, 1926), and *Principles of Successful Church Advertizing* (New York: Fleming H. Revell Co., 1908). On Stelzle, see George H. Nash, "Charles Stelzle: Social Gospel Pioneer," *Journal of Presbyterian History* 50 (1972), pp. 206–228, and John Duncan, "Charles Stelzle and the Labor Temple: Showplace for Presbyterian Concern," unpublished paper, 1984.

48. See John Piper, "Robert E. Speer on Christianity and Race," *Journal of Presbyterian History* 61 (1983) pp. 227–247; and my "Francis J. Grimké: Racism, World War I, and the Christian Life," *Journal of Presbyterian History* 51 (1973), pp. 471–488.

49. Julius Melton, *Presbyterian Worship in America* (Atlanta: John Knox Press, 1967), pp. 107–111. Hugh T. Kerr, "The 1906 Book of Common Worship: An Amusing Footnote," *Journal of Presbyterian History* 58 (1980), pp. 182–184, quotes one minister's speech opposing adoption: "We accept canned meat, canned milk, canned fruit, and canned vegetables, but we can't stand for canned prayers."

Kerr also quotes the poem of one William Lampton in reply:
"It's up to preachers everywhere,
     To drop the long and rambling prayer
 And try the best and latest brand
     Although the mossbacks called it 'canned.' "

50. Eugene Carson Blake, Stated Clerk of the UPCUSA, perhaps best illustrates the point, though pressures have existed on every one of them. See R. Douglas Brackenridge, *Eugene Carson Blake: Prophet with Portfolio* (New York: Seabury Press, 1977).

51. GA, PCUSA, 1902, pp. 10–26, for example, listed all Board of Home Missions locations in Alaska, the Synod of Indian Territory, and elsewhere. The list proved lengthy indeed. See also William E. Nelson, *The Roots of American Bureaucracy, 1830–1900* (Cambridge, Mass.: Harvard University Press, 1982), for a wider analysis of the same phenomenon.

52. In early decades, it may have been men's and women's Bible classes. More recently, singles groups and service bodies might function in a similar, semiautonomous fashion. Of late, friends have pointed to several congregations now designating one minister as the "executive pastor."

53. Richard Hutcheson, *The Wheel Within a Wheel* (Atlanta: John Knox Press, 1978), p. 229.

54. Ibid.

2: Managing the Mission: Church Restructuring in the Twentieth Century

1. Many of the issues discussed in this chapter are given fuller treatment in my dissertation, "The Reorganizational Impulse in American Protestantism: The Presbyterian Church (U.S.A.) as a Case Study (1788–1983)" (Ph.D. dissertation, Princeton Theological Seminary, 1984). Ben Primer, *Protestants and American Business Methods* (Ann Arbor, Mich.: UMI Research Press, 1979) explores organizational change in four denominations.

2. *Minutes of the General Assembly of the Presbyterian Church in the United States of America* [cited hereafter in text as GA, PCUSA], 1923, pp. 52, 58–88.

Although the term "bureaucracy" often has a negative connotation, I mean nothing pejorative by it. I use bureaucracy in the sense of Max Weber, to mean a rational authority which administers according to set rules and procedures, which involves hierarchical subordination of duties, and which presupposes specialized functions performed by qualified and trained experts. Bureaucracy, in Weber's model, is characteristic of a modern society, as opposed to societies or institutions relying on traditional or charismatic authority. See H. H. Gerth and C. Wright Mills, eds., *From Max Weber: Essays in Sociology* (New York: Oxford University Press, 1958), pp. 196–244.

3. Bruce David Forbes, "William Henry Roberts: Resistance to Change and Bureaucratic Adaptation," *Journal of Presbyterian History* 54 (Winter 1976): 405–421; GA, PCUSA, 1879, pp. 621–623; 1881, pp. 569–571; 1882, pp. 52–53.

4. Robert H. Wiebe, *The Search for Order, 1877–1920* (New York: Hill & Wang, 1967), pp. 11–43, gives an excellent treatment of social forces that impacted the church in significant ways.

5. For several excellent treatments of the efficiency movement see Samuel Haber, *Efficiency and Uplift: Scientific Management in the Progressive Era, 1890–1920* (Chicago: University of Chicago Press, 1964); Samuel P. Hays, *Conservation and the Gospel of Efficiency: The Progressive Conservation Movement, 1890–1920* (New York: Atheneum, 1975); and Alan Trachtenberg, *The Incorporation of America: Culture and Society in the Gilded Age* (New York: Hill & Wang, 1982).

6. Rolf Lunden, *Business and Religion in the American 1920s* (Westport, Conn.: Greenwood Press, 1988), pp. 5–56; William G. Shepherd, "John Timothy Stone: A Business Man in Religion," *The Christian Herald* 46 (January 27, 1923): 67, 79.

7. See GA, PCUSA, 1920, p. 250; General Assembly, Presbyterian Church in the U.S.A., Special Committee on the Reorganization and Consolidation of Boards and Agencies, 1920–23, *Minutes,* November 10, 1920, and December 14, 1920, Presbyterian Office of History, Philadelphia, Pa. [hereafter cited as SCRCBA *Minutes* and date]. On Speer, see William Reginald Wheeler, *A Man Sent from God: A Biography of Robert E. Speer* (Westwood, N.J.: Fleming H. Revell Co., 1956) and James A. Patterson, "Robert E. Speer and the Crisis of the American Prot-

estant Missionary Movement, 1920–1937" (Ph.D. dissertation, Princeton Theological Seminary, 1980), pp. 1–35.

8. Robert E. Speer to John Timothy Stone, November 6, 1920; Stone to Speer, November 12, 1920, correspondence and papers relating to the General Assembly's Special Committee on the Reorganization and Consolidation of Boards and Agencies, 1920–23, John Timothy Stone, MS, Presbyterian Office of History, Philadelphia, Pa. (hereafter, Stone papers).

9. "Conclusions of Robert E. Speer touching the subject of Board Consolidation," SCRCBA papers; Stone to Speer, November 12, 1920, Stone papers.

10. SCRCBA *Minutes,* February 24–25, 1921; GA, PCUSA, 1921, pp. 64–89; *The Continent,* May 26, 1921, pp. 640–650.

11. SCRCBA *Minutes,* October 4–5, 1921.

12. Statement presented by the Board of the Church Erection Fund to the SCRCBA, January 24, 1922, SCRCBA papers; statement presented by the Permanent Committee on Sabbath Observance to the SCRCBA, January 24, 1922, SCRCBA papers; transcript of interview with Dr. J. M. Gaston, January 24, 1922, SCRCBA papers; SCRCBA *Minutes,* December 6–7, 1921.

13. SCRCBA *Minutes,* December 6, 1921; transcript of interview with Margaret Hodge, January 24, 1922, SCRCBA papers; "Statement of the Woman's Board of Home Missions to the SCRCBA," January 24, 1922, SCRCBA papers; transcript of interview with Lucy Dawson, January 24, 1922, SCRCBA papers. See also Janet Harbison Penfield, "Women in the Presbyterian Church: An Historical Overview," *Journal of Presbyterian History* 55 (Summer 1977), pp. 118–121, and R. Douglas Brackenridge and Lois A. Boyd, "United Presbyterian Policy on Women and the Church: An Historical Overview," *Journal of Presbyterian History* 59 (Fall 1981), pp. 383–407.

14. Although in one sense the reorganization was a setback for women in eliminating a visible locus of women's responsibility and authority for mission, in another sense the reorganization provided a catalyst for fuller participation. Men and women worked together on a General Assembly board elected by the General Assembly, in which women could not vote. The incongruity of this situation undoubtedly accelerated constitutional changes that allowed women to be ordained as elders. For a different interpretation, see Elizabeth Howell Gripe, "Women, Restructuring, and Unrest in the 1920s," *Journal of Presbyterian History* 52 (Summer 1974), pp. 188–199.

15. See *The Presbyterian,* April 13, 1922, pp. 7, 9; *The Continent,* June 1, 1922, pp. 704–705; *The Presbyterian Banner,* June 8, 1922, p. 5; June 15, 1922, pp. 6–7.

16. Alfred D. Chandler, Jr., *Strategy and Structure: Chapters in the History of the Industrial Enterprise* (Cambridge, Mass.: M.I.T. Press, 1962), pp. 1–51; transcript of interview of the SCRCBA with David Wylie, January 24, 1922, SCRCBA papers.

17. I am indebted to Dr. Scott Brunger of the department of economics at Maryville College for insight into these parallels.

18. *The Presbyterian,* April 13, 1922, pp. 7, 9; *The Presbyterian Banner,* June 8, 1922, p. 5; John Timothy Stone to Frederick W. Hinitt, June 23, 1922; John Timothy Stone to John W. DeWitt, January 21, 1923, SCRCBA papers.

19. Gerth and Mills, *From Max Weber,* pp. 196–198; Robert Lee, "The Organizational Dilemma in American Protestantism," in *The Dilemma of Organizational Society,* Hendrik M. Ruitenbeek, ed. (New York: E.P. Dutton, 1963), pp. 147–175.

20. Donald Black, *Merging Mission and Unity* (Philadelphia: The Geneva Press, 1984), pp. 7–26; William Stanley Rycroft, *The Ecumenical Witness of The United Presbyterian Church in the U.S.A.* (Philadelphia: The Board of Christian Education, 1968); interview with Donald Black, New York, August 5, 1988; interview with George L. Hunt, Richmond, July 25, 1988; Philadelphia, Presbyterian Office of History, taped interview with John Coventry Smith, conducted by Gerald W. Gillette, October 5, 1978.

21. Ernest Trice Thompson, *Presbyterians in the South,* 3 vols. (Richmond: John Knox Press, 1963–1973), III, p. 210.

22. David W. A. Taylor, "A History of PCUS Program Structures," unpublished paper, May 6, 1981, pp. 1–7.

23. Thompson, *Presbyterians in the South,* III, pp. 365–371.

24. Thompson, *Presbyterians in the South,* III, pp. 371–373; Taylor, p. 8.

25. *Minutes of the General Assembly of the Presbyterian Church in the United States* [hereafter GA, PCUS], 1949, pp. 130–171. Thompson, *Presbyterians in the South,* III, pp. 373–377; Lois A. Boyd and R. Douglas Brackenridge, *Presbyterian Women in America: Two Centuries of a Quest for Status* (Westport, Conn.: Greenwood Press, 1983), pp. 207–224.

26. Sydney E. Ahlstrom, "The Radical Turn in Theology and Ethics: Why it Occurred in the 1960s," in *Religion in American History: Interpretive Essays,* John M. Mulder and John F. Wil-

son, eds. (Englewood Cliffs, N.J.: Prentice-Hall, 1978), pp. 445–456; Robert Wuthnow, *The Restructuring of American Religion: Society and Faith Since World War II* (Princeton, N.J.: Princeton University Press, 1988), pp. 3–13.

27. Interviews with Kenneth Neigh, Princeton, N.J., July 8, 1988; Earl Larson, Huntington, N.Y., December 4, 1987; Philadelphia, Presbyterian Office of History, taped interview with Max E. Browning, conducted by Charles E. Quirk, August 12, 1981.

28. *Minutes of the General Assembly of the United Presbyterian Church in the United States of America* (cited hereafter in text as GA, UPCUSA), 1963, pp. 45, 122; interview with William C. Schram, telephone, September 6, 1988.

29. *General Assembly Daily News,* May 26, 1965, p. 1.

30. John R. Fry, *The Trivialization of the United Presbyterian Church* (New York: Harper & Row, 1975), p. 18; Lewis Seymour Mudge, Jr., *Why Is the Church in the World?* (Philadelphia: The Board of Christian Education, 1967), pp. 7–12, 71–73.

31. Arthur M. Adams, "Communication and Decision in the United Presbyterian Church: Reflections on Administrative Principles and Practices," unpublished paper, Philadelphia, Office of History; GA, UPCUSA, 1968, pp. 245–290; 1969, pp. 476–515.

32. Wuthnow, *The Restructuring of American Religion,* pp. 132–172. Wuthnow argues that the strong hold of denominational ties waned and divisions appeared within each denomination regarding theological and ethical perspectives which were far more significant than distinctions between the denominations.

33. Alfred D. Chandler, Jr., *The Visible Hand: The Managerial Revolution in American Business* (Cambridge, Mass.: The Belknap Press of Harvard University Press, 1977), p. 1; Peter F. Drucker, *The Practice of Management* (New York: Harper & Brothers, 1954), pp. 3–17; Peter F. Drucker, *The New Society: The Anatomy of the Industrial Order* (New York: Harper & Brothers, 1949), pp. 203–212; interview with Neigh.

34. Richard G. Hutcheson, Jr., *Wheel Within the Wheel: Confronting the Management Crisis of the Pluralistic Church* (Atlanta: John Knox Press, 1979), pp. 15–22, 37–59; interview with Schram. Schram indicated that the committee undertook no formal study of management principles.

35. Interviews with Theophilus Taylor, telephone, August 17, 1988; William P. Thompson, New York, July 22, 1988; interviews with Neigh, Smith.

36. GA, UPCUSA, 1969, pp. 499–505; "Equipping the Saints for the Work of Ministry: Provisional Proposal Concerning Reorganization of the General Assembly Agencies," prepared for the Special Committee on Regional Synods and Church Administration by the subcommittee on National Agencies, January 14, 1969; interviews with James I. McCord, Princeton, May 24, 1988, Neigh, and Smith. The story about the reaction to Smith and Neigh's initiative is told in varying forms but with the same basic meaning.

37. Interviews with James Gailey, telephone, August 13, 1988, and Black. John Coventry Smith, in a taped interview with Gerald Gillette, October 5, 1978, indicated he had written a paper for the Mason Committee on January 8, 1970, emphasizing the importance of their spending time with the boards and not only working with the SCGAA. He felt it was ignored and he was never invited back to the committee.

38. "Minutes of the Special Committee on General Assembly Agencies, United Presbyterian Church in the U.S.A.," August 27–28, 1970; G. Mason Cadwell, Jr., "Functional Analysis: United Presbyterian Church in the U.S.A. Final Summary— Boards and Agencies," August 26, 1970; interviews with Black and McCord.

39. Interviews with Neigh and McCord.

40. *General Assembly Daily News,* May 20, 1972; May 24, 1972, p. 1; Dennis E. Shoemaker, "Ecclesiastical Future Shock: The Ordeal of Restructuring," *The Christian Century* 90 (March 14, 1973): 312–315. No one seems to be clear on who made the decision to terminate the entire staff, which everyone agrees was unfortunate.

41. The quoted comment was made to Kenneth Neigh by an administrator in response to Neigh's inquiry about why a particular man was not hired in the new structure. Neigh's colleague Max Browning, who later headed the Council on Administrative Services, later commented, "We've really lost . . . leadership that combines creativity with know-how to carry them out and the guts to do it. I think we're paying the price of a personnel process that will not give us that kind of leadership. I suspect at some point we're going to have to revise our whole approach to this open hiring thing because it is keeping us from getting the right people in." Taped interview with Charles E. Quirk.

42. G. Daniel Little, "Ten Years of GAMC," unpublished paper, March 18, 1983.

43. GA, PCUS, 1972, pp. 85–89. Interviews with William Fogleman, telephone, August 15, 1988; John F. Anderson, Jr., telephone, August 17, 1988; Sara Bernice Moseley, telephone, September 13, 1988.

44. Letter from James A. Millard, Jr., July 20, 1988; interviews with Fogleman; Robert Worley, telephone, November 29, 1988; and Lawrence Bottoms, Atlanta, August 1, 1988.

45. "Agentry" seems to be a word coined by the PCUS to refer to all the GA mission structures.

46. Interviews with Worley, Fogleman, and Moseley.

47. Fry, *The Trivialization of the United Presbyterian Church,* pp. 53–64; Janet Harbison Penfield, "Presbyterian Prognosis: Guarded," *The Christian Century* 95 (February 15, 1978): 158–163; interview with G. Daniel Little, telephone, August 12, 1988.

48. Interviews with McCord; Little; Frank Heinze, Fort Washington, Pa., August 3, 1988; and Margaret Thomas, telephone, September 10, 1988.

49. Interviews with Thomas and Larson; Margrethe B. J. Brown, "Restructuring as a Response to a New Era in Mission," *International Review of Missions* 61 (October 1972), pp. 382–383.

50. Fry, *Trivialization,* pp. 50–56; interview with Little. There was some passionate feeling about the spending of reserves. Smith says he differed with Neigh over the wisdom of spending the boards' reserves before they went out of existence.

51. Fry, *Trivialization,* pp. 53–64; interviews with Little and McCord.

52. Interviews with Heinze, Black, and Robert Rodisch, telephone, November 14, 1988.

53. Interviews with Little, Black, and Thomas.

54. Interviews with Moseley and Anderson.

55. Interviews with Fogleman, Moseley, and G. Thompson Brown, Atlanta, August 1, 1988.

56. *GA Minutes,* PCUS, 1976, pp. 112–127; interviews with Moseley and Patricia McClurg, telephone, September 7, 1988.

57. Interview with Little; interview with McCord.

58. Fry, *Trivialization,* p. 55.

59. *Minutes of the General Assembly of the Presbyterian Church (U.S.A.)* (cited hereafter as GA, PC(USA), [year]), 1986, p. 367.

60. George L. Hunt, "Another Part of the Problem," *The Presbyterian Outlook,* March 28, 1988: 8.

61. *The Plan for Reunion of the Presbyterian Church in the*

United States and the United Presbyterian Church in the United States of America to form the Presbyterian Church (U.S.A.) (New York and Atlanta: Joint Committee on Presbyterian Union, 1981), pp. 13–31; interviews with Fogleman and Thomas; GA, PCUS, 1983, p. 648.

62. *The Presbyterian Outlook,* April 23, 1984; interviews with Black and Moseley.

63. *The Presbyterian Outlook,* September 5–12, 1983; September 26, 1983; and October 10, 1983.

64. *The Presbyterian Outlook,* May 28, 1984; June 18, 1984; and June 25, 1984; GA, PC(USA), 1984, pp. 151–161; interviews with Hunt and McClurg.

65. GA, PC(USA), 1985, pp. 48–51, 186–188, 240–249; Jack Rogers, "Renewal of the Church," in *A Call to Renewal,* William P. Showalter, ed. (Orleans, Mass.: Paraclete Press, 1989), pp. 21–31.

66. GA, PC(USA), 1986, pp. 57–58, 68–73, 362–418; *The Presbyterian Outlook,* September 9, 1985, pp. 2–4; November 11, 1985, pp. 8–9.

67. Interviews with Oscar McCloud, New York, September 21, 1988; S. David Stoner, September 14, 1988; and Brown; Rogers, "Renewal of the Church," p. 25.

68. GA, PC(USA), 1987, pp. 28–29, 62–65, 190; interview with Hunt.

69. Interviews with Anderson, Moseley, Black, Fogleman, Thomas, and Stoner.

70. *The Presbyterian Outlook,* May 4, 1987; April 24, 1989, pp. 3–4; May 15, 1989, p. 11.

71. Church organization theorist and consultant Robert C. Worley argues that leaders have to learn how to build their own mandates, since they are not built into the structure. There has been a rebellion against an elitist style of leadership, but the church has not developed satisfactory alternatives. Leaders in the church will be those who take the structures and build their own legitimacy. Interview with Worley.

72. Interview with Fogleman; *The Presbyterian Outlook,* May 1, 1989, pp. 3–4.

73. Leonard I. Sweet, "From Catacombs to Basilica: The Dilemma of Oldline Protestantism," *The Christian Century* 105 (November 2, 1988): 981–984.

74. Peter F. Drucker, *The Practice of Management,* p. 194; Wuthnow, *The Restructuring of American Religion,* pp. 132–172.

75. John H. Leith, *The Reformed Imperative: What the Church Has to Say that No One Else Can Say* (Philadelphia: Westminster Press, 1988).

3: The American Presbytery in the Twentieth Century

1. These churches include those founded as a result of British and American Presbyterian missions in Asia, Africa, and Latin America.

2. In the Netherlands, the comparable body is called a "classis." German Reformed and other churches use the term "*Presbyterium*" to designate congregational entities.

3. Few interpreters of Presbyterian polity have looked carefully at the canon law tradition of the Western church catholic, which is itself indebted to older traditions of the Roman *jus publicum.* A Presbyterian who reads the latest revision of *The Code of Canon Law in English Translation* (London: Collins, 1983) will discover many similarities between the revised constitution of the Roman Catholic Church and the architecture, form, and content of Presbyterian constitutional documents. When Presbyterians refer to a congregation as a "particular church," when they use "powers of order" and "powers of jurisdiction" as a basic distinction to describe office and ordination, and when they ordain persons to three offices (minister, elder, deacon), they are operating within the framework of Western canon law.

Presbyterians and Roman Catholics also agree that constitutional ordering of the church is a way of doing the church's theology, a social embodiment of authoritative church teaching, and therefore a necessary and consistent companion to the church's confessions of faith. Cf. John Paul II, "Apostolic Constitution" given at Rome, January 25, 1983, upon the promulgation of the revised *Code* cited above, xiii–xiv.

4. The title "bishop" for pastors of congregations was reserved in the Scottish *First Book of Discipline* (FBD 1560) to the pastor of the principal kirk in the largest town of a "diocese" or "province" (used interchangeably), whom the General Assembly designated to function as a bishop or superintendent. The *Second Book of Discipline* (SBD 1578) defined *episkopos* as "all one with the ministers, as before was declared. For it is not a name of superiority and lordship, but of office and watching" (SBD XI, 10). The Westminster *Form of Presbyterial Church Government*

(WFPG 1645) uses "pastor" but not bishop, and uses the well-known *episkopos* texts from the New Testament (especially from Timothy and Titus) to proof-text its list of pastoral functions. The first American Presbyterian Form of Government (FG 1788) is entitled "Chapter III. Of Bishops or Pastors," and inserts here its only explanatory footnote:

"As the office and character of the gospel minister is particularly and fully described, in the holy scriptures, under the title of Bishop, and as this term is particularly expressive of his duty as a overseer of the flock, it ought not to be rejected."

These varying patterns of usage reflect changing polemical contexts in which Presbyterians sought to pursue their vision for rightly ordering the church and ministry. The title "bishop" for the pastor of a congregation was maintained in American Presbyterian constitutions until FG 1983.

5. The term "judicatory" was replaced in the 1983 Form of Government by "governing body." In most contexts in this essay, usage of the newer language would be anachronistic.

6. Representative lay participation in church government was original and universal in Reformed churches. Entitling the lay representatives as "elders," electing them for life, and ordaining them to an office developed gradually and differently in various Reformed churches.

7. Elders did not lay on hands in the ordination of ministers in the Presbyterian Church U.S.A. until after the formation of The United Presbyterian Church U.S.A. in 1958. See James Frederick Holper, "Presbyterial Office and Ordination in American Presbyterianism: A Liturgical-Historical Study," Ph.D. dissertation, University of Notre Dame, 1988 (Ann Arbor, Mich.: University Microfilms International, 1982), 442ff.

8. The requirement that three ministers lay on hands to ordain parallels the canon-law provision that three bishops be present to ordain or consecrate a bishop. The purpose of these provisions in both systems was to ensure continuity of ministry in the succession of the apostles, a concern that Presbyterians and other English-speaking Protestants shared even though their theories of ministerial legitimacy were nonsacramental.

9. Lewis Langley Wilkins, Jr., "The Presbytery: Gift and Problem" (D.Min. major project, McCormick Theological Seminary, 1978), pp. 63ff.

10. The polity was codified in 1689 by Walter Steuart (of Pardovan), *Collections and Observations methodized; concerning*

the worship, discipline and government of the Church of Scotland. In four books by Walter Steuart . . . To which is added, the form of process in the judicatories of the Church of Scotland as also, an abridgment of the acts of Parliament, relating to the Church of Scotland (Aberdeen: J. Findlay, 1802); usually cited as Pardovan's *Collections.*

11. See Robert S. Paul, *The Assembly of the Lord* (Edinburgh: T. & T. Clark, 1985).

12. Presbyterians did not draw parish boundaries; however, they organized congregations in the same way parishes had been organized in Great Britain. A very important new reframing of current historical views of religion in the American colonies before the Revolution is Jon Butler's *Awash in a Sea of Faith: Christianizing the American People,* Cambridge, Mass.: Harvard University Press, 1990. Butler shows that efforts to establish the church according to a European parish model in colonial America were more extensive and successful than has previously been recognized; see especially chapter 4, "The Renewal of Christian Authority," pp. 99–128.

13. FG 1788, Chapter IX. "Of the Presbyterial Assembly."

14. For the Southern frontier, but with larger implications, see Grady McWhiney, *Cracker Culture, Celtic Ways in the Old South* (Tuscaloosa, Ala., and London: The University of Alabama Press, 1988).

15. Holper, *"Presbyterial Office,"* p. 66.

16. Richard W. Reifsnyder, "The Reorganizational Impulse in American Protestantism: The Presbyterian Church (U.S.A.) as a Case Study (1783–1983)," Ph.D. dissertation, Princeton Theological Seminary, 1984, pp. 135ff.

17. The consequences of this delay are still to be seen in the demographics of American Presbyterianism. The states with the highest concentrations of Presbyterians within their borders, both in numbers and as a percentage of the population, are all east of the Appalachians. Lewis Wilkins, "The Present Profile of Ecumenical Relations in the Presbyterian Church U.S.," *Midstream* XV:1 (1976) 28ff.

18. See H. Richard Niebuhr, *The Social Sources of Denominationalism* (Magnolia, Mass.: Peter Smith Publishers, 1984).

19. "Mission" and a doctrine of the Holy Spirit were added to the Presbyterian Church U.S.A. version of the Westminster Confession at the time of union with the Cumberland Presbyterian Church in 1906.

20. As used in this paper, "northern" refers to those parts of the American Presbyterian Church that united to form The United Presbyterian Church in the United States of America (UPCUSA) prior to 1983: (1) the Presbyterian Church U.S.A. (1861–1958); (2) about two thirds of the Cumberland Presbyterian Church (1906–1983); (3) the United Presbyterian Church of North America (UPNA; part of UPCUSA 1958–1983). "Southern" refers to the church called the Presbyterian Church in the Confederate States of America (1861–1865) and the Presbyterian Church in the United States (PCUS, 1865–1983). Except for a few congregations in Pennsylvania and New Mexico, all the members of the PCUS lived in the Southeast, between Texas and Virginia. In 1983, about 10 percent of the members of the UPCUSA lived in the southeastern United States.

21. Reifsnyder, "Reorganizational Impulse," pp. 176f.

22. Reifsnyder, "Reorganizational Impulse," pp. 187f., and Holper, *Presbyterial Office,* pp. 245ff., deal in detail with different aspects of the Hodge-Thornwell debates.

23. There is an interesting parallel between Thornwell's view of "mission" in the church and Emil Brunner's ecumenically important 1930s slogan, "The Church exists by mission as fire exists by burning."

24. The "Address" was written by Thornwell. It was his last word on the points he had so long disputed with Hodge. *Minutes of the General Assembly of the Presbyterian Church in the Confederate States of America,* 1860, pp. 51–60.

25. *Minutes of the General Assembly of the Presbyterian Church in the United States of America* [cited hereafter in text as GA, PCUSA], 1901, Report of the Board of Missions.

26. *Minutes of the General Assembly of the Presbyterian Church in the United States,* 1901, Report of the Executive Committee of Home Missions.

27. After 1972 these funds were much reduced and lumped with other causes of the General Assembly Mission Board.

28. GA, PCUSA, 1901, Report of the Board of Home Missions.

29. Data for the Old School and New School churches are summarized in *Presbyterian Reunion: A Memorial Volume, 1837–1871* (New York: De Witt C. Lent & Company, 1870), pp. 493–504. Data for PCUSA and UPCUSA and PCUS, 1900–1980, are from General Assembly *Minutes.* The average presbytery in the North was almost three times as large in 1980 as in 1900 (264

percent); in the South, it was more than four times as large (405 percent). Presbyteries' average geographic size also increased as the number of presbyteries was reduced: from 293 in 1930 to 186 in 1980 in the North and from 92 in 1930 to 59 in 1980 in the South. Improved communication and transportation made larger presbyteries possible; mission and organizational efficiency made them desirable.

30. GA, PCUSA, 1921, Report of the Board of Publication and Sunday School Work, p. 320, describes one of these field staff systems.

31. See Reifsnyder, "Reorganizational Impulse," pp. 327ff.

32. GA, PCUSA, 1923, p. 72.

33. The largest synod in 1920 had 335,600 members and an average presbytery size of 16,800; the smallest had 1,366 members and an average presbytery size of 455.

34. Wilkins, "The Presbytery: Gift and Problem." In the following summary, the descriptions of the four types in my 1978 study are assumed to be valid. The account of their emergence and the names given to them are revised.

35. The "Stated Clerk Presbytery" in "The Presbytery: Gift and Problem."

36. The "Home Mission Superintendent Presbytery" in "The Presbytery: Gift and Problem."

37. E. T. Thompson, *Presbyterians in the South,* vol. 3 (Richmond: John Knox Press, 1973), p. 424, summarizes the various organizational incarnations of the domestic mission enterprise of the PCUS General Assembly. "As the South rose from the ashes, surplus funds were directed into the growing West, toward the frontiers of the church. With the growth of industry and the rise of the 'New South' [funds were] channeled . . . to promising areas in the South as a whole."

38. It is ironic that some of the presbytery home missions committees in southern presbyteries acquired the status of Hodge's boards when they formed corporations distinct from the presbytery, held sizable funds which they managed independently of the presbytery for practical purposes, and employed their own executive staff who were not accountable to the presbytery as a whole, but to the home missions committee.

39. If growth in numbers of congregations is taken as a sign of vitality in mission, it should be noted that the new church development boom after World War II actually reflects a decline from the levels of activity in organizing new churches in the "old fron-

tier" in the first half of the century. PCUS congregations grew 18 percent, from 2,959 to 3,487 between 1900 and 1940, despite a net decline of 77 churches in the Depression decade 1930–1940, the only decade of numerical decline in the history of the PCUS. Comparable statistics for the two churches in the decade of the 1970s are impossible because of changes in statistical reporting occasioned by the formation of union presbyteries. Suburban new church development continued to produce net growth in Presbyterian membership in the South through the 1960s, because most of the South's urban areas were "new cities" in which postwar suburban gains were not offset by the massive changing neighborhood losses that afflicted Presbyterian congregations in the older cities of the North. The number of PCUS churches peaked at 4,067 in 1980.

40. The membership of the UPCUSA in 1960, two years after the merger with the United Presbyterian Church of North America, was 3,260,000. The membership loss in the 1970s was approximately equivalent to the gain that resulted from the 1958 union. Throughout the twentieth century, the number of congregations in the northern church has declined in every decade except those in which unions occurred:

1900	7,779	
1910	10,051	+2,272 after Cumberland union
1920	9,842	− 209
1930	9,242	− 600
1940	8,733	− 509
1950	8,552	− 181
1960	9,383	+ 831 after UPNA union
1970	8,813	− 570
1980	8,832	+ 19 after Union presbyteries

41. For many years until the late 1960s, about 25 percent of all Presbyterian giving went to mission outside congregations and 75 percent was spent by the congregations. Congregations now spend close to 90 percent of every dollar and give 10 percent to mission at all levels.

42. See Reifsnyder, "Reorganizational Impulse," for an account of the processes that led to these changes.

43. The "Executive Presbyter Presbytery" in "The Presbytery: Gift and Problem."

44. Ten of twenty-nine presbytery directors of Christian education listed in 1930 *Minutes,* GA, PCUS, were in Texas.

45. Lewis Wilkins, "Nomocracy Versus Telocracy: An Institu-

tionalized Conflict in Presbyterian Polity" (unpublished paper, 1980) interprets conflicts between presbytery stated clerks and executive presbyters in the broad historical context of Presbyterian ecclesiology and government.

46. The "General Presbyter Presbytery" in "The Presbytery: Gift and Problem."

47. The losses of congregations to the Presbyterian Church in America and the Evangelical Presbyterian Church in the 1970s proved that these concerns were not misplaced.

48. Paul Donald Young, "A Clergy Recruitment System for Palo Duro Union Presbytery" (D.Min. major project, McCormick Theological Seminary, 1978), p. 5.

49. Wade Clark Roof and William McKinney, *American Mainline Religion: Its Changing Shape and Future* (New Brunswick, N.J., and London: Rutgers University Press, 1987), and Robert Wuthnow, *The Restructuring of American Religion: Society and Faith Since World War II* (Princeton, N.J.: Princeton University Press, 1988), convincingly dissect the corpse. Though Roof has said recently that new data on membership trends in mainline churches may modify his book's grim demographic projections in the next two or three years, there is no reason to believe that improvement in membership and giving alone will restore the mainline denominations to their former mission potency.

4: A Financial History of American Presbyterian Giving, 1923–1983

1. The inspiration for this equation is a prediction of charitable contributions in John J. McAuley, *Economic Forecasting for Business: Concepts and Applications* (Englewood Cliffs, N.J.: Prentice-Hall, 1986), pp. 402–403.

2. Council of Economic Advisers, *Economic Report of the President 1987* (Washington, D.C.: U.S. Government Printing Office) and U.S. Bureau of the Census, *Historical Statistics of the United States: Colonial Times to 1970* (Washington, D.C.: U.S. Government Printing Office).

3. Data and regression results are available on request from the authors or the library of Louisville Presbyterian Theological Seminary.

4. The authors of this paper have contributed separate studies of the allocations of funds within the denominations. See Robin Klay, "Changing Priorities: Allocation of Giving in the Presbyterian Church in the U.S.," p. 132, and Scott Brunger, "Global and Local Mission: Allocation of Giving in the Presbyterian Church in the U.S.A. and The United Presbyterian Church in the U.S.A., 1923–1982," p. 153 in this volume.

5: Changing Priorities: Allocation of Giving in the Presbyterian Church in the U.S.

1. An outline of the terminology used in this essay:
   A. Total member *contributions* are all offerings received by congregations.
   B. *Local congregation expenses* include all monies used by local churches for staff, program, and buildings.
      (1) *Current* expenses, except where noted otherwise, include:
         (a) ministers' salaries and benefits
         (b) other operational expenses
      (2) *Building* expenses
   C. *Benevolences* include that portion of contributions not used for local expenses.
      (1) Giving used for local and miscellaneous mission
         (a) *local congregational mission*—mission projects carried out by local congregations
         (b) *miscellaneous*—gifts made by local congregations to non-Presbyterian causes (that is, programs not officially sponsored by any level of the denomination)
      (2) Giving sent by congregations to *presbyteries* for their mission and administration
      (3) Giving sent by congregations to *synods* for their mission and administration
      (4) Giving sent by congregations to the *General Assembly* for its mission ("causes") and the denominational administration

2. All the data used are taken from annual *Minutes of the General Assembly of the Presbyterian Church in the United States* [cited hereafter in text as GA, PCUS]. Additional data on which

this essay is based are available from the author or the library of Louisville Presbyterian Theological Seminary.

3. A look at the underlying inflation, giving, and membership data for these years suggests that the bulge may have been related to a temporary slowdown in membership loss rates. Perhaps congregations had successfully been urged to meet various budgets despite rapid membership losses (8 percent between 1972 and 1976), and the momentum carried over into the 1976–1980 period, when membership losses had slowed somewhat. If so, this is remarkable, since real per capita income growth nationally was actually slower in this period of increased individual giving.

4. Some people who remember the era well cite disagreement between denominational leaders and parishioners about social policy as key examples of different priorities.

5. Interviews were conducted with a number of present and former presbytery and General Assembly officers, including John Kittle, G. B. Strickler, Flynn V. Long, James Andrews, and William Adams. These conversations helped identify some financial procedures used in the periods under study, as well as feelings about changes made in those procedures.

6. The imbalance of representation in the General Assembly (and other church courts) between laity and clergy can certainly lessen membership confidence in their decisions when divisive issues are at hand. Fifty percent of delegates to the General Assembly are clergy, though they represent only about 1 percent of the total Presbyterian membership. The principle of equal representation between clergy and laity in the courts of the church has been a basic feature of Presbyterian and Reformed polity. Despite this long tradition, it may have contributed to alienation and divisiveness, especially when clergy and laity have held significantly different visions of the priorities of the church. That division on many issues has been confirmed by the polls published in the *Presbyterian Panel* and by other studies. See Jeffrey K. Hadden, *The Gathering Storm in the Churches* (Garden City, N.Y.: Doubleday & Co., 1969), and Wade Clark Roof and William McKinney, *American Mainline Religion: Its Changing Shape and Future* (New Brunswick, N.J.: Rutgers University Press, 1987).

7. Michael Novak, *The Spirit of Democratic Capitalism* (New York: American Enterprise Institute/Simon & Schuster, 1982), p. 210.

**6: Global and Local Mission: Allocation of Giving in
the Presbyterian Church in the U.S.A. and The
United Presbyterian Church in the U.S.A.,
1923–1982**

1. Robin Klay, "Changing Priorities: Allocation of Giving in the Presbyterian Church in the U.S." in this volume, p. 132.

2. *Minutes of the General Assembly of the Presbyterian Church in the United States of America* [cited hereafter in text as GA, PCUSA], *1950,* Part I, pp. 274–282.

3. "Giving Trends and Funding Patterns in the Presbyterian Church (U.S.A.), 1973–88," a report by the Mission Funding Team, Stewardship and Communication Development Unit, Presbyterian Church (U.S.A.), July, 1989, p. 3.

4. The United Presbyterian Foundation, as it was named after 1973, originated in 1799 as The Trustees of the General Assembly of the Presbyterian Church in the United States of America. Instead of being reorganized like the other church structures in 1923, it was not until 1953 that it assumed the name of The Foundation of the Presbyterian Church in the U.S.A. in conformity with the Nonprofit Corporation Law of 1933. *Minutes of the General Assembly of The United Presbyterian Church in the United States of America,* Part I, pp. 475–476, 735.

5. See Richard W. Reifsnyder, "Managing the Mission: Church Restructuring in the Twentieth Century," in this volume, p. 55.

6. A. D. Chandler, *Strategy and Structure: Chapters in the History of American Industrial Enterprise* (Cambridge, Mass.: M.I.T. Press, 1962).

7. Steven Hymer, "The Efficiency (Contradictions) of Multinational Corporations," *American Economic Review,* Vol. 60, May 1970.

8. Clinton A. McCoy, Jr., "How This Mustard Seed Grew: The Origin and Impact of the Per Capita Apportionment as a Means of Financing the General Assembly," *American Presbyterians,* Vol. 66, Spring 1988.

9. This conclusion is similar to the report cited in note 3. The report states, "The percentage increase for non-Presbyterian giving over the past ten years is about the same as the percentage for church-wide mission."

10. Benton Johnson, "On Dropping the Subject: Presbyterians and Sabbath Observance in the Twentieth Century," in Milton J Coalter, John M. Mulder, and Louis Weeks, eds., *The Presbyte-*

rian Predicament: Six Perspectives (Louisville, Ky.: Westminster/ John Knox Press, 1990), pp. 90–108, and Benton Johnson, "From Old to New Agendas: Presbyterians and Social Issues in the Twentieth Century," in Coalter, Mulder, Weeks, eds., *The Confessional Mosaic: Presbyterians and Twentieth Century Theology* (Louisville, Ky.: Westminster/John Knox Press, 1990), p. 208.

11. The Rev. Canon Burgess Carr of Liberia spoke in a publicity film for the All-Africa Conference of Churches assembly in Zambia in the early 1970s.

7: A Financial History of Presbyterian Congregations Since World War II

1. It should be noted that the focus of this study is the congregation. Thus, statistics will be given for the average congregation, and explanations will be offered as they affect either congregational receipts or expenditures. Specifically, this approach differs from other studies in this volume, by Brunger and Klay, which analyze financial trends from the point of view of denominational structures.

2. Total congregational receipts are defined as "the total of all moneys received from January 1 to December 31 by all treasurers including the church treasurer and the treasurers of all boards and organizations of the congregation."

These statistics were derived from the *General Assembly Minutes* as follows:

1950–1970: The total of the three columns marked "Finances," which included the categories "Current Receipts," "Special Receipts," and "Benevolences"

1975: Column 12, marked "Total Receipts"

1980–1985: The sum of the columns under the major heading of "Receipts" minus "Subsidy or Aid," thus leaving the sum of contributions from "Living Donors" and "Bequests and Other Non-Living Donors"

3. The title Presbyterian Church (U.S.A.), or PC(USA), is used anachronistically to refer to the combined totals of the UPCUSA and the PCUS.

4. Dollar values were adjusted to offset the effects of inflation by using the consumer price index (CPI-U) for each year. The conversion is made as:

$$\text{Adjusted value} = \text{Current value} \times 100 \, / \, \text{CPI}$$

The resulting adjusted value is measured in 1967 real dollars. CPI values are taken from *World Book Almanac 1985.*

5. The membership of the average congregation was deduced by dividing the sum of the total membership of the PCUS and UPCUSA by the sum of the total number of congregations in each. For the years 1975 and 1980 data were taken from tables which accounted for union churches and union presbyteries. See, for example, the Research Division of the Support Agency, *Comparative Statistics 1984* (New York: Presbyterian Church (U.S.A.), p. 5, Table #1).

6. The level of personal contributions was calculated for each year by dividing the adjusted total receipts of the churches in the combined PC(USA) by the total number of their members.

7. These values were calculated by dividing personal contributions by per capita personal income (fig. 7.3 / fig. 7.5). It should be noted that this graph does not necessarily correspond exactly to the percentage of income given by the average member. Rather, per capita personal income simply modulates personal contributions to accommodate the increase in real earnings over time. Furthermore, the fact that per capita income for Presbyterians is typically higher than the national average does not affect the shape of this graph, because Presbyterians are taken to be more wealthy throughout the period of study.

8. Per capita personal income as measured by the United States Department of Commerce, Bureau of Economic Analysis, "Survey of Current Business," 44:8 (August 1964), 16; 56:8 (August 1976), 17; 67:8 (August 1987), 45.

9. Nathan Weber, ed., *Giving USA (1987),* (New York: American Association of Fund-Raising Counsel Trust for Philanthropy, 1988), pp. 11, 15, 72.

10. Some have suggested that sources of income other than personal contributions, particularly bequests, are the reason that total receipts increased. Although the number of congregations in the UPCUSA receiving bequests rose from 1,011 in 1960 to 1,657 in 1980, the average amount per bequest (adjusted for inflation) peaked around 1970 such that total bequest income for the denomination fell after 1975 (*Comparative Statistics 1982,* Table #17, p. 23). Because there is reason to believe that this data, gleaned from The United Presbyterian Foundation, is accurate but may not be complete (meaning that many bequests may go unreported), it was decided not to base any conclusions on these values.

A study in Southern California suggested that additional

sources of income may play a larger role in finances. In that region, it was found that some congregations were using the proceeds from business ventures such as a nursery school or property rental to augment the contributions of individuals. Again, no national conclusions can be drawn from such a small data set. D. Scott Cormode, "A Financial History of Southern California Presbyterian Congregations" (unpublished paper, 1988).

11. The data on expenditures apply only to UPCUSA congregations because detailed records of the various spending categories were not available for the PCUS.

12. This conclusion was based on comparing treasurers' reports to their congregations with the General Assembly statistics which were supposed to be based on them.

13. *Comparative Statistics 1975,* Table #10, 18; *Comparative Statistics 1982,* Table #12, 19.

14. The data ends in 1981 because the portion of these categories that came from former UPCUSA congregations after reunion could not be separated from PC(USA) data.

15. Values adjusted to counteract the effects of inflation.

16. See, for example, Robert Wuthnow, *The Restructuring of American Religion: Society and Faith Since World War II* (Princeton, N.J.: Princeton University Press, 1988), pp. 218–222.

17. This is an issue in which perception may be more poignant than reality. Although national leaders continue to point out that the UPCUSA General Assembly never gave any money to Angela Davis's defense, many Presbyterians assume it did.

18. Dean R. Hoge, *Division in the Protestant House: The Basic Reasons Behind Intra-Church Conflicts* (Philadelphia: Westminster Press, 1976), pp. 106–115, 118.

19. This discussion will focus on salaries of pastors from the former UPCUSA because specific data are available for this group that could not be found for their PCUS counterparts.

20. Median salary information was gleaned from *Monday Morning* as follows:

Average salaries as of 8/15/1960 and 8/1/1965: September 27, 1965

Average salaries as of 8/1/1965 and 8/1/1970: October 5, 1970

Median effective salary for calendar year 1975: December 17, 1979

Average salaries as of 8/1/1980 and 8/1/1985: November 18, 1985

The author would like to thank archivist Susan W. Miller of the Presbyterian Department of History for locating these figures.

21. Constant H. Jacquet, Jr., "Clergy Salaries and Income in 1982 in Eleven U.S. Denominations," *Yearbook of American and Canadian Churches, 1984,* Nashville: Abingdon Press, 1984, pp. 265–269. Robert L. Bonn, "Ministerial Income—1973," in *Yearbook of American and Canadian Churches, 1975* (Nashville: Abingdon Press, 1975), pp. 246–251.

22. Parish clergy are defined as those classified as either pastors, co-pastors, associate pastors, assistant pastors, or stated supply pastors, interim pastors, or temporary supply pastors. *Comparative Statistics 1975,* Table #7, 9. *Comparative Statistics 1980,* Table #11, 14. *Comparative Statistics 1986,* Table #10, 15.

23. Average pastoral expense per congregation (fig. 7.11) = Adjusted pastoral salary (fig. 7.9) × number of parish clergy per congregation (fig. 7.10).

24. The values used to describe adjusted total receipts will not correspond to those in figure 7.1 because, while figure 7.1 represents the combination of both the UPCUSA and the PCUS, the present discussion deals only with UPCUSA data.

25. Although the mission that the church is most likely to support is its own local program.

26. Such logic was employed in this essay to show that neither the Angela Davis affair nor Overture H altered the spending habits of congregations.

27. For further explanation of contextual and institutional factors at both the local and national levels, see Dean R. Hoge and David A. Roozen, "Some Sociological Conclusions About Church Trends," in *Understanding Church Growth and Decline (1950–1978),* Dean R. Hoge and David A. Roozen, eds. (New York: Pilgrim Press, 1979), pp. 321–325.

28. Steve Sangkwon Shim, *Korean Immigrant Churches Today in Southern California* (San Francisco: R&E Research Associates, 1977), p. 68.

29. Ibid., 70.

30. Hyung Sug Kim, "Young Nak Presbyterian Church in Los Angeles," 1987.

31. *Comparative Statistics 1985,* p. 13.

32. Hyung Sug Kim, "Young Nak Presbyterian Church," p. 1.

33. For further discussion of the ways in which a variety of local contexts have affected congregations, see Douglas A. Walrath, "Social Change and Local Churches: 1951–75" in *Under-*

standing Church Growth and Decline (1950–1978), Dean R. Hoge and David A. Roozen, eds., pp. 248–269.

34. R. Stephen Warner, *New Wine in Old Wineskins* (Berkeley, Calif.: University of California Press, 1988), p. 174.

35. Ibid., pp. 277–280. Denominational support is defined by Warner as the sum of per capita, general mission, and special offerings.

36. For further discussion on why Presbyterians contribute, see Research Division of the Support Agency, Presbyterian Church (U.S.A.), "Presbyterians and Stewardship," *Presbyterian Panel* (June 1987).

37. The particular causes an individual or group might hold dear vary widely. For a discussion of the ways in which these causes can be categorized into two major groups, see: Wuthnow, *The Restructuring of American Religion,* p. 131.

38. D. G. Reid, R. D. Linder, B. L. Shelly, and H. S. Stout, *Dictionary of Christianity in America* (Downers Grove, Ill.: Inter-Varsity Press, 1990), pp. 1227, 1228.

39. Henry K. Rowe quoted in Wade Clark Roof and William McKinney, *American Mainline Religion: Its Changing Shape and Future* (New Brunswick, N.J.: Rutgers University Press, 1987), p. 40. For a discussion of the relationship between localism and this intrinsic voluntarism, see William H. Swatos, Jr., "Beyond Denominationalism? Community and Culture in American Religion," *Journal for the Scientific Study of Religion* (September 1981): 218–227.

40. Ibid., p. 44.

41. Ibid., p. 41.

42. Wuthnow, *Restructuring of American Religion,* pp. 71–99, 218–222.

43. Ibid., p. 221. For an application of these conclusions directly to the Presbyterian Church, see Robert Wuthnow, "The Restructuring of American Presbyterianism: Turmoil in One Denomination," in *The Presbyterian Predicament: Six Perspectives,* Milton J Coalter, John M. Mulder, Louis B. Weeks, eds. (Louisville: Westminster/John Knox Press, 1990), pp. 27–48.

44. Ibid., pp. 100–131.

45. Sidney E. Mead, *The Lively Experiment: The Shaping of Christianity in America* (New York: Harper & Row, 1963), p. 104, quoted in Roof and McKinney, *American Mainline Religion,* p. 44. (Italics mine.)

46. Roof and McKinney, *American Mainline Religion,* p. 44.

47. Ibid., p. 50.

48. Ibid., pp. 63–67. One implication of this concept for mission interpretation and stewardship development is that pleas that focus on the institution, such as the fiftieth anniversary of the founding of a church, will have less appeal than those which describe the necessity of funds to accomplish a particular activity, such as new church development or feeding the hungry.

49. The "mission of the church" refers, theologically, to the task(s) intrinsic to the church universal. Mission is the acting out of the church's purpose in the world, all that the church does and is called to do.

50. Wuthnow, *Restructuring of American Religion,* p. 218.

51. For further development of the concept of identity, see Barbara Brown Zikmund, "Liberal Protestantism and the Language of Faith," in *Liberal Protestantism: Realities and Possibilities,* Robert S. Michaelsen and Wade Clark Roof, eds. (New York: Pilgrim Press, 1988), pp. 183–187. See also Phillip Hammond, "Religion and the Persistence of Identity," *Journal for the Scientific Study of Religion,* 27:1 (March 1988): 1–11.

52. Such a statement is meant neither to justify nor to indict, but only to call attention to a present reality.

53. Robert Bellah et al., *Habits of the Heart: Individualism and Commitment in American Life* (New York: Harper & Row, 1985). The concept of "communities of memory" (pp. 152ff.) is tremendously helpful in understanding how shared identity is worked out in everyday life. The present discussion of common history and language grows out of the concepts of "constructive narrative" and "second language" (p. 153).

54. Wuthnow, *Restructuring of American Religion,* p. 129.

55. Phillip E. Hammond, "In Search of a Protestant Twentieth Century: American Religion and Power Since 1900," *Review of Religion,* 24:4 (June 1983): 286–288.

56. John H. Leith, *The Reformed Imperative: What the Church Has to Say That No One Else Can Say* (Philadelphia: Westminster Press, 1988).

8: Money and Power: Presbyterian Women's Organizations in the Twentieth Century

1. This study encompasses the twentieth-century history of women's organizations in the Presbyterian Church in the United States (PCUS), the Presbyterian Church in the U.S.A. (PCUSA),

The United Presbyterian Church in the U.S.A. (UPCUSA), and the new PC(USA). The histories of women's organizations in the Cumberland Presbyterian Church and the United Presbyterian Church of North America (UPNA) have not been included.

2. Lois A. Boyd and R. Douglas Brackenridge, *Presbyterian Women in America: Two Centuries of a Quest for Status* (Westport, Conn.: Greenwood Press, 1983), pp. 56, 59, and 60.

3. Katherine McAfee Parker, transcript of interviews by Barbara Roche (Philadelphia: Presbyterian Historical Society, MS, C272, 614–621, folder 1, 1972–73), 3.

4. Boyd and Brackenridge, *Presbyterian Women,* p. 87; *Minutes of the General Assembly of the Presbyterian Church in the United States* [cited hereafter as GA, PCUS], 1957, Board of Women's Work, p. 9.

5. Wade Clark Roof and William McKinney, *American Mainline Religion: Its Changing Shape and Future* (New Brunswick, N.J.: Rutgers University Press, 1987), pp. 152–155.

6. The breakdown of attendance by ages at the July 1988 Churchwide Gathering was: 6% under 35; 26.5%, 35–50; 38%, 51–65; 24% over 65; 5.5%, unknown. Also of note, 38% were elders and 3.5% were clergy (Barbara A. Roche, "Drawn by the Water of Life," *Horizons* [September/October, 1988], 3).

These statistics show that 62% of those attending were age 51 or older. In 1987, 49% of all Presbyterians were age 55 or older (Presbyterian Panel, *Background Report for 1988–1990 Panel* [Louisville: Presbyterian Panel, 1988], Table 7: Age Distribution, 8). The average age of those attending the 1988 women's meeting was significantly higher than for the denomination as a whole.

7. *Minutes of the General Assembly of the Presbyterian Church in the United States of America,* 1890, p. 43.

8. Florence Hayes, *Daughters of Dorcas: The Story of the Work of Women for Home Missions since 1802* (New York: Presbyterian Church in the U.S.A., 1952), p. 123, quoted in Elizabeth Verdesi, *In but Still Out: Women in the Church* (Philadelphia: Westminster Press, 1976), p. 63, n. 19.

9. Boyd and Brackenridge, *Presbyterian Women,* pp. 50–54.

10. Ibid., p. 59.

11. *The Home Mission Monthly* (September 1923), p. 253, quoted in Verdesi, *In but Still Out,* pp. 193–194, n. 45.

12. Margaret Gibson Hummel, *The Amazing Heritage,* with references and resources assembled by Mildred Roe (Philadelphia: The Geneva Press, 1970), p. 52.

13. *Minutes of Woman's Board of Home Missions,* January 1922, p. 147, quoted in Verdesi, *In but Still Out,* p. 72, n. 40.

14. Discussion of the Woman's Conference of the Boards of Missions of a Woman's Organization, April 30–May 1, 1925: 14, 15, and 49 (Philadelphia: Presbyterian Historical Society, Record Group 81-41-15), quoted in Boyd and Brackenridge, 1983, p. 68, n. 38.

15. Hummel, *Amazing Heritage,* p. 73.

16. Ibid., pp. 82–83.

17. Parker, transcript, p. 56.

18. Ibid., pp. 45–46, 49, 50.

19. *Minutes of the General Assembly of The United Presbyterian Church in the United States of America* [cited hereafter in text as GA, UPCUSA], 1967, Part I, p. 80.

20. Hummel, *Amazing Heritage,* p. 93.

21. Elizabeth Howell Verdesi and Lillian McCulloch Taylor, *Our Rightful Place: The Story of Presbyterian Women 1970–1983* (New York and Atlanta: The Council on Women and the Church, the General Assembly Mission Board, and the Program Agency, Presbyterian Church (U.S.A.), 1985), pp. 31–33.

22. Ibid., pp. 33–34.

23. Ibid., pp. 36–37.

24. *Central Presbyterian,* December 16, 1885, quoted in Ernest Trice Thompson, *Presbyterians in the South* (Richmond: John Knox Press, 1973), vol. 3, p. 384, n. 1.

25. Hallie Paxson Winsborough, as told to Rosa Gibbins, *Yesteryears* (Atlanta: Assembly Committee on Woman's Work, 1937), pp. 22–23.

26. Mary D. Irvine and Alice L. Eastwood, *Pioneer Women of the Presbyterian Church, United States* (Richmond: Presbyterian Committee of Publication, 1923), pp. 51–52.

27. In 1913, the General Assemblies of the PCUS, PCUSA, and UPNA met concurrently in Atlanta. Evidently, union of the churches was being discussed, and an alarmed representative of the UPNA's Women's General Missionary Board sent a telegram to her Moderator asking him not to consider union with the southern church, because their women had chosen to have an auxiliary women's board rather than an independent board like the UPNA and PCUSA churches. The southern women, excited over their new national organization, were demoralized by the incident, which was publicized in the Atlanta newspapers. Winsborough wrote, "Truly, we seemed destined for criticism from

both the liberals and the conservatives!" (Winsborough, *Yesteryears,* p. 54).

28. Hallie Paxson Winsborough, *Report of the Woman's Auxiliary of the PCUS for the Seven Months Ending March 31, 1913* (Montreat, N.C.: The Presbyterian Study Center [Development of Women's Work, 1887–1972, box 1]).

29. Hallie Paxson Winsborough to the president of the Missionary Society, December 1912 (Montreat, N.C.: The Presbyterian Study Center [Development of Women's Work, 1887–1972, box 1]).

30. Winsborough, *Yesteryears,* p. 124.

31. Ibid., p. 128.

32. Ibid., p. 129.

33. Janie W. McGaughey, *On the Crest of the Present: A History of Women's Work* (Atlanta: PCUS, Board of Women's Work, 1961), p. 94.

34. Verdesi and Taylor, *Our Rightful Place,* p. 65.

35. Dorothy Barnard to Lillian McCulloch Taylor, March 7, 1985, quoted in Verdesi and Taylor, *Our Rightful Place,* p. 73, n. 12.

36. "Two Goodly Heritages," *Concern,* February 1977, p. 4.

37. Barnard to Taylor (see n. 35).

38. "Plan for Reunion of UPC and PCUS Rejected by UPC Women's Committee," *Presbyterian Survey,* April 1982, p. 39.

39. *The Manual for Presbyterian Women* (The National Executive Committee of United Presbyterian Women and the Women of the Church Committee), VI-3.

40. Lois A. Boyd and Douglas R. Brackenridge, "Reflections on Presbyterian Women's Quest for Equality," paper presented at the conference of the American Society of Church History, Louisville, April 29, 1989.

41. Marian Casper, address delivered at the General Assembly Mission Council, February 1974, quoted in Verdesi and Taylor, *Our Rightful Place,* p. 42.

42. "Two Goodly Heritages," pp. 3–4.

43. Verdesi and Taylor, *Our Rightful Place,* p. 66.

9: Men and Mission: The Shifting Fortunes of Presbyterian Men's Organizations in the Twentieth Century

1. Robert Wuthnow, *The Restructuring of American Religion: Society and Faith Since World War II* (Princeton, N.J.: Princeton

University Press, 1988). Most of the material relating to the history of men's work is found at the Historical Foundation for the Presbyterian Church U.S. in Montreat, N.C.; material for the Presbyterian Church U.S.A. and the United Presbyterian Church is located in the Presbyterian Historical Society in Philadelphia, Pa. Hereafter, material will be referred to as located in Historical Foundation, Montreat, or Historical Society, Philadelphia. Men's organizations often reported directly to their respective General Assemblies, and periodically would briefly summarize key historical developments. Most instructive are the following: Daniel W. Martin, "The United Presbyterian Church Policy on Men's Movement—an Historical Survey," *Journal of Presbyterian History* 59:3 (Fall 1981), 408–439; a brief historical summary is found in the pamphlet *A New Song: A Design for Presbyterian Men in Ministry* (prepared for the Core Working Group Presbyterian Men, 1985).

2. The best work to date relating the work of urban reform to a vision of moral righteousness is Paul Boyer, *Urban Masses and Moral Order in America 1820–1920* (Cambridge, Mass.: Harvard University Press, 1978). The literature on the social gospel movement is voluminous; the classic treatments are Charles Hopkins, *The Rise of the Social Gospel Movement in American Protestantism, 1865–1915* (New Haven: Yale University Press, 1967); and Henry F. May, *Protestant Churches and Industrial America* (New York: Harper & Brothers, 1949).

3. *Minutes of the General Assembly of the Presbyterian Church in the United States of America* [cited hereafter as GA, PCUSA], 1906, p. 57; *Report of the Brotherhood Convention, 1906,* Presbyterian Board of Publication, 1907, p. 8, Historical Society, Philadelphia.

4. GA, PCUSA, 1906, p. 60; *Report of the Brotherhood Convention, 1906,* pp. 10–12, 94, Historical Society, Philadelphia.

5. *Reports of the Brotherhood Convention, 1906–1911,* Historical Society, Philadelphia; Paul H. Heidebrecht, "Chicago Presbyterians and the Businessman's Religion, 1900–1920," *American Presbyterians,* Vol. 64 (Spring 1986), 39–48.

6. *Report of the Brotherhood Convention, 1906,* p. 100, Historical Society, Philadelphia; William B. Patterson, *Modern Church Brotherhoods* (New York: Fleming H. Revell Co., 1911).

7. G. W. Butler, "The Brotherhood and Civic Improvement," *Presbyterian Brotherhood,* Vol. 1 (February 1909), Historical Soci-

ety, Philadelphia; (statistics) GA, PCUSA, 1908, p. 60; Heide-brecht, "Chicago Presbyterians," p. 41.

8. "Report of the United Presbyterian Men's Movement," *Minutes of the General Assembly of the United Presbyterian Church of North America* [hereafter cited as GA, UPNA], 1908, pp. 164–168.

9. John Mott, *Five Decades and a Forward View* (New York: Harper & Brothers, 1939) (History of Laymen's Missionary Movement); Letter, Charles Rowland to James Jackson, May 28, 1954, Box 35-10 Men's Work, Historical Foundation, Montreat; Proceedings of Men's National Missionary Congress (New York Laymen's Missionary Movement, 1910), Historical Society, Phil-adelphia.

10. More recently, attention has been paid to "masculine" Christianity early in the twentieth century because of the work of Ann Douglas in her *The Feminization of American Culture* (New York: Alfred A. Knopf, 1977). Douglas asserted that in the nine-teenth century Protestantism became connected with a more feminine image and clergy participated in the sentimentalizing of American culture. In response, clergy from around the country pushed for a more masculine identity for Christianity, and Mark Matthews was among the most prominent. See Dale Soden, "Mark Allison Matthews: Seattle's Minister Rediscovered," *Pacific Northwest Quarterly,* 74 (April 1983), 50–58.

11. Schenectady, New York, Union Presbyterian Church, men's club minutes 1911–1915, Historical Society, Philadelphia.

12. William Weir, the general secretary for Men's Work for the PCUSA between 1916 and 1931, wrote several articles detailing some of the history and articulating his personal philosophy: "Men's Work in the Local Church," *Union Seminary Review* 40 (1929): 389–398; "The Men's Work of the Presbyterian Church U.S.A.," *Union Seminary Review* 40 (1929): 310–320; "Religious Movements Among Men," *Union Seminary Review* 41 (1929): 52–57. See also "Report of the General Committee of Home Missions," GA, UPNA, 1912, p. 35; GA, PCUSA, 1913, p. 124.

13. Interdenominational Men's Congress Program, December 11–12, 1930; Historical Society, Philadelphia.

14. See Minutes of Brotherhood of Andrew and Philip at Beth-any Church Philadelphia, 1911–1915; Historical Society, Phila-delphia.

15. Program Helps 1926–1935, Vol. I, Box 5-35 (Men's Work), Historical Foundation, Montreat; William Kennedy, "History of

Men's Work," November 8, 1966, Box 16–35, Historical Foundation, Montreat.

16. Program Helps 1926–1935, Vol. I, Box 5–35 (Men's Work), Historical Foundation, Montreat.

17. Assembly Men's Council Minutes, MSS Montreat; *Minutes of the General Assembly of the Presbyterian Church in the United States,* 1946, p. 74.

18. Presbyterian Men's Convention book, 1957. Prepared for national convention Miami, Florida, p. 29.

19. GA, PCUSA, 1944 report; *The Report of the Meeting of Presbyterian Men,* Palmer House, Chicago, 1948, prepared for the National Council of Presbyterian Men in the United States of America, pp. 25–31, Historical Society, Philadelphia.

20. Robert Bellah, "American Civil Religion," *Daedalus,* Journal of the American Academy of Arts and Sciences, 96 (Winter 1967): 1–21; Martin Marty, *The Shape of American Religion* (New York: Harper & Brothers, 1958), pp. 6–30; Robert Wuthnow, *The Restructuring of American Religion,* pp. 241–267.

21. Program Helps 1942–1947, Box 16–35 (Men's Work), MSS Montreat.

22. Ibid.

23. Ibid.

24. GA, PCUSA, 1948, pp. 49–50; *Minutes of the General Assembly of The United Presbyterian Church in the United States of America* [hereafter cited as GA, UPCUSA], 1958, pp. 214–215.

25. *A Progress Report: Presbyterian Men 1948–1956.* Prepared for the National Council of Presbyterian Men, Historical Society, Philadelphia.

26. *The Christian Century,* 74 (April 3, 1957): 412.

27. *Bulletin: United Presbyterian Men,* September 1959, p. 4.

28. Interview with Andy Andrews, June 2, 1988; Andy Andrews, "Report to General Assembly, Division of Men's Work," 1963, Historical Foundation, Montreat.

29. William Kennedy, "History of Men's Work," November 8, 1966, Box 16–35, Historical Foundation, Montreat.

30. *The Future Involvement of Men in the Presbyterian Church in the United States,* Report by a Special Study Committee to the Board of Christian Education, 1968, Box 19–35, Historical Foundation, Montreat.

31. Ibid.

32. *Presbyterian Layman,* May 1968; *Presbyterian Layman,* January 1969: 8.

33. *A New Song: A Design for Presbyterian Men in Ministry.* Prepared for Core Working Group Presbyterian Men, 1985, p. 6.

10: Special-Interest Groups and American Presbyterianism

1. This scene from "First Presbyterian" is a composite drawn from sessions' responses to the report "Presbyterians and Peacemaking," which were shared with me during 1987.

2. Since the number of special organizations continues to grow and the complexity of the issues involved in enormous, I cannot address every group or all of their concerns. Events included in this essay extend through the 202nd General Assembly in 1990.

3. For Calvin's views on the relation of the church to the state see *The Institutes of the Christian Religion,* John T. McNeill, ed. (Philadelphia: Westminster Press, 1960), IV, XX, 1–32. An excellent analysis is provided by John T. McNeill, "Calvin and Civil Government," in *Readings in Calvin's Theology,* Donald K. McKim, ed. (Grand Rapids, Mich.: Baker Book House, 1984), pp. 260–74.

4. A popular survey of American Presbyterianism that describes these years is Lefferts A. Loetscher, *A Brief History of the Presbyterians,* 4th ed. (Philadelphia: Westminster Press, 1983). See also Robert T. Handy, *A Christian America: Protestant Hopes and Historical Realities* (New York: Oxford University Press, 1971).

5. For an account of the multiplication of benevolent societies in America during the nineteenth and twentieth centuries, see Robert Wuthnow, *The Restructuring of American Religion: Society and Faith Since World War II* (Princeton, N.J.: Princeton University Press, 1988), pp. 101–112.

6. A brief review of the history of special-purpose groups in the Presbyterian Church can be found in "Guidelines for Special Organizations Reporting Under G-9.0600," which was prepared by the Advisory Council on Discipleship and Worship of the PC(USA) in 1985.

7. See: "Guidelines for Special Organizations," 5–7.

8. *Minutes of the General Assembly of the Presbyterian Church (U.S.A.)* [cited hereafter in text as GA, PC(USA)], 1989, Part I, p. 739. The annual report of each Chapter Nine group can be found in the Assembly *Minutes;* however, these reports lack key information such as audited financial statements.

9. Editorial, "Loving, Not Leaving It," *The Presbyterian Layman,* Vol. 22, No. 6 (November–December 1989): 2.

10. The statement comes from a new member's brochure produced and circulated by the Witherspoon Society in 1987. The same brochure offers the information on causes supported by the Society.

11. For the Mission Statement of PNAODA see: *Alcohol-Drug Network News,* Vol. 13, No. 2 (Winter 1990): 2.

12. Wuthnow, *The Restructuring of American Religion,* pp. 100–131.

13. There are a host of studies that make essentially this same point. See especially Robert Wuthnow, *The Struggle for America's Soul: Evangelicals, Liberals, and Secularism* (Grand Rapids: William B. Eerdmans Publishing Co., 1989), pp. 72–76. Chapter 4, "Struggle in One Denomination," is an excellent resource on Presbyterian conflicts.

14. Wade Clark Roof, "The Church in the Centrifuge," *The Christian Century* 106 (November 8, 1989): 1012–1014.

15. Jack B. Rogers, "Renewal in the Church" (paper presented at the Presbyterians for Renewal meeting, St. Louis, Missouri, April 21, 1989).

16. Dwight A. White, "PBC Endorses PFR: Ends 24 Year Life," *The Presbyterian Communique* (May–June 1989): 1.

17. This material comes from a brochure entitled "How Can God Use You to Renew Our Denomination?" published and circulated by the Presbyterians United for Biblical Concerns, 1987.

18. White, "PBC Endorses PFR," 2.

19. William A. Brafford, "The Covenant Fellowship of Presbyterians, 1969–1989," *The Open Letter,* Vol. 20 (November–December 1989): 1. A detailed monograph tracing the early years of CFP has been written by Harry S. Hassall and is available through Highland Park Presbyterian Church, Dallas, Texas.

20. Ibid.

21. Ibid., 4.

22. From summary sheet of the conference, "A Call to Renewal," Dallas, Texas, May 18, 1988.

23. Ibid.

24. Ibid.

25. Jerry Van Marter, "Over 1,000 Are Present for the Birth of Renewal," *The News of the Presbyterian Church (U.S.A.)* (April 5, 1989): 5. Van Marter is quoting the Reverend Paul Watermulder

of Burlingame, California, chair of the temporary steering committee that planned the St. Louis meeting.

26. Jack B. Rogers, "The Renewal of the Church," *The Presbyterian Communique* (May–June 1989): 11–14.

27. See: "A Covenant for Renewal," *The Open Letter,* Vol. 20 (May–June 1989): 4.

28. Van Marter, "Over 1,000 Are Present for the Birth of Renewal," 5.

29. *Minutes of the 200th General Assembly of the Presbyterian Church (U.S.A.),* Part I, 1988, Report of the Task Force on Theological Pluralism Within the Presbyterian Community of Faith, p. 826.

30. Ibid., p. 839.

31. Ibid., p. 834.

32. Ibid., p. 829.

33. Ibid., p. 840.

34. Ibid.

35. Ibid., p. 849.

36. Wuthnow, *The Struggle for America's Soul,* p. 81.

37. Ibid., p. 89.

11: The Emerging Importance of Presbyterian Polity

1. Presbyterian Panel, *Background Report for 1988–1990 Panel* (Louisville: Presbyterian Panel, 1988), 1, 3.

2. Robert Wuthnow, *The Restructuring of American Religion: Society and Faith Since World War II,* Studies in Church and State, John F. Wilson, editor (Princeton, N.J.: Princeton University Press, 1988), pp. 87ff.

3. Minutes of the General Synod, in *Minutes of the Presbyterian Church in America (1706–1788),* Guy S. Klett, ed. (Philadelphia: Presbyterian Historical Society, 1976), p. 104.

4. Minutes of the Synod of New York and Philadelphia, in *Minutes of the Presbyterian Church in America (1706–1788),* pp. 628, 636.

5. For an account of this decline of confessionalism in the Presbyterian churches and the subsequent legitimation of theological pluralism, see David B. McCarthy, "The Distinctiveness of the Presbyterian Church: Polity as Theology" (M.Div. senior thesis, Harvard Divinity School, 1985), pp. 5–33.

6. Wuthnow, *Restructuring,* p. 69.

7. Dean R. Hoge et al., *Divisions in the Protestant House: The Basic Reasons Behind Intra-Church Conflicts* (Philadelphia: Westminster Press, 1976), p. 107.

8. *Minutes of the General Assembly of the UPCUSA* [cited hereafter in text as GA, UPCUSA], 1971, Part I, pp. 296, 506, and 512.

9. Hoge et al., *Divisions,* pp. 106–115.

10. John R. Fry, *The Trivialization of the United Presbyterian Church* (New York: Harper & Row, 1975), p. 41.

11. Ibid., p. 40.

12. Lois H. Stair to the Session Members of the Apostle United Presbyterian Church, July 13, 1971, Waukesha, Wisconsin (Philadelphia: Presbyterian Historical Society), 1.

13. See also Vic Jameson, news release (New York: Presbyterian Office of Information, November 27, 1975) and John H. Gerstner, "Disturbing Decision: Candidate Denied Ordination," *The Presbyterian Layman* 8 (February 1975): 1–3.

14. Joseph M. Hopkins, *Christianity Today,* 19 (March 28): 36–37.

15. "Lay committee head hits decision in Kenyon case," *A.D.* (Presbyterian edition), 4 (September 1975): 58–59.

16. "Ordination denied opponent of eldership for women," *A.D.* (Presbyterian edition), 4 (March 1975): 58.

17. William R. Hayes et al., *Report of the Sub-committee on the Question of Candidates for the Ministry who hold that it is Unscriptural to Ordain Women as an Elder or Minister* (Subcommittee of the UPC General Assembly Candidates and Credentials Committee, May 13, 1974), p. 12.

18. Mrs. Richard L. Kjos, "Letter to the editor," *A.D.* (Presbyterian edition), 4 (June 1975): 10; and Taffy Tarbell, "Letter to the editor," ibid.

19. Mayo Y. Smith, "Comment: On Conscience and Law," *A.D.* (Presbyterian edition), 4 (July–August 1975): 35.

20. Gerstner, "Disturbing Decision," 2.

21. See Lewis S. Mudge, ed., *Model for Ministry: A Report for Study Issued by the General Assembly Special Committee on the Theology of the Call* (Philadelphia: Office of the General Assembly of the United Presbyterian Church in the United States of America, 1970), pp. 17–19, 29–34.

22. *The Book of Order, 1990–91* (Louisville: The Office of the General Assembly), G-1.0306.

23. James Montgomery Boice, *Christianity Today,* 19 (June 6, 1975): 42–43.

24. William P. Thompson to Larry M. Hoyt [Executive Secretary, Presbyterians United for Biblical Concerns], February 5, 1975 (photocopy).

25. Robert Clyde Johnson, "The Reformation and the Ministry," in *The Church and Its Changing Ministry,* Robert Clyde Johnson, ed. (New York: The General Assembly of The United Presbyterian Church in the U.S.A.), pp. 53–62. Reprinted in part in "Ordination and Ministry," *Church and Society,* 67 (May–June 1977): 47–51.

26. See John H. Leith, *Introduction to the Reformed Tradition: A Way of Being the Christian Community,* rev. ed. (Atlanta: John Knox Press, 1981), p. 50.

27. See Mayo Y. Smith, "Comment."

28. Ted Menke, "Letter to the editor," *A.D.* (Presbyterian edition), 4 (June 1975): 10.

29. "Lay committee head" (see note 15), 58.

30. "Ordination of Women," *Presbyterian Outlook,* 159 (July 25, 1977): 6.

31. *An Open Letter to the United Presbyterian Church* (Presbyterians United for Biblical Concerns, February 1975).

32. Richard Lovelace to participants in a meeting of evangelical Presbyterians in Pittsburgh [apparently immediately following the 1975 UPCUSA General Assembly], n.d. (photocopy), p. 2.

33. *An Open Letter to Boston Presbytery* (Boston: Boston Presbytery, United Presbyterian Church in the United States of America, February, 1975), p. 1.

34. Richard Lovelace to members of the Boston Presbytery Special Committee on the Kenyon Case, April 28, 1975 (photocopy), p. 1.

35. Thompson to Hoyt, February 5, 1975.

36. Task Force to Study the Community of Jesus, *Report to General Council from the Task Force to Study the Community of Jesus,* adopted by Boston Presbytery on October 24, 1982, for recommendation to the General Assembly (Boston, Mass.: Boston Presbytery, 1982), p. 2.

37. Leon Howell, "The Controversial Community of Jesus," *The Christian Century,* 100 (April 6, 1983): 307.

38. Task Force, *Report to General Council,* 5.

39. Ibid., 3.

40. Howell, "Controversial Community," 303.

41. Quoted in Howell, "Controversial Community," 311, 312.

42. Task Force, *Report to General Council,* 3–4.

43. Synod of the Northeast, *Minutes of the Thirteenth Annual Meeting of the Synod of the Northeast of the Presbyterian Church (U.S.A.),* June 24–26, 1987 (Syracuse: Synod of the Northeast, 1987), pp. 33, 403–410.

44. Task Force, *Report to General Council,* 4–5.

45. *Minutes of the General Assembly of the Presbyterian Church in the United States* [cited hereafter as GA, PCUS], 1977, p. 112.

46. Presbytery of Atlanta, *Minutes of the Presbytery of Atlanta, 1975, 1976* (Atlanta: Presbytery of Atlanta, 1976), p. 84.

47. Ibid., pp. 88–89.

48. Synod of the Southeast, *Minutes, Synod of the Southeast, Fourth Session, Presbyterian College, Clinton, South Carolina, May 18–19, 1976,* pp. 64–65.

49. "High Court Sustains Preliminary Judgments In Ellis, Lyle Cases," *Presbyterian Survey* 67 (July 1977): 15.

50. Janet Harbison Penfield, "Presbyterian Prognosis: Guarded," *The Christian Century* 95 (1978): 159.

51. A few years later, in 1982, the PCUS reaffirmed the distinction it had drawn in the Ellis case between views and actions: the Fayetteville Presbytery (*Minutes,* 1981, p. 152; 1982, n.p.) had received the Reverend John Douglas Mark from the Presbyterian Church of Ireland, despite his views on "admitting baptized children to the Table and the ordination of women," which were deemed to be "not presently consistent" with the *Book of Church Order.* Several members of the presbytery filed a complaint, and the Synod of North Carolina subsequently sustained the presbytery, "noting the similarity of this case and that of the Reverend Thomas T. Ellis by the Presbytery of Atlanta" (*Minutes of the One Hundred and Seventieth Annual Session of the Synod of North Carolina (Presbyterian Church in the United States)* meeting at Richmond, Virginia, May 24–25, 1982, pp. 151–152). Although the General Assembly PJC sent the matter back to the presbytery to reexamine Mr. Mark and to clarify his answers, the Commission recognized "the right of individuals to hold views contrary to the Constitution of the PCUS but, for the sake of order, actions contrary to the Constitution are not sanctioned" (GA, PCUS, 1983, p. 44).

52. Richard Lovelace, "Conscience and Women's Ordination: A Difficult Issue to Resolve," manuscript, n.d. (later published in

the P.U.B.C. *Communique* [apparently written between 1978 and 1979, subsequent to the passage of Overture L by the General Assembly in 1978 but prior to its ratification by the presbyteries]), p. 3.

53. "Judicial Commission to Hear Kaseman Case January 24," *Presbyterian Outlook,* 163 (January 26, 1981): 4.

54. "Kaseman Upheld Again," *Presbyterian Survey,* 71 (April 1981): 32.

55. Examination, quoted in "Kaseman Sustained and Received Into Presbytery," *Presbyterian Outlook,* 162 (April 7, 1980): 3.

56. Ibid.

57. National Capital Union Presbytery, *Minutes,* Vol. III (Washington, D.C.: National Capital Union Presbytery, March 18, 1980), p. 22.

58. Synod of the Piedmont, "The Decision of the Permanent Judicial Commission in the Appeal of the Reception of Mansfield M. Kaseman by National Capital Union Presbytery (decision rendered January 21)," quoted in *Presbyterian Outlook,* 162 (February 18, 1980): 3–4.

59. *Book of Order, 1990–91,* G-14.0405e.

60. *Minutes of the General Assembly of the Presbyterian Church (U.S.A.)* [cited hereafter in text as GA, PC(USA)], 1985, p. 115.

61. XX.2 or XXII.2.

62. Wallace M. Alston, Jr., *Guides to the Reformed Tradition: The Church* (Atlanta: John Knox Press, 1984), p. 96.

63. "Historic Principles, Conscience and Church Government," report adopted by the 195th General Assembly (1983) of the Presbyterian Church (U.S.A.), (in GA, UPCUSA, 1983, Part I), p. 145.

64. John Calvin, *Institutes of the Christian Religion,* John T. McNeill, ed., trans. by Ford Lewis Battles, The Library of Christian Classics, vols. 20 and 21 (Philadelphia: Westminster Press, 1960), IV.7.15.

65. Ibid., IV.10.30.

66. See ibid., IV.3.10., IV.10.27.

67. John Calvin, *Draft Ecclesiastical Ordinances,* in *Calvin: Theological Treatises,* J. S. K. Reid, ed., The Library of Christian Classics, vol. 22 (Philadelphia: Westminster Press, 1964), p. 58.

68. Lewis Wilkins, "A Crucial Distinction," *Presbyterian Outlook,* 167 (March 6, 1985): 9.

69. Calvin, *Institutes,* IV.1.5.

70. See Leith, *Introduction to the Reformed Tradition,* pp. 155–158, 162–163.

71. Minutes of the Synod of New York and Philadelphia, p. 341.

72. *Book of Order, 1990–91,* G-6.0108.

73. "Historic Principles," pp. 157–158.

74. *Book of Order, 1990–91,* G-14.0405e.

75. John Calvin, *Draft Ecclesiastical Ordinances,* pp. 70–71.

76. John Calvin, *Draft Order of Visitation of the Country Churches,* in *Calvin: Theological Treatises,* pp. 74–75.

77. John Calvin, *Reply to Sadolet,* in *Calvin: Theological Treatises,* p. 232.

78. Martin Bucer, *De Regno Christi,* in *Melanchthon and Bucer,* Wilhelm Pauck, ed., The Library of Christian Classics, vol. 19 (Philadelphia: Westminster Press, 1969), I.v., 232.

79. Scots Confession, chapter XVIII.

80. "Historic Principles," p. 156.

81. Ibid.

12: The National Organizational Structures of Protestant Denominations: An Invitation to a Conversation

1. Sidney E. Mead, "From Coercion to Persuasion: Another Look at the Rise of Religious Liberty and the Emergence of Denominationalism," *Church History* 25 (1956): 317–337.

2. To cite but one set of such organizations, the American Baptist Foreign Mission Society formed in 1814, and similar societies for publications and home missions founded in 1824 and 1832, respectively, were not under denominational control. In fact, the formation of a general denominational body of northern Baptists did not take place until 1907. Even then, the issue of what relation those mission and publications boards had to the denomination would be problematic for another decade.

3. Sidney E. Mead, "Denominationalism: The Shape of Protestantism in America," *Church History* 23 (1954): 291–321.

4. James D. Beumler, "Church and State at the Turn of the Century: Missions and Imperialism, Bureaucratization, and War, 1898–1920," in *Church and State in America,* ed. John F. Wilson (Westport, Conn.: Greenwood Press, 1987), p. 159.

5. Timothy L. Smith, "Religious Denominations as Ethnic

Communities: A Regional Case Study," in Russell E. Richey, ed., *Denominationalism* (Nashville: Abingdon Press, 1977), pp. 195–196.

6. Shailer Mathews, *The Standard* (Chicago), October 8, 1910.

7. For a more fully developed exposition of the theme of "incorporation" in denominational life, see Louis Weeks, "The Incorporation of American Religion: The Case of the Presbyterians," *Religion and American Culture* 1/1 (Winter 1991): 101–118, and in this volume, pp. 37–54.

8. As Robert Wuthnow has commented, the jury is still out as to whether religious special interest groups provide more of a release valve or an irritant to their denominations. Robert Wuthnow, *The Struggle for America's Soul* (Grand Rapids: William B. Eerdmans Publishing Co., 1989), pp. 80ff.

9. Theda Skocpol, "Political Response to the Capitalist Crisis—Neo-Marxist Theories of the State and the Case of the New Deal," *Politics & Society* 10/2 (1980): 155–201.

10. See Peter Berger, "American Religion: Conservative Upsurge, Liberal Prospects," in *Liberal Protestantism,* ed. Robert S. Michaelsen and Wade Clark Roof, (New York: Pilgrim Press, 1986), pp. 34ff.

Index

A.D., 285, 286
Ad Interim Committee on
  Restructuring Boards and
  Agencies (CRBA), 75–76,
  82
Adams, Arthur M., 69, 72
Advisory Council on
  Discipleship and Worship,
  257
affirmative action, 80
Africa, 137
agency structure, 70–74
agenda, 194–198
Alban Institute, 320
Alexander, Maitland, 59
All-Africa Conference of
  Churches, 169
American Bible Society, 156,
  256
American Board of
  Commissioners for Foreign
  Missions, 314
American Sabbath School
  Union, 45

American Sunday School
  Union, 256
American Tract Society, 256
Anderson, John, 75
Andrews, E. A., Jr. (Andy),
  244, 248
Angela Davis legal defense
  controversy, 73, 78, 122,
  124–125, 130, 183–184,
  189, 198, 281–284,
  291–292, 305
Anglicans, 98–99, 309–310
Annett, Hugh, 73
Asbury, Francis, 310
Association of Presbyterians
  in Cross-Cultural Mission,
  264

baby boom, 66, 267
Baptist Church, 100, 309,
  314. *See also* Southern
  Baptist Convention
Barnard, Dorothy, 226
Beeman, Josiah, 87, 89